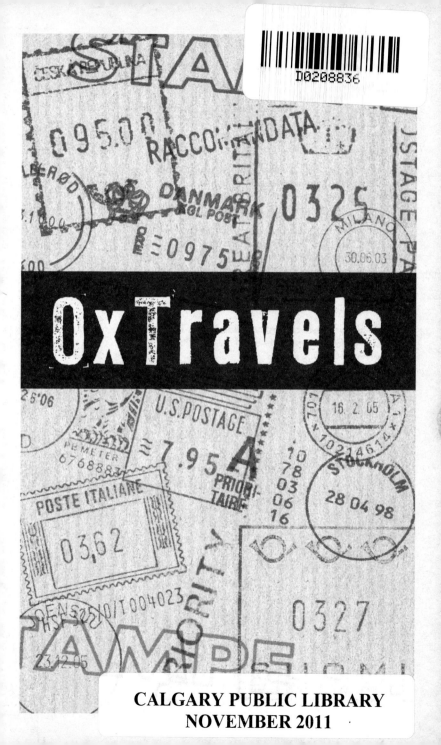

Thanks

OxTravels was developed by Mark Ellingham of Profile Books (www.profilebooks.com), Barnaby Rogerson of Eland Books (www.travelbooks.co.uk) and Peter Florence of Hay Festival (www.hayfestival.com), together with Tom Childs of Oxfam.

Thanks from each of us to the authors who generously donated their stories – and time – to the book, and to the photographers who allowed us to use their work, in support of Oxfam. Thanks also to their publishers and agents for their support of the project.

At Profile, special thanks to Peter Dyer for the inspired cover design. At Oxfam, thanks to Brian Harley, Sara Griffiths, Rose Marsh, Matt Kurton and David McCullough.

OxTravels © 2011 Profile Books.

All individual stories © the authors (see 'Permissions', following)

Set in Sabon, Bradon and LLRubberGrotesque
Page design by Henry Iles

First published in 2011 by
Profile Books
3A Exmouth House
Pine Street, Exmouth Market
London EC1R OJH

Printed and bound in Great Britain by CPI Bookmarque, Croydon CR0 4TD, on Forest Stewardship Council (mixed sources) certified paper

A CIP catalogue record for this book is available from the British Library.

ISBN 978-184668 496 8
eISBN 978-184765 745 9

OxTravels

MEETINGS OF REMARKABLE TRAVEL WRITERS

INTRODUCED BY

MICHAEL PALIN

EDITED BY

MARK ELLINGHAM, PETER FLORENCE
AND BARNABY ROGERSON

P

PROFILE BOOKS

PERMISSIONS

ABOUT OxTravels

OxTravels is a very simple idea. We asked the best travel writers based in Britain – and a few further afield – for a story loosely based around a meeting. There were no rules except that the story should be true – and the meeting real. The book follows on from *Ox-Tales*, our collection of stories from fiction writers, published in 2009, and again its purpose is primarily to raise funds for Oxfam's work. All of the authors have again donated their royalties to Oxfam.

The original concept was for a book of about 250 pages, with contributions from twenty writers. We had imagined only about half the travel writers that we approached would find time to contribute. They tend to be away travelling, after all. But the response was almost unanimous, both from the established authors and from those we identified as an emerging new wave of travel writers. Almost all have contributed original material, though a handful of authors, for whom that was impossible due to immediate commitments, have adapted previously published pieces.

So here they are: thirty-six compelling stories, together with an introduction from Michael Palin and an afterword by Oxfam's own chief traveller, Barbara Stocking.

Mark Ellingham, Peter Florence and Barnaby Rogerson
Editors, OxTravels

CONTENTS

Michael Palin	**Introduction**	9
Nicholas Shakespeare	**Return of the Native**	13
Sonia Faleiro	**Madam Say Go**	31
Paul Theroux	**The Monk's Luggage**	43
Peter Godwin	**Blood Diamonds**	53
Ruth Padel	**Arifin**	69
William Dalrymple	**The Nun's Tale**	83
Oliver Bullough	**The Last Man Alive**	103
Lloyd Jones	**The Penguin and the Tree**	115
Victoria Hislop	**Manoli**	123
John Julius Norwich	**Costa**	129
John Gimlette	**The Other World**	143
Dervla Murphy	**Three Tibetans in Ireland**	157
Jason Webster	**Rafaelillo**	173
Shehan Karunatilaka	**The Piece of String**	181
Sara Wheeler	**The End of the Bolster**	193
Hugh Thomson	**Encounter in the Amazon**	199
Rory MacLean	**Love in a Hot Climate**	209
Jasper Winn	**A Confederacy of Ghosts**	223

Aminatta Forna	The Beggar King	237
Ian Thomson	The Fall and Rise of a Rome Patient	245
Chris Stewart	Cures for Serpents	259
Michael Jacobs	On the Way to Timbuktu	273
Tiffany Murray	Big Yellow Taxi	283
Robin Hanbury-Tenison	The Orchid Lady	291
Raja Shehadeh	With Eyes Wide Open	301
Janine di Giovanni	Decide To Be Bold	311
Anthony Sattin	The Man Who Laughed in a Tomb	321
Horatio Clare	A Villain	331
Tom Bullough	The Zoo from the Outside	341
Sarah Maguire	Meetings with Remarkable Poets	353
Tim Butcher	Letting Greene Go	359
David Shukman	Heat of Darkness	371
Jan Morris	The Fourth World	381
Rory Stewart	The Wrestler	387
Colin Thubron	In Mandalay	403
Patrick Leigh Fermor	A Cave on the Black Sea	411
Barbara Stocking	Afterword	429

MICHAEL PALIN (born Broomhill, Sheffield, 1943) established his reputation with **Monty Python's Flying Circus** and **Ripping Yarns**. His work also includes several Python films, **The Missionary, A Private Function** and **A Fish Called Wanda**. He has written books to accompany his seven travel series – **Around the World in Eighty Days, Pole to Pole, Full Circle, Hemingway Adventure, Sahara, Himalaya** and **New Europe** – as well as a novel, **Hemingway's Chair**. He is currently President of the Royal Geographical Society.

Introduction

MICHAEL PALIN

G'athered here, for the benefit of Oxfam and its work, are a series of vivid accounts of people and places which not only show the wonder of the world but also the wealth of fine travel writers working today. The theme behind each contribution is, quite loosely, meetings, or to put it more poetically, encounters.

When I set out on my BBC series *Around the World in Eighty Days* in 1988 I was nervous. Not so much of the world outside, but of what I would make of it. Ahead of me were the giants of broadcast travel – the James Camerons, Charles Wheelers and the Alan Whickers. Masters of the concise and the memorable. I had also been commissioned to write a book of my experiences on the journey, and all I could think of was the daunting legacy of great descriptive writers like Bruce Chatwin and Jan Morris, and my personal favourite, Norman Lewis, who used bone-dry humour to lure his readers into all sorts of weird and dangerous places. As if this literary legacy wasn't intimidating enough, there was also Jules Verne, who'd written *Around the World in Eighty Days* already.

As my journey went on and I struggled to find a single fresh word to apply to sunsets, Venice or another morning on the Mediterranean, it struck me that perhaps I'd been born just too late and that everything that could be said had already been said. Then, in the third week of the journey, everything changed. We found ourselves far from well-trodden Europe, confined for seven days and nights on a dhow on the Persian Gulf. It had no radar or radio and of the crew of fifteen Gujaratis, only one had a smattering of English. It was wonderful. I couldn't fill the pages of my notebook fast enough. The unfolding relationship between our BBC crew, high-tech and largely helpless, and the dhow crew, low-tech and indispensable, was one of the most extraordinary and unusual encounters of the *Eighty Days* journey, and indeed of my six subsequent television journeys. It was the story of two groups of people from almost diametrically opposed backgrounds finding common ground through a common endeavour. In the absence of a shared language, shared food and physical tasks became our currency. Expressions, gestures and laughter became invaluable points of contact. Thanks to the connections I was able to make with the crew of the *Al Sharma*, I knew that I had a story to tell, both on and off camera, that was recognisably my own. Sunsets and sunrises would always be there but what made them special was who you were watching them with at the time.

From then on I've relied on human encounters to bring to life the places I've visited. As far as possible I've tried to avoid formal interviews or rehearsed interactions in favour of the accidental and the unexpected. It doesn't always work. Whilst filming my *Pole to Pole* journey, I remember being instructed to make friends with a morose lighthouse keeper on the Hurtigruten boat service up the Norwegian coast. He was returning to the most northerly lighthouse in Europe. My magic moment of contact rather fell apart when I asked him, with great concern, how he survived six months of Arctic ice and darkness. 'Oh,' he said, brightening up considerably, 'we watch your programmes on the television'.

The Tibetan plateau can be an intimidating stretch of the globe, and I would remember it as an abstract and impersonal space had it not been for an encounter with Sonam, a yak herder, who I met at a horse fair near Yushu. Sonam and I ended up in his tent, beside a yak-dung fire, talking about family life in two quite incompatible languages but with as much laughter and understanding as if I were back in my kitchen at home.

Over a roast goat supper in the heart of the Sahara, I and a group of Touareg cameleers were reduced to hysterics whilst trying to teach each other words from our separate languages. My greatest achievement was to get one of the Touareg to say 'Bottoms Up' in an accent that would not have disgraced David Niven. That one evening of human intercourse in the middle of a hostile wilderness gave me a special and particular memory of the biggest desert on earth.

It is those chance relationships we make along the way that unites this collection of thirty-five travellers' tales. These stories carry us right across the globe, from Brazil to Burma and Antarctica to Orissa. Lloyd Jones shares Scott's Hut with a legendary snorer. A raki-fuelled Patrick Leigh Fermor watches a Greek fisherman doing a Turkish bellydance in a Bulgarian cave. Victoria Hislop is moved and inspired by her friendship with a former resident of the leper colony of Spinalonga. Colin Thubron is pedalled about by a rickshaw driver called Tun, who has a powerful and sobering story to tell. Ian Thomson revisits Rome to meet Professor Milza (or, as he helpfully translates for us, Professor Spleen), the surgeon who saved his life twenty-five years earlier. John Gimlette, visiting the forests of Orissa in India to investigate the story of tribesmen who wanted to eat their teacher, encounters the small but fearsome men of the Bonda tribe who would kill anyone who tried to take a photo of them. Russell Crowe and Naomi Campbell are clearly not the only ones.

From Sarah Wheeler and Rory MacLean come stories of travel experiences enhanced by love and lust. Robin Hanbury-Tenison sets out on a river journey from one end of South America to another with a companion who has to be regularly injected in the bottom. Janine di Giovanni describes how her meeting with a Jewish lawyer in Jerusalem changed her life.

The great strength of these encounters is that the personal illuminates the general, so through Dervla Murphy's fondly described encounters with three Tibetans, one of them a dog she adopted, we gain a powerful insight into the history and predicament of the Tibetans in exile. Similarly, the chance that sat Sonia Faleiro next to an Indian maid returning from the Gulf, on the wrong plane as it turns out, gives us a brief but poignant glimpse of what millions of poor Indians will put up with to earn money from rich employers abroad. Through William Dalrymple's meeting with a Jainist nun I learn more than I ever knew about the extreme asceticism of one of the world's oldest living religions.

And there are many more stories that make up this fascinating and irresistible assortment. I'll not spoil the treats ahead of you by giving away any more. Suffice to say, *OxTravels* is a uniquely readable and entertaining travel anthology. It ranges right across the world and will hopefully restore your faith in the human race.

Just like Oxfam, in fact.

Michael Palin, London, 2011

Return of the Native

NICHOLAS SHAKESPEARE (born Worcester, 1957) grew up in the Far East and South America. After a stint as a BBC journalist, he joined The Times and then became literary editor for The Daily Telegraph and the Sunday Telegraph. His novels have been translated into twenty languages. They include **The Vision of Elena Silves**, winner of the Somerset Maugham Award, the Booker-longlisted **Snowleg**, and **The Dancer Upstairs**, which was made into a film by John Malkovich. He is also the author of an acclaimed biography of **Bruce Chatwin**, and a travel memoir, **In Tasmania**. He lives in Oxford.

Return of the Native

NICHOLAS SHAKESPEARE

My sister and I grew up in Brazil during the 1960s. Thirty years later, my sister went back to work with street children in the Pelhourinho district of Bahia, where she fell in love with a former street boy, a carefree Rastafarian called Rasbutta da Silva.

In 1994, research for a book took me to Bahia and I stayed with them. While my sister occupied herself feeding and teaching the children, Rasbutta showed me around the cobbled streets of the Pelhourinho, where, I could tell, he enjoyed some status. He strummed the mandolin and guitar, composed ballads and sang in a band, the Lions of Jehovah. (His drummer, he told me with a hint of pride, had played with the Lemonheads).

Rasbutta had been born into an impoverished black family who lived in a *favela* overlooking the bay. Built on layers of moist garbage, this was no second Troy: what the imagination reconstructed from the stinking mounds were generations of malnourishment and poverty. The shit dripped down stilts that were held together by rags. Water leaked from a single spout and the children who rinsed their hair in the dribble risked hepatitis or cholera.

Pinched between ocean and highway, Rasbutta's community survived on fishing for *vermelho* and *enguia*. Unable to afford outboard engines, the fishermen paddled huge distances to find the shoals. In the dawn, they crouched exhausted on the dirty sand, slicing eels that they had stunned with dynamite.

Shoeless, in overlarge shorts, the children of the *favela* were forced like Rasbutta in the opposite direction, onto a maniacal highway called the Contorno. They stood in small, excited groups, reaching out their hands to the traffic whirling past. But it was a perilous business, begging on the Contorno, and sometimes a car knocked one of them down.

Rasbutta had made it across the Contorno to become a musician. His songs divided into two: laments for the children of the *favela* who grew up to be drug addicts and child prostitutes (that is to say, those whom my sister attempted to care for), and homesick, repetitive melodies about 'Mama Africa' and 'Africa Diaspora'. Rasbutta had little idea what these phrases meant. The way he talked, the words had been leeched of their original sad power, like a national anthem which is sung but not felt.

'I don't know where my family comes from, what my origins are. Why *does* Bahia have so many blacks?'

Nor could Rasbutta's community enlighten him. His family lacked an oral tradition. One of very few scraps his mother had passed on was how white Portuguese from Brazil went with guns to Africa and carried off the blacks. But nothing more. Africa, for Rasbutta, was simply the source of his blackness, part of a hazy nostalgia. It was not something he questioned or discussed. It was something he sang about.

He didn't even believe in voodoo. Once, I stood with Rasbutta inside the shrine belonging to his austere elder brother, a priest of *candomblé*. The shrine – a stifling shed in a garden – contained a red plastic doll with a lascivious smile, a bar of black soap and an empty champagne bottle. Outside, a tortoise clambered over the roots of a *loko* tree. The roots, suggested Rasbutta's brother, stretched under the Pacific to the land of Rasbutta's ancestors: to Itu-Auyé, to Africa, home of the gods.

Hocus pocus, said Rasbutta out of earshot. 'If voodoo's so powerful, why were we slaves for 400 years?'

At dusk we walked along the waterfront. Close to the *favela* was a white-limed building planted about with banana palms – a chic restaurant, the Solar do Unhao, which tormented the warm air with the tantalising odour of fish stew. Two centuries ago this restaurant was the warehouse where they unloaded slaves from the Gulf of Benin.

In the Pelhourinho, my sister indicated a smooth flagstone the size of a grey handkerchief. 'This was where the pillory stood. That's where they sold the slaves.'

The most sought after slaves, I had read, came from a West African port called Ouidah, in the kingdom of Dahomey. '*Do Ouidah!*' the slavers yelled, as if selling horses, and prised lips apart to show the fine teeth. The words slurred into the single word '*Ajuda*', meaning 'God help me'. Many of the slaves died of '*banzo*', a longing for Africa which cracked the brain. They ate earth, drank copious quantities of brandy and masturbated excessively.

Rasbutta had never heard of '*banzo*'.

I INVITED MY SISTER and Rasbutta to travel with me, later that year, to Africa. I had a reason. I was researching a biography of Bruce Chatwin whose second book, *The Viceroy of Ouidah*, dramatised the slave trade between Bahia and Dahomey. The book's protagonist was based on a white Portuguese slaver from Bahia who, around 1800, settled in Ouidah, where he helped his friend King Ghézo onto the throne. Ghézo rewarded him with the title of Viceroy and the monopoly on the sale of slaves. The Viceroy accumulated innumerable wives, eighty documented children and grew rich on his pickings. And there is this coincidence. In the book, Chatwin gave his hero the same surname as Rasbutta: da Silva.

The coincidence was satisfying, if not astonishing: Bahia's telephone directory listed twenty-four pages of da Silvas. But it left this tantalising question, no less tormenting than the aromas surrounding the Solar do Unhao. Was Rasbutta da Silva descended from one of the millions of Africans shipped from Ouidah to Bahia and traditionally given the name of their owner? Or was his forebear the prodigiously wealthy Bahian slaver José-Rodrigues da Silva? Aside from not possessing any oral tradition, Rasbutta had no documentary evidence: in 1891 the Brazilian government burnt all records of 'this vile trade'.

ON OUR SECOND DAY in Africa, a taxi drives us along the coast road to Porto Novo, the capital of Benin (as Dahomey is now called). The windscreen is obscured by stickers of Christ hammered to the cross, and between the stickers the thin palms of the Slave Coast flash by.

At last, in a backstreet, we find the address. The place is guarded by a tall grey metal gate. Rasbutta bangs it open, squeezes through and emerges into a courtyard of red earth. Squatting by a flame in one corner is an old black lady. She glances from her pan where something dark boils away. Rasbutta goes over and explains himself in Portuguese.

She stares at him, mouth open. Her eyes are strangely blue around the pupils and there is a hole visible in her tongue. She struggles to her feet, scattering two plucked-looking chickens. 'A da Silva!' Then, louder: 'A da Silva *from Brazil*!' Her cry pierces the open doors and windows of the Maison Familiale da Silva.

Here, in a jumble of decrepit rooms, live sixteen families all called da Silva. The clan descend from the Portuguese merchant who shipped Africans to Brazil in the middle of the eighteenth century. His fortune sprang from a simple barter: Bahia, where he lived on the north-east coast of Brazil, had tobacco but required slaves to work the plantations. Dahomey had the slaves and wanted tobacco. José-Rodrigues da Silva kept his holds full.

The da Silvas of Porto Novo continue to take pride in their descent from the white slaver who built this house. Few visitors come from the land that they associate with his wealth. Not in living memory has anyone from Brazil walked through that gate – further, someone who bears their name. Faces appear at the grilles, drawn by the old woman's cry. Children hurtle naked into the heat. They converge on Rasbutta, fascinated by his dreadlocks. Hands dart out to touch his hair. A whisper passes among them. Somebody says something in French. The refrain is taken up. Not knowing French, Rasbutta wonders what they are saying. My sister tells him: 'When are you going to take us to your big house in Brazil?'

Confused, Rasbutta responds in the best way he knows: unstraps his mandolin and strikes up a tune from Bahia. The effect is instantaneous: seventy people clapping hands, bumping hips, singing. But here's the odd thing: they are not singing in French (Benin's official language), nor in Yoruba. They are singing in Rasbutta's language, Portuguese. More extraordinary, they are singing the words of his song. They seem to know it by heart.

The song over, the old woman stumbles up and speaks animatedly to Rasbutta. Her skin is blacker than whatever boils in her pan. In the high-pitched roll of her dialogue, like one of her teeth, a Portuguese word here and there pokes out. Her name, she says, is Amoudatou and she was born twelve years after the last consignment of slaves left Dahomey. When she has finished addressing Rasbutta, she snatches hold of his shoulders and kisses him.

Overcome, Rasbutta starts another song. The dancers mince barefoot on the earth, dancing to the words '*Bravo! Bouryan Brasileira*'. Their movements mimic carnival and horses. Rasbutta, dressed in a white jellaba lent him by one of the da Silvas, will sing for two hours in the heat.

IT'S LATE AFTERNOON when we return to Cotonou. Rasbutta remains silent in the back of the taxi.

That night we dine under an African tulip tree facing the port. Rasbutta sits at the end of the table, holding down his head. Tears stream from his eyes and his shoulders beneath his dreadlocks heave with silent sobs.

He gets up, wanders off.

'*C'est normal*,' says a woman at the table. 'He *must* cry.' She has seen it before. 'They leave as slaves, then come back three generations later to retrieve their past. They come back knowing no one, not speaking the language, unable to communicate. *Ça c'est terrible*.' She glances over to where Rasbutta leans on his upstretched arms against a tree. 'He wants to speak and he can't. But he has his eyes. All he can do is cry. It's very good. And,' she says, 'it's not finished.'

Rasbutta sobs through that night and into the next. 'I didn't know I had so many tears.' When the old woman, Amoudatou, kissed him it was, he says, the most powerful experience of his life. He hadn't realised there was a da Silva house, a beginning to everything. 'I went to that house as a visitor, not as a member of the family, but she treated me as my mother would treat me if I came home. And then I had this sensation, like a dream, that I'd already been there. It reminded me of something *I'd already experienced.*' For the very first time, he says, he felt linked, personally, to what he was singing about.

Our evening peters out at the So What! nightclub where a band from Zaire performs to an empty room. Rasbutta plucks at my arm. He wants me to repeat what the old woman Amoudatou had said, what everyone in the courtyard was saying.

'They were saying: "Take me to Brazil. Take me to your big house in Brazil. When are you taking us?"'

Rasbutta shakes his head. 'As if they think I live in a big house. As if where I live is better. *Why do they think this?*'

MORE UNRAVELS WHEN we meet the head of the da Silva clan. Karim Elisio-Urbain da Silva Kamar-Deen II is a secretive man who lives in one of the largest houses in Port Novo. He styles himself an author/editor and hotel-owner, but his deeper ambitions are political. In 1968, he ran for president. Foiled in the attempt, he exudes the impatience of his guard-dog, a Great Dane. Something about Karim suggests that, one day soon, he might run again for office. Meanwhile, he represents the interests of a far-flung country. Among his incarnations, Karim is Brazil's honorary consul to Benin.

Karim sits fidgeting in a throne-like chair in the centre of his courtyard, dressed in a long new pink shirt, a new straw hat, and pale babouches stitched with the insignia of a python. Lizards perform press-ups on the soil by his feet and every few minutes a boy runs up with a message written on a yellow square of paper that Karim inspects and crumples.

'Our relations with Brazil are very dear to us,' he says to Rasbutta. Solicitous, he taps him on his arm. How might he assist?

My sister translates for Rasbutta – since Karim, despite the dignity of his office, does not speak Portuguese. 'Rasbutta wants to know, if possible, who he's descended from.'

Karim raises his straw hat to scratch a pitch-dark bald head. 'Impossible.' The story is the same as in Brazil. In 1924, to the 'great regret' of the family historian, all da Silva papers were destroyed by fire.

'Then who are *you* descended from?' I ask.

'Our ancestor was a white, José-Rodrigues da Silva. He came here in 1736, from Portugal. *Il est de l'aristocratie portugaise.*'

'What did he do?'

'He was involved in commercial activities in Ouidah.'

'You mean slaves?'

'He was a slaver, yes. But if you were white, you couldn't easily avoid that.'

'Then isn't it likely that Rasbutta's family were slaves who took his name?'

Karim's head-shake is vigorous. 'Those who are da Silva – and you're a *da* Silva, right? – are descended originally from the aristocracy. You could not take the name of your master. It was too sacred! You took his first name. If you were called simply "Silva", no "da", you might have been a slave, but when it's "da Silva"... *c'est la noblesse.*' He taps Rasbutta's arm and looks pleased. 'Let's have a drink.'

We go inside. Karim's house, topped with a huge satellite dish, is organised about a room in which everything is larger than life: the billiard table, the elephant tusks, the six-foot video screen. Larger in proportion to anything else are the outsized portraits of our host dressed in a fez. Karim, it turns out, also heads Porto Novo's Muslim community.

Karim claps his hands and a girl appears. From a cabinet he brings out champagne glasses and a Lanvin ice bucket. He fills a glass with melted water from the bucket and hands it to Rasbutta.

We realise, talking to Karim, how mistaken it is to suppose that the abolition of the trade in 1838 led to the end of slavery. The last shipments of slaves left Ouidah in 1901. And yet as recently as 2001 there were reports of children being sold in Porto Novo. 'When I was young,' Karim reminisces, 'there was a slave market in this town. Children who didn't have parents, they were offered to people who would feed them.'

Before we leave, Karim casts his eyes about the room for something to commemorate this unscheduled visit by a Brazilian da Silva. He hovers over a scrap of printed cotton before settling on a yellow rosette, a leftover from a three-year-old voodoo festival. He pins the rosette to the chest of his putative distant cousin and Rasbutta is thanking him when his eyes lock on something across the room. On the crimson carpet, beside an exercise platform, is a man's skeleton.

Karim chuckles. He bought the skeleton in Paris where he has another house.

'That's George.'

WE DRIVE NORTH to the former capital, Abomey, where skulls once covered the mud walls of the Palace.

'We are in black Africa. With us the dead are not dead,' intones a guide before a metal-framed bed of the sort you find in English boarding schools. The sheet is patterned with teddy bears and ducks, and where the pillow ought to be is a blue cooking pot. The guide removes the lid for us to make a donation. 'The dead are with us and their souls are venerated by the sacrifice of animals.'

The bed is the chief feature of a tomb to one of the Kings of Dahomey, who pledged to leave their people richer with each reign. This ambitious promise led Dahomey's rulers to sacrifice humans as well as animals, hunting their victims in season like pheasants. 'The warlike spirit,' an English traveller, A.B. Ellis, reported in 1883, 'was kept alive by a yearly war which commenced in April.' The crack troops were women who fought with a ferocity 'that most resembled the blind rage of beasts'. Foreigners were forbidden to set eyes on these 'Soldieresses', but Ellis, risking a snatched look through his fingers, survived to describe them as physically plain: 'all of them looked wiry and muscular and were covered with the cicatrices of old wounds.'

The royal Amazons beheaded their prisoners out of sight in the Palace compound. Ellis was told that they poured the blood into pools three feet square and set miniature canoes afloat on it. Afterwards, apparently, they mixed the blood with gold dust, sea-foam and rags, and patted the mixture, along with the skulls, into the temple walls.

'How many sacrifices a year?' I ask the guide.

'It's been exaggerated,' he shrugs. 'About eighty.'

There's not much to see in Abomey's Royal Palace save for a collection of Dutch clay pipes and a pair of wooden thrones. The larger, four feet high, is carved from a *fromager* tree and belonged to the Viceroy's patron, King Ghézo. The backless stool rests, beneath an open civil servant's umbrella, on four cracked human skulls lacquered to a nicotine hue.

'He must have looked a bit stupid sitting there,' reflects Rasbutta.

'I don't suppose many people told him that,' my sister responds.

The second stool, embellished by two skulls, is the throne once squatted on by Ghézo's mother, Princess Agontimé.

'She was sold by her stepson to Bahia,' says the guide.

The majority of prisoners were not beheaded, but exchanged like Princess Agontimé for pipe tobacco. Rasbutta finds the concept a slippery one to grasp. Between us, my sister and I try to explain: The Portuguese in his native Brazil refused to smoke tobacco picked from the lowest leaves of the plant. Rather than waste the leaves, merchants in Bahia experimented by lacing them with cane molasses which, reasonably pleasant tasting, had the advantage of adding weight. This sweetened pipe tobacco, known as *soca*, found an unanticipated market in West Africa. One after another the Kings of Dahomey became addicted, preferring *soca* to all superior brands. To finance their craving, they offered in exchange an erratic supply of slaves. By 1750, Bahia was sending fifteen ships a year to Ouidah. Each cargo contained up to 2,000 rolls of the syrupy-smelling tobacco and carried back to Brazil up to 700 Africans, from all ranks of society, who were put to work on the plantations.

RASBUTTA BUYS A DRUM in Abomey's voodoo market. He beats on it for the rest of the day. His song is morose, unvarying.

Nao sei de onde eu sou
Nem de onde eu vim...
I don't know who I am,
I don't know where I came from...

A thought torments him. Could it be, as Karim da Silva suggested, that he descends from the slaver's family? Already several people have remarked on Rasbutta's resemblance to Amoudatou. And there is a curious incident. In a poorly lit house beside a church, we interrupt three brothers seated around a Bacardi bottle. One of them, noticing Rasbutta, flings out a hand. 'Hey! Are you a da Silva? You *look* like a da Silva. *Ooh là là, il ne parle pas français.*'

The man can have no idea who Rasbutta is: we have walked in out of the blue. But he has guessed right. '*C'est incroyable,*' he cackles when we tell him. '*Et c'est vrai.*'

Rasbutta's thoughts grow wilder. If you have no documented proof of ancestry, all ancestors become possible. Why should he not be descended from a Portuguese slaver? Or someone more aristocratic? His daydream helps me to understand, among American blacks, the widespread affection for names like Earl, Count, Duke, Prince, King and Caesar.

The grandfather of Haiti's Toussaint Louverture was, before his sale into slavery, a Prince of Dahomey. And what about Princess Agontimé who was sent to Brazil, right up the coast from Rasbutta's village. Rasbutta, his mind dwelling on her ghoulish stool, is obsessed. 'What do you think? *Maybe I'm descended from a king?*'

WE DRIVE TO OUIDAH, a coastal town of small mud houses and large boards advertising 'London cigarettes' and 'Black King' schnapps.

José-Rodrigues da Silva disposed of his slaves from a fort that today houses the ramshackle museum. Set in a concrete plinth is the charred steering wheel of the last governor's Citroën. Also on exhibit are a rusty ankle shackle, a photocopied print of an Amazon and Dahomey's first flag. Embroidered in 1811 and framed by three cutlasses, the centrepiece is a figure holding aloft a basket of fresh-severed heads.

The museum contains no portrait of da Silva, but on one wall there hangs a painting of his more famous successor, known locally as Chacha.

Ouidah's most prominent slaver, and the model for Bruce Chatwin's Viceroy, was a curly-haired Brazilian called Francisco Felix da Souza. His wealth, Chatwin wrote, was a curse: 'Prince de Joinville, a son of Louis Philippe, came to call and described fantastic displays of opulence – silver services, gaming saloons, billiard saloons – and the Chacha himself wandering about distractedly in a dirty caftan.'

Exactly as da Silva's birth is celebrated in the Maison Familiale in Porto Novo so, on 4 October every year, the da Souza clan gather in Ouidah to honour their ancestor with dances and songs in Portuguese, and dishes of *feijoada* and *pirao*. 'We fete his birth, but not his death because he lives always,' the head of the clan tells me.

Honoré da Souza, a lawyer who owns the aluminium concession for Togo, is the new Viceroy of Ouidah, an honorific title with no political power attached but lashings of sentiment. Two weeks before our arrival, in the spacious pink da Souza courtyard, Honoré was crowned before several hundred members of the da Souza family. They assembled beside Francisco Felix's ebony Brazilian bed. Prayers were muttered, a bottle of Royal Stork gin passed round, and afterwards Honoré, wearing a replica of the tasselled cap of his ancestor, was lifted three times on and off a wooden elephant throne. After a 21-gun salute, his uncle Norberto handed him the cane of command.

I speak to Norberto. 'Let me get this straight. You, a black, are celebrating the life and continued existence of a white

Brazilian who was responsible for sending your people into slavery?'

Norberto nods. 'He had to earn his living. Then, slavery was the fashion. Now it's rice.'

THE AUCTIONS TOOK PLACE outside the da Souza house, beneath a large ancient tree. The tree is still growing, still casting a specked shade. Its roots protrude from the earth like the bones on the back of one's hand, plunging underground just a few feet shy of a metal sign printed with the words *Route des esclaves*. As had da Silva's slaves half a century before, da Souza's slaves filed from under these same branches clustered with yellow berries, through the Quartier de Brésil, past crumbling merchants' houses of luminous apricot, along a red dirt track.

Martine da Souza is Chacha's great-great-granddaughter and works as a guide at the museum. She leads us onto the Slave Road. It cuts for three miles through cane plantations and rice fields. We walk in the footsteps of the estimated twenty million Africans who trod this path between 1530 and 1901, with gags in their mouths and their feet in metal hoops.

After a mile we come to a statue commemorating the Place de l'Oubli, where each and every slave circulated a tree four times to say goodbye to their country. The ceremony was intended to obliterate a person's origins and cultural identity – which makes it all the more noteworthy that Rasbutta should abruptly remember, a few yards after leaving this place, a detail which has slipped his memory; and which suggests that Rasbutta da Silva is descended not from a slaver, nor a king.

Rasbutta recalls in his fishing village how his grandmother described the marks on *her* grandfather's ankles. Marks left by a chain.

Another mile on, we reach the Casa de Zomai, 'the house of darkness'. The slaves were locked for three months in this room, into which no light penetrated, to subdue them for the trip in the hold – an inferno described by one historian as 'week after week of shitting, starving, shrieking hell'.

'After three months in darkness,' says Martine, 'they were no more Dahomeans, no more human beings.'

Back in the sun, Rasbutta speaks to my sister in a low urgent voice. 'I feel I've been on this road before. I feel this is *my* road. We're going to come to a river and a bridge.'

'How do you know?' she says. There is nothing in sight, only the dirt road.

'I just *feel* it.'

Right at that moment, we observe a three-headed statue on the verge. 'Tohosu,' explains Martine: the water divinity. And points. 'There's a bridge over there, crossing the river.'

We walk over in silence.

The beach is furrowed by black pigs with sandy noses foraging for shrimps.

No one swims from this shore. There are so many sharks that, in 1879, the canoeists went on strike: too many had been eaten. As well, there's a dangerous undertow. 'Don't go into the sea – ever,' our honorary consul has warned. 'We're sending back one person a month in a box.'

Close to the water's edge, five men prepare to launch their pirogue. They run down the sand and paddle like mad. The waves engulf the grey dugout, overturning it. Nothing is whiter than the foam that hisses in a broad, bubbling band towards us.

We watch the men flounder back through the crashing surf, cursing.

There's no shade and we are sweating. A local poet imagined this stretch of coastline as the doorway to hell. 'It opens onto a blue sea. There is a woman with bare breasts who walks towards the prison of the waves. It's my mother.'

Today, the men who right the canoe and retrieve the glass floats are fishermen. In the past they ferried a human cargo to the ships. How much, I wonder, were Rasbutta's ancestors bartered for? Sixteen Dutch clay pipes? Twelve Pondichéry handkerchiefs? Sixty pounds of *soca*?

It has taken time to absorb this shocking thing. The people whom Rasbutta has met in Mama Africa are not, ancestrally speaking, his family, but his enemies. The Africans who stayed behind, the da Silvas, the da Souzas, the Kings of Abomey, were those who had connived in flogging his forebears for sweetened pipe tobacco.

'Rasbutta, what do you feel?' I ask.

He goes on staring out to sea, towards Brazil, towards the young Rasbutta, the fisherman's son who had no clue what he was singing about.

'I don't feel anything,' he says after a long time. '*They* should be feeling something.'

SONIA FALEIRO (born Goa, India, 1977) is an award-winning reporter and the author of **Beautiful Thing** (Canongate, 2011), a non-fiction narrative about the secretive world of Bombay's dance bars. She lives in San Francisco and Bombay. **www.soniafaleiro.com**

Madam Say Go

SONIA FALEIRO

'Madam say, "Go!"'

She scraped her scarf back on her head and I saw she was in her twenties, that her face was only large enough to accommodate her features. That one kohl-lined eye was swollen shut.

'Madam?' I said, trying not to stare.

She nodded, tilting her good eye towards me. 'Where going?'

'Bombay,' I said.

'You?' I asked tentatively.

'Hyderabad,' she replied. 'This flight Hyderabad,' she said decidedly.

I shook my head. 'This flight Bombay.'

She turned to the window; it was dark outside.

'You do want to go to Bombay?'

She rummaged inside the box-like handbag on her lap, and retrieving her ticket handed it to me. She'd started her journey in Abu Dhabi and was to end it in Bombay.

'Hindi?' I asked, handing it back to her.

She shook her head. 'Telugu?'

I shook my head.

'English,' she sighed. 'Okay.' She stuck her hand out. It was small, limp, and covered with scabs. 'Padmavati Kadali, village Rameswaram, Andhra Pradesh. How are you?'

'Good,' I replied, shaking her hand gingerly. 'How are you?'

Kadali shrugged. 'Last week job, today nothing. Madam say, "You stealer! Go!"' Her face broke into a grin. 'Madam cheat Padma out of salary and madam say "Stealer!"'

She shrugged as though to say 'the irony'.

'Hyderabad going?'

I pressed the call button for the flight attendant.

'Just a minute,' I told Kadali.

She nodded.

The cabin lights were dim, the other passengers reduced to shapes and sounds. The shape of a woman covered entirely by a thin grey blanket; the sound of a man's rasping snores; the shape of a baby burrowing restlessly into its mother's breast; the sound of the mother's determined 'Shhhs'.

I'D BOARDED THIS FLIGHT in the UAE; it was a connection from Bahrain. I'd flown into Bahrain from Kuwait, Kuwait from Qatar. Technically, I'd started my journey in Bombay, but really, it had been months before that when I'd been in Kerala, taking a vacation from writing. I'd become intrigued by the adverts offering work in the Gulf that covered every public wall, alongside chalk paintings of gods and goddesses and life-sized, colourful posters declaring the latest *Super Hit!* film. Alongside these *Help Wanted! In Dubai! Call Now!* adverts were plastered cheaply printed offers of help with procuring a visa, and acquiring skills to be *Best Maid!* and *Top Mechanic!*.

Later, I learnt that Kerala sent more than two million, or one in six, of its people to the Gulf, the most of any state in India, and that remittances from these men, women, and even children young as sixteen, boosted the state's economy by thirty-five per cent. Five million Indians, many barely literate construction workers and domestic help, had been making this journey since the 1970s, signing on for a hard life, far harder than they might even have had in India, but one that was also meant to be far more lucrative.

I wondered not just who these people were, but also, why they kept going back. For although their remittances, estimated at over fifty billion dollars annually, were life altering, so too was the abuse many suffered. In India government officials shared police reports – of a maid burnt with an iron for damaging a shirt, of a cook rescued from a home where he slept at midnight, woke up at 3 a.m., and was given dog food to eat.

In Qatar, an official at the Indian Embassy said it wasn't unusual for an employer who couldn't be bothered to buy his employee's ticket home to drive her to the border with Saudi Arabia and abandon her. There was the story of a worker 'encouraged' to give up a kidney to his sick employer, of the maid whose ears were sliced off, of the IT employee promised an IT job, but who instead found himself herding sheep.

The abuse didn't start in the Gulf. Recruitment agents in India charged exorbitant sums; money that was borrowed, sometimes from a half dozen places, at a high rate of interest, sometimes in exchange for pledging a home as security; because the job seeker believed he would earn that amount back quickly. But the job he was given was, more often than not, not just different from the one promised, it was low paying and binding. Breaking a contract could nullify one's visa.

Agents were also responsible for what was known as 'pushing'. An agent whose client had been rejected for a visa would pay off immigration officials, ensuring that when his client's passport was to be examined, it wouldn't be. He'd be 'pushed' through, turning him, instantly, into an illegal immigrant.

Once in the Gulf, semi-skilled or unskilled workers were forced to live isolated lives. They submitted their passport to their sponsor or employer, and because the visa and work permit system in the Gulf was skewed to entirely favour nationals, it was virtually impossible for them to break a contract, even one that broke the initial commitment made to them by a recruitment agent, or that underpaid and over-worked them, or made their life a previously unimaginable misery. To leave the country without the consent of their sponsor could result in them being charged with absconding; leading to arrest and deportation, ruining any chance they might have had to renew their visa and apply for a better job. The comparatively lucky ones experienced the 'Taxi System': an 'absconder' who'd made his way to the Indian Embassy was heard out, fed, and given legal counselling. He was then placed in a taxi and sent to the deportation centre where he would stay until his case was resolved and the embassy could buy his ticket home.

While workmen were confined to their places of work and sleep, evidence of their toil was everywhere. In the perfect smoothness, length and curve of freeways, in the shimmering chrome and glass beauty of skyscrapers, in indoor ski slopes and outdoor Venetian-inspired water canals.

At the Al Hajeri labour camp in Doha lived three thousand Indians who worked at the Ras Laffan Industrial City, one of the world's largest LNG exporting facilities. The day I was invited to visit just happened to be the day the contractor decided that workers must put in an extra shift. When I arrived, the sprawling camp was empty except for a supervisor and kitchen staff. I was welcome to inspect the sleeping areas, the supervisor said, and the kitchen. Vegetables were imported from Kerala, he assured me; workers even ate fish and chicken. The men, I said, can I see them tomorrow? The supervisor shook his head glumly. 'Out of question.'

At least I'd seen workmen. Not at the camp, but almost everywhere else, drilling, digging, paving roads. They toiled in the steam of the hottest day, in the swirl of wind and dust storms; security guards oversaw their every move. But at least I could verify their existence with my own eyes.

Domestic workers were entirely invisible.

The homes they worked in were enormous domed villas with walls so thick, so high, one could only imagine what lay beyond. When contacted, the owners of these villas would invite me for a meal at an expensive restaurant, and they'd be courteous, recommending shopping malls, and because I was a writer, one of the few bookstores in town, and they would talk of how they couldn't live without their help, how she was so clean, so loyal, and it was so sad I couldn't meet her because she was currently unwell/on vacation/in India.

My best bet, if I wanted to speak freely with a domestic worker, I was told by another official at the Indian Embassy, this time in Kuwait, was a deportation centre. Or, the flight home.

THE ATTENDANT BENT over me. 'Can I help you?'

'She thinks she's going to Hyderabad,' I said, nodding at Kadali.

Kadali looked up at the attendant eagerly. 'Hyderabad?' she said.

The attendant was sympathetic. 'Her madam packed her off to the wrong city, I suppose. Happens all the time.'

The man in the seat in front of me swivelled his head. 'Gulfie people are all rogues. Muslim sheikh mafia, I tell you!'

'Let me talk to the chief attendant,' the attendant said. 'We'll take care of her, don't worry.'

'We should boycott the Gulf!' the man spluttered, his face bulging. 'Why don't we do it? I'll tell you why. Because we Indians have no pride, that's why – NO PRIDE WHATSOEVER!'

The attendant gave him a look.

'Blanket?' he beseeched.

Kadali turned to me. 'My husband told this would happen. They always send home long way. Wrong way. "But never mind, madam," he told me. "You can look after yourself."'

'He's right,' I said. 'I'm sure you can. I mean, you have.'

Kadali's eyes lit up. 'I told madam first time, "You beat!"' She grabbed my wrist. '"You beat, I take police. Straight police!"'

I burst out laughing. So did she. 'Straight police!' she giggled, slapping my knee.

'But wait, what about your eye?' I asked.

She was sheepish. 'Fell down airport rushing, rushing. So happy to go home.'

I didn't know whether to believe her.

'You fell down?'

'Uh huh,' she nodded.

The chief attendant came over. He appeared solicitous. 'We'll drop her off with the ground staff in Bombay,' he said. 'They'll do the needful.'

Nothing about Kadali's expression changed. She was serene, like all she'd needed was a confirmation of her suspicions, and now she knew she'd been duped, she could move on.

'What do you do?' she asked, not appearing to give her own situation another thought.

'I'm a writer,' I said.

'Housemaid,' she pointed to herself. Digging into her handbag, she retrieved a plastic sandwich bag, and from it, a passport stored safely within. 'Take a look.'

Kadali posed with a wide smile, a gold chain at her neck, gold earrings in her ears, a dot of red on her forehead. Her dark eyes focused intently ahead, a mixture of curiosity and impatience. It was clear that she was, at whatever age the photograph had been taken, already a fully formed personality, who might be moved by the world, but would not be swayed by it.

'How long were you in Abu Dhabi?' I asked, handing back the passport.

'First, Oman. Two years after, visa expire, come home, work hard, earn thirty thousand rupees, then only Abu Dhabi.'

'Thirty thousand for the agent?' I asked.

She nodded.

'In Abu Dhabi,' she continued. 'Madam sleep. Mister drink. He travel a lot and madam, oh so fat, so grumpy I can't tell, every time mister travel she lose mind; walk up and down house like ghost talking non-stop crazy to herself. Four children she had, four big-big children, and who look after them tell?'

'You did,' I said.

'Yes,' she smiled fondly. 'I wash, I fed, I school bus took. I told stories of India. The children liked my stories. See my hands? So much work, hands need hospital!'

'Were you happy?' I asked.

She thought about this. 'The food was good ... Because I cooked!'

She grinned. 'Cook well, eat well!'

'But money? Some month 500 dirhams*, some month zero dirhams. And madam so crazy, I can't tell.' She tapped the side of her head meaningfully. 'When my husband call from India, if madam hear, she pull my hair and scream, "Boyfriend?!" What boyfriend? Mister has been my husband for eleven years.' She giggled naughtily. 'Too much time!

'But when madam go out, I call husband. I say, "Too much difficult without you. Too much sadness." And he say, "You be okay, Padma, you be fine. Stay strong for me, for children." "Okay, alright," I answer. "I'm okay." But inside not okay. I think of husband. Of children without mother. I think, when I go home after three years, maybe four, they will call me "Aunty". Not Mummy, Aunty. And then, after all this, madam say me, "Stealer!" "What did I steal?" I ask her. "Tell me!" "Like you don't know!" she reply. So I said, "I don't know, right. But I know you crazy woman." Madam get so angry she come towards me to slap but I say, "Uh uh, remember, police!" That make her more angry than anytime! So angry she was, she make me clean full house, fill full fridge, iron all clothes, and then, only then, she say, "Go! I buy ticket, go!" When I was leaving, madam's children how they cry. And why not? I love them too much. But madam? Madam watch TV and when I say, "Madam, goodbye," she say, "Huh!" Huh?! Two years I clean after her and she say, "Huh!"'

Kadali tut-tutted. 'Too much bad manners.'

*500 dirhams is about £85.

'What will you do now?' I asked. 'Will you go back?'

'Never!' she said. 'Never go Abu Dhabi. Go home.'

'To your village?'

Kadali leaned in. 'My home in village have one room. Bathroom, kitchen, one bed four peoples all same room. At evening time, 5 p.m, lights go. Padma light candles, send children to rich neighbour with more candles, so children can study well. Padma's husband has bicycle. He has chickens, goat, cow, also mother but she live in other village so no problem for Padma. In village nothing fancy like Abu Dhabi. No money like Abu Dhabi. That's why I go Abu Dhabi. To buy for children things I never had – schooling in English medium, clothes, shoes, nice food. One boy of mine so crazy for film star Nagarjuna, must watch Nagarjuna film at least once month. Once month! Crazy boy!'

'He our Baby Nag!' She laughed fondly.

'But who say to me if you go work there you get beat, you get shouting, they call "Stealer"? No one. People who stay say, "Ai Padma, when you come home get some gold for me also." People who go say, "Come quick, this place better than USA." Hah. Like in Abu Dhabi all eat gold. Eat gold, yes, but all? I'll tell if someone ask. But no one ask, because no one want believe.'

She shook her head sadly. 'Everyone like to dream.'

'I thought you said you fell down.'

Kadali shrugged. 'Fell down, get pushed by driver in hurry for me to get in airport. Same thing. Fell. Hurt eye.'

'I'm so sorry,' I said.

The attendant was leaning over me again. 'Everything okay?'

I looked at Kadali.

She bobbed her head. 'Fully okay.'

Kadali watched the attendant walk away. 'Now on, Padma stay home,' she said. 'If Padma cook, for family. If clean, for family. No crazy madam stealing money then calling Padma stealer. Enough! Maybe less money, okay. Even no money, okay. Sell chickens. Sell goat. Something.'

'Good for you,' I said, meaning it. 'Good luck.'

'Thank you,' Kadali smiled. 'But not required. Going home.'

PAUL THEROUX

The Monk's Luggage

PAUL THEROUX (born Medford, MA, USA 1941) worked as a Peace Corps teacher in Malawi and as a university lecturer in Uganda and Singapore before becoming a full-time writer. He is the author of more than forty books, including the novels **A Dead Hand** and **The Mosquito Coast**, and the travel books **The Great Railway Bazaar**, **The Old Patagonian Express** and **Ghost Train to the Eastern Star** – from which he has adapted 'The Monk's Luggage'. His latest book is **The Tao of Travel** – 'a distillation of travellers' visions and pleasures'. He lives in Hawaii and on Cape Cod. **www.paultheroux.com**

The Monk's Luggage

PAUL THEROUX

I remembered from long ago the Mandalay train as basic, the trip an ordeal. This train was in better shape, but it was no less a ghost train, a decaying relic of the past, taking me from Rangoon, the skeletal city still haunted by the military, to the northerly ghost town of Mandalay. I felt that strongly as we set off. I had no idea how accurate that vision of Mandalay was, as a city of wraiths and the living dead, and people being screamed at by the demonic soldiers.

In the sleeping compartment a young Frenchman was lolling in his berth, his sinuous Thai girlfriend, still in her teens, wrapped around him. I said hello and then went to the platform to buy some oranges.

A monk with a bundle slung over his shoulder was being pestered by a ragged Burmese man. The monk was speaking English and trying to give the man some money – some folded ragged bills.

'No, two dollah,' the Burmese man said.

'This same, these kyats,' the monk said.

'Two dollah,' the Burmese man said again.

I said, 'What's the problem?'

The ragged man was a scooter-rickshaw driver, who had taken the monk to the station. He insisted, as many Burmese did of foreigners, on being paid in American dollars.

'Here,' I said, giving the man the two dollars. The man took them with both hands, fingers extended, then touched them to his forehead.

'You're a stranger,' the monk said. 'You don't know me.'

I had been reading a Buddhist text, The Diamond Sutra, as background for a story I was calling 'The Gateway of India', so I was able to say, 'The Diamond Sutra says that you should give and not think about anything else. You don't speak Burmese?'

'I'm from Korea.' And it turned out that he too was on this train to Mandalay, the fourth person in my compartment. He said hello to the Frenchman and the Thai girl, and soon after, with a clang of couplings, the train started to move.

I looked out the window and marvelled again, as I had on arriving in Yangon. Nothing had changed in the outskirts, either – after the decaying bungalows and the creekside villages, it was just dry fields, goats cropping grass on the tracks, ducks on murky ponds, burdened women walking, looking haughty because they were balancing bundles on their heads, slender sarong-wearing Burmese, and befouled ditches.

I dozed, I woke up; the Frenchman and his girlfriend had separated and dozed in the upper berths. The monk sat opposite me.

He was a Zen monk, his name was Tapa Snim ('*snim* means monk in Korean'). He had just arrived in Myanmar. He was fifty years old. He had shifted his small bundle; it was now in the corner of his berth. He was a slender man, slightly built, very tidy, with clean brownish robes and a neatly shaved head that gave him a grey skull. He was not the smiling evasive monk I was used to seeing, who walked several inches above the ground, but an animated and watchful man who met my gaze and answered my questions.

'How long have you been a monk?' I asked.

'I became a monk at twenty-one,' Tapa Snim said. 'I have been meditating for twenty-nine years, but also travelling, I have been in a monastery here in Yangon for a few days, but I want to stay in a monastery in Mandalay.'

'How long will you be here?'

'Meditation for six months, then I will go to Laos and Cambodia – same, to meditate in a monastery.'

'You just show up and say, "Here I am".'

'Yes. I show some papers to prove who I am. They are Theravada Buddhist. I am Mahayana. We believe that we can obtain full enlightenment.'

'Like the Buddha?'

'We can become Buddha, totally and completely.'

'Your English is very good,' I said.

'I have travelled in fifteen Buddhist countries. You know something about Buddhism – you mentioned The Diamond Sutra.'

'I read it recently. I like the part of it that describes what life on earth is:

A falling star, a bubble in a stream.

A flame in the wind. Frost in the sun.

A flash of lightning in a summer cloud.'

'A phantom in a dream,' Tapa Snim said, the line I'd forgotten. 'That's the poem at the end. Have you read The Sixth Patriarch's Sutra?'

I said no, and he wrote the name in my notebook.

'All Zen Buddhists know this,' he said, tapping the name.

We travelled for a while in silence. Seeing me scribbling in my notebook, the Frenchman said, 'You must be a writer.'

He had a box of food, mainly potato chips, pumpkin seeds and peanuts. He shared a bag of pumpkin seeds with us.

Up the great flat plain of Pegu Province, dusty-white in the sun, the wide river valley, baking in the dry season. Small simple huts and villages, temples in the distance, cows reclining in the scrappy shade of slender trees. Tall solitary stupas, some like enormous whitewashed pawns on a distant chessboard, others like oversize lamp finials, under a blue and cloudless sky.

The bamboo here had the shape of giant antlers, and here and there pigs trotted through brambles to drink at ponds filled with lotuses. It was a vision of the past, undeveloped, serene at a distance, and up close harsh and unforgiving.

Miles and miles of drained and harvested paddy fields, the rice stalks cut and rolled into bundles and propped up to await collection. No sign of a tractor, or any mechanisation – only a woman with a big bundle on her head, a pair of yoked oxen – remarkable sights for being so old-fashioned. And then an ox cart loaded with bales of cotton, and across a mile of paddy fields a gold stupa.

I walked to the vestibule of the train, for the exercise, and talked a while with an old toothless man going to Taungoo. When I asked him about the past he seemed a little vague.

'I'm fifty-two,' he said, and I was reminded how poverty aged people prematurely.

When I came back to the compartment, Tapa Snim was rummaging in his bag. I watched him take out an envelope, and then he began knotting the two strands that made this simple square of cotton cloth into a bag.

'Do you have another bag?' I asked, because the smallness of this one seemed an improbable size for a long-distance traveller.

'No. These are all my possessions.'

Everything, not just for a year of travel, but everything he owned in the world, in a bag he easily slung under one arm. True, this was a warm climate, but the bag was smaller than a supermarket shopping bag.

'May I ask you what's inside?'

Tapa Snim, tugging the knot loose, gladly showed me the entire contents.

'My bowl, very important,' he said, taking out the first item. It was a small black plastic soup bowl with a close-fitting lid. He used it for begging alms, but he also used it for rice.

In a small bag: a piece of soap in a container, sunglasses, a flashlight, a tube of mosquito repellent, a tin of aspirin.

In a small plastic box: a spool of grey thread, a pair of scissors, nail clippers, Q-tips, a thimble, needles, rubber bands, a two inch mirror, a tube of cream to prevent foot fungus, ChapStick, nasal spray, and razor blades.

'Also very important,' he said, showing me the razor blades. 'I shave my head every fifteen days.'

Neatly folded, one thin wool sweater, a shawl he called a *kasaya*, a change of clothes. In a document pouch, he had a notebook and some papers, a photograph showing him posed with a dozen other monks ('to introduce myself') and a large certificate in Chinese characters he called his *bikkhu* certificate, the official proof he was a monk, with signatures and seals and brushwork.

And a Sharp electronic dictionary that allowed him to translate from many languages; and a string of beads – 108 beads, the spiritual number.

As I was writing down the list, he said, 'And this' – his straw hat – 'and this' – his fan.

'Nothing else?'

'Nothing.'

'What about money?'

'That's my secret.' And then carefully he placed it all on the opened cloth, and drew the cloth together into a sack, everything he owned on earth.

'Tell me how you meditate.'

'You know the Japanese word *koan*,' he said. It wasn't a question. 'For example, in ancient China, a student asked an important Zen monk, "What is Buddha?" The monk answered, "One pine-cone tree in front of a garden."'

Out the train window I could see a village set in a bower of dense trees, offering shade, scattered groves of bananas and coconut, more lotus ponds, people on bikes. And here before me the shaven-headed and gently smiling Tapa Snim.

'I meditate on that. "One pine-cone tree in front of a garden." It is a particular tree.'

'How long have you been using this *koan*?'

'Years. Years. Years.' He smiled again. 'Twelve hours a day.'

'Is it working?'

'I will understand eventually. Everyone has Buddha-spirit in their mind. By reason of sufferings and desires and anger we can't find it.' He rocked a little on the seat, and then went on. 'If we get rid of suffering and desire and anger, we can become a Buddha.'

'How do I get rid of them?'

'Meditate. Empty your mind – your mind must be vacant. Non-mind is the deepest stage of the deep stage.' He asked to borrow my pen, and the little notebook I'd been using. He said, 'Every night I have a serious question in my head – every day and night. Look.'

He set down six Chinese characters, inscribing them slowly, each slash and dot. Then he poked at them, translating.

'Sun-faced Buddha, moon-faced Buddha,' he said. 'For twenty-six years I have thought about this. If I solve this I will know truth. It is my destination, my whole life, to solve this problem.'

'But how did you happen to choose these images?'

'One day, a famous monk, Ma Tsou, was asked, "How are you?" This was his reply.'

'Why did you come here to meditate? You could have stayed in Korea.'

He said, 'Buddha travelled! So I travel. I am looking for enlightenment.'

'What do you think about Burma?'

He laughed and told me that on the day of his arrival he had gone to the railway station, but the ticket window was closed. So he waited on a bench and, waiting there, had fallen asleep. When he woke up he discovered that the pouch at his waist had been razored open by – literally, a cutpurse – and some of his money stolen.

'But small money! Big money is in a secret place.'

'You've been to India?'

'India can be dangerous,' he said. 'But I have a theory about India.' He sat forward, eager to explain. 'I see many poor people there, and I think, What is their karma? They are the poorest people in the world. Why do they receive this big suffering? Eh?'

I said I had no idea, and that the people here – right out the window – seemed miserably poor, living in bamboo huts and steadying wooden ploughs pulled by oxen, and labouring under the load of heavy bales.

'India is worse,' he said. 'This is my ridiculous thought. I know it is silly, but...' But, he implied that it was not ridiculous at all and that I should not be too quick to judge him. 'Indian people have many bad karmas. In their history, they created violence, they destroyed Buddhist stupas and persecuted monks. They all the time blame Muslims, but Hindus have been just as bad. In my Indian travel I think this is the deep reason for the suffering there.'

'What about Korea – any suffering?'

'Suffering everywhere! In Korea we have mad crazy Christians, because we are under the influence of the United States.'

'Reverend Moon?'

'Many people like him!' Tapa Snim said. 'I am glad to be here.'

In the setting sun, the muted pinks and browns, the subdued light, the long shadows of the labouring bent-over harvesters. And in the dusk, the unmistakable sign of rural poverty – no lights in the villages, only the lampglow in small huts, or the small flare of cooking fires at ground level, the smell of woodsmoke. All the train windows were open to insects and smoke and, passing a swamp or a pond, a dampness in the air, the malodorous uprush of the hum of stagnant water.

Peter Godwin

Blood Diamonds

PETER GODWIN (born Zimbabwe, 1957) is the author of **The Fear** (from which 'Blood Diamonds' is adapted), **When a Crocodile Eats the Sun**, and **Mukiwa**. Raised in Zimbabwe, he was educated at Cambridge and Oxford and became a foreign correspondent, reporting for the Sunday Times, and the BBC, from more than sixty countries. Since moving to New York, he has written for National Geographic, the New York Times magazine and Vanity Fair. He has taught at Princeton and Columbia, and is a recipient of a 2010 Guggenheim fellowship.
www.petergodwin.com

Blood Diamonds

PETER GODWIN

Georgina and I are waiting outside Meikles Park in the town of Mutare early on Saturday morning, waiting to meet the Hon. Lynette Kore-Karenyi, another of the new crop of opposition MPs. She thinks she may be able to sneak us into the Marange diamond fields. Control of these diamond fields is now the key to Zimbabwe's future. With the economy shattered, the farms looted, and the death of the Zimbabwe dollar snuffing out the black market in foreign currency, diamonds – *ngoda* – are one of the very few remaining sources of wealth. Robert Mugabe and his men need to keep control of them to finance their political machine.

The granite obelisk in the centre of the park is plastered with AIDS sensitivity posters, part of the 'Zimbabwe National Behavioural Change Strategy: 2006–2010'. I rummage beneath the accretion of posters, to find the original carved inscription, 'For King and Empire 1914–1918'. Above us, the Bvumba Mountains are still wreathed with cool morning *guti*. Yet, here, along the central island of Herbert Chitepo Avenue, deferential ilala palms sough softly in the sunny breeze. Georgina is window-shopping across the road in the tragically under-stocked Meikles Department Store. Behind the glass, frozen in time, stand naked white mannequins under twirling yellow smiley-faced cardboard discs declaring, 'Going Summer!'

A soldier strolls down the road and stops at the bus stop. He is tall and straight-backed, in his early thirties, wearing a sharply ironed one-piece camouflage jump suit with the insignia of a Zimbabwe bird within a laurel wreath looped through his epaulettes.

'How are things in the army, Major?' I ask tentatively.

'We are happy since yesterday' – he grins – 'when we were paid for the first time in *USAhs*. We got US$100 each.'

He has trekked all the way from Harare to give some of his hard-currency bounty to his grandmother, who lives in Zimunya, the arid communal land at the foot of the Bvumba. In Harare, he is in charge of a Yugoslav-made artillery battery. 'It has forty missiles,' he says proudly, 'with a range of twenty kilometres.'

Lynette's husband drops her off, and we drive south, past Sakubva township. Its roadside market, where mounds of donated clothes end up for sale, is just cranking up. We drop down into Zimunya. On the left, freshly painted, is the New Cannibal Inn and Butchery. 'What kind of flesh do you think they sell?' Georgina asks Lynette, and she giggles.

LYNETTE IS THIRTY-FOUR and wears cork wedges, a calf-length brown corduroy skirt, glasses, and straightened hair. Georgina is complaining to her about the sexist policies of the Mutare Club, where women are banned from the bar.

'Shona men have a saying,' replies Lynette. '*Mhamba inonaka navamai mudhuze*. It means "Beer tastes better with a woman by your side".'

Lynette was educated at a Catholic mission school, St Patrick's, Nyanyadzi, worked as a doctor's PA and, in 2003, became the opposition Movement for Democratic Change's first woman local councillor. It was Roy Bennett, the MDC's fiery treasurer, who suggested she stand for national office. She comes from a political family – her mother had worked for Ndabaningi Sithole's party, for years the sole opposition voice in parliament, but still, she had reservations about Lynette's candidature, 'in case I lost, and people laughed at me'. But Lynette didn't lose, and she was reelected in the recent elections.

She's had a tough time of it, though. As well as fighting various recounts and court challenges, she's been arrested four times, and beaten up by the police. She's had to send her three kids – the youngest, a girl of eight – away to boarding school, for their own safety. 'They're proud of me becoming an MP,' she says, 'but scared that I will be killed.' The last time she visited her fourteen-year-old son at school, he said it was lovely to see her, but he'd rather she didn't come in her official MDC vehicle, in case he got into trouble.

Things got particularly bad for her two years ago, she says, when Mugabe's feared spying agency, the Central Intelligence Organization, the CIO, raided her house, hunting for her, so she fled for a while to South Africa. She crossed the Limpopo and then climbed through the razor-wire border fence – ripping her clothes and slicing her back; she still has the scars – and then walked five miles, with a guide Roy Bennett had sent to assist them. Three times they had to fight off *magumaguma*, robbers, armed with knives and iron bars, who prey on border-jumpers. 'I had no idea getting across would be so horrible,' she says. Finally, torn and terrified, she met up with Roy at a service station at 2 a.m.

Before Wengezi, we arrive at the roadblock that marks the entrance to the diamond district, the first of five roadblocks we will encounter. Lynette leans across me to talk to the soldier sweating at my window. 'I am visiting my constituency,' she tells him. 'And these ones are my guests.'

This seems to do the trick. As he jots down the vehicle details, I ask him, 'Why don't you guys erect some kind of shelter from the sun?'

He shakes his head. 'Ah, it is a shortage.'

'A shortage of what?'

'A shortage of initiative,' he says, without missing a beat, and waves us through.

As we head south, the land is parched and goat-wrenched, stony and thorn-treed. It's too dry for maize, and sorghum, the ancient grain, is still grown. Many people here are only alive because of emergency feeding by Christian Care, says Lynette, though Mugabe interrupted that during the elections.

'How is the irrigation scheme?' I ask. The nearby village of Nyanyadzi used to have an ambitious project for black farmers, growing back-to-back crops. 'It is no longer functioning,' she says. 'All is diamonds now.'

We start to pass trading stores that service the diamond diggers. Babylon Investments, Luckyfields Enterprises, New Gift Store. But many seem in ruins. 'During the run-off elections shop-owners in Nyanyadzi had vehicles burned, and houses,' says Lynette. 'The Nyanyadzi Training Centre was turned into a ZANU torture base.'

The way Lynette tells it, in 2006, a diamond-miner made his way home to Chiadzwa from the massive alluvial diamond fields of Namibia, known as the Sperrgebiet, 'the Forbidden Territory'. It's an area stretching more than two hundred miles along the Skeleton Coast (so called because it is strewn with the ribs of ships, wrecked in the lethal fog band caused when the cold Atlantic current laps the desert shore) and up to sixty miles inland that is off-limits to all but NamDeb, the Namibia De Beers Diamond Corp. Even carrier pigeons were banned as they've been used to smuggle out diamonds.

This returning worker saw something shining on the ground in Chiadzwa, recognised it as a diamond, and started looking for more. 'Nobody believed that what he had found were really diamonds, there were no buyers and people were just throwing them away,' she recalls. 'But after six months, West Africans and Lebanese and Israelis came to buy them. Initially anyone could come and dig, then the syndicates started. The police would allow digging in return for half of the diamonds found.'

Legally, the diamond rights belonged to African Consolidated Resources (who took them over from De Beers), but in 2006, once the rush began, the police chased them away, and they haven't got back since, despite High Court orders. Mugabe's ministers moved in and were soon making personal fortunes through the digging syndicates. Estimates put the potential haul as high as US \$1.2 billion a year. So it was unsurprising that people swarmed here from all over this paupered country, to try their luck. As many as thirty thousand miners were digging at any one time, working the main hundred-and-seventy-acre diamond fields. Conditions were appalling, with women and children digging too, often for a pittance.

'There were lots of deaths from malaria,' says Lynette. 'No sanitation, no water supply – the diggers would buy water with diamonds!'

ALLUVIAL DIAMONDS, like the ones at Chiadzwa, have been eroded from their original kimberlite pipes and scattered close to the surface by rivers. In Africa, such deposits almost always result in conflict (hence the term 'blood diamonds'), from the diamond fields of Kimberley itself, which helped cause the Anglo-Boer War, to the protracted war in Namibia, before South Africa would relinquish control, to Angola, Liberia, Sierra Leone, and the Congo. Zimbabwe has proved to be no exception.

In October 2008, just after his blood-soaked election, Mugabe decided to end the free-for-all in Chiadzwa and to control the diamond revenue more tightly. He ordered the army in, and they launched Operation Hakudzokwi, 'No Return'. Hundreds of soldiers, some on horseback, descended on the diggers at Chiadzwa, backed by helicopter gunships. Even by Zimbabwe's appalling standards, it was a scene of egregious brutality. They fired tear gas into the shallow diggings and when the miners emerged choking, they gunned them down, or released attack dogs to tear them apart.

In charge of the operation? Air Marshal Perence Shiri, the same man who oversaw the Matabeleland massacres, twenty-five years before, ably assisted now by General Constantine Chiwenga.

In a fit of nostalgia, perhaps, Shiri even shipped in some soldiers from the notorious North Korean-trained Fifth Brigade, to reprise their main skill set: how bravely they can kill civilians. Human Rights Watch confirmed at least two hundred deaths, but the real toll is probably more than twice that number. Most were buried in mass graves in Chiadzwa and in Mutare. Thousands more were injured. Twenty-two thousand people were arrested, not just miners, but dealers and middle-men and smugglers too – anyone who was found with foreign currency or a nice car.

Now the army has taken control of the main Chiadzwa diamond fields, rotating new units through every two months, to keep them happy. They still use civilians to do the actual burrowing, including children, many of whom are used as forced labour – diamond slaves. The soldiers have cordoned off the entry points, and sealed the area to outsiders.

But Lynette knows of a new, subsidiary field, east of Chiadzwa, in a wild corner of her constituency where the army has not penetrated yet. To get to it, we turn down a very rough dirt road toward Mhakwe, past Chikwizi School, and after ten miles or so, we pull over at a kraal. Women are bent over, hoeing in the fields, babies bound to their backs.

Lynette hails them, and they squeal with delight at seeing her. 'This is my area,' she says proudly.

Here we pick up a young man, who introduces himself as Ediclozi. It is only much, much later, when I ask him how it's spelled, that he says, 'It is my nickname. Because my friends say I am clever, they call me after Ediclozi, who is too clever.' I continue to look perplexed, so he spells it out for me: 'Eddie Cross.'

'Oh, of course!' I say, defeated once more by the Shona aversion to Rs. Eddie Cross is an MDC senator, and one of their chief strategists.

EDICLOZI IS EIGHTEEN, and has been mining, off and on, for more than a year now. In that time, he has found sixteen industrial diamonds. But his friend found a big gem-quality stone, what they call here a *maglass*, and got US $2,000 for it. Four years' pay at the average annual income. 'On this side,' he says, 'there are only police, but we bribe them.'

We drive another few miles, past the rock they call Buwere Vasikana, 'The Stone for Girls', where six girls were killed by lightning, and park at the bottom of a steep, conical mountain. Ediclozi points to the summit, where the ground is broken and piled with loose rock, the main diamond diggings. You can see ant-like figures up there. Georgina and Lynette take one look at the ascent, and decline to accompany us, so Ediclozi and I set off alone.

'The digging syndicates are usually three to six men strong, and we must trust each other because we share whatever we find,' explains Ediclozi, as we clamber up in the pulsing heat. He has just finished a session up there, and has rotated out of his syndicate, but others have substituted for him, so the syndicate doesn't lose its digging place.

Once we gain height the view opens out onto a primordial topography of jagged mountains, furrowed with ridges like mastiff brows, thickly vegetated with gurugushi bird bush and mupangara thorn trees, and, in the Nyadokwe River valley, wide-girthed baobabs, silvered in the sun. From across the coulee, baboons bark.

'There are too many animals here,' says Ediclozi. 'Leopard and kudu, mambas and puff adders.'

We climb on, passing exploratory, zigzag trenches, about the depth of a man. These are called *hambakachana* – 'the path you travel finding nothing'.

As we climb we start to hear the *magweja* – the working diamond-diggers. The violent chime of pickaxes and sledge-hammers as they strike rock. And behind that I can hear snatches of song. I squint upward into the sun, but I can't see anyone, nothing but wisps of smoke rising from the summit. When the diggers reach a boulder too big to break, Ediclozi explains, they light fires on it to crack it.

Not long ago, says Ediclozi, there was an attempt to flush the diggers from here too. A convoy of police paramilitaries arrived with guns and tear gas, he says. They started up the mountain, just as we are now. At that time, he estimates, there were four to five hundred diggers working up here. When the alarm call went up that the police were on their way up, the diggers, like defenders of a medieval castle, came to their ramparts and began hurling rocks down. The police fired back but the topography was against them.

The diggers levered boulders that bounced lethally down the hill, and set off landslides. They taunted the policemen, shouting down, '*Muri imbwa dzaMugabe*' [You're just Mugabe's dogs], '*voetsak*' [fuck off].

The policemen took fright, 'And they ran away,' says Ediclozi.

ON THE RIDGE across from us, we now see the first syndicates, standing on the rim of their workings, silhouetted against the sun. They shout over to us. 'They think you are a *mabhaya*,' a diamond-buyer, says Ediclozi. Word goes from group to group up the mountain. Finally we reach the summit – which opens out into two extensive digs. As we arrive, men run over.

'You wanna buy diamond, mister?' they call out. They are rough, wild-looking. Their hands horned with carapaces of callus from swinging their smooth-shafted sledgehammers and picks. Many are dreadlocked, shirtless, reeking of ganja.

Soon we are surrounded. Ediclozi shadows his eyes with his hand against the sun, scanning the scree mounds for his syndicate. 'My friends are not here,' he says quietly. 'These are new ones, *makorokoza* – gold-panners from Mberengwa. They are dangerous, these ones.'

One of the men, his already considerable height augmented by a Medusa's nest of fat dreads, comes to the front. He is the boss of one of the syndicates, he says, and his name is Dread. He snaps his fingers and calls Jealous, who is improbably wearing a houndstooth jacket and little else. From somewhere inside the shiny, sweat-infused lining, Jealous produces a tiny package, which he slowly unwraps. It's a billion Zimbabwe dollar note. He indicates that I should open my hand, and from the crumpled note, he drops into my palm a translucent stone. Jagged and irregular, it reflects the sharp Manica sun. The diggers' ranks draw closer.

'This is *maglass*, three, maybe four carat,' says Dread, 'the biggest stone we find here. The best opportunity you ever get – better even than Kimberley.' He smiles brilliantly, though his eyes remain hard.

I admire the stone. It seems only polite to do so.

'How much do you think it is worth?' asks Dread.

'Well . . .' I glance over at Ediclozi, who is looking nervously at his feet. I can't decide which is more dangerous, to talk money, only to have to break it to them later that I don't actually have the money on me. Or to tell them up front that I don't have cash, that I'm not here to buy.

'I'm, I'm on a recce, just looking. I don't have money. I'm not buying today,' I say.

'How much you think this one, it is worth?' insists Dread, his eyes narrowing. It's as though I haven't spoken. I've heard the going rate is about $2,000 a carat, but this doesn't look like three carats to me – two, maybe.

'Well, I think it's probably worth about US $2,000,' I say.

There is wild jeering and shrill whistles of derision at my estimate, and the diggers' ranks contract again.

'Maybe $3,000?' I venture, uncertainly.

Dread looms. 'A big one like this is worth at least 6,000 USAhs,' he says. His tone is openly menacing now. 'There are many of us and we have been digging a long time, and it is dangerous here. The army and the police, they shoot us and rob us.'

'I understand. Then maybe it is worth $6,000, as you say.' I reach out to hand the diamond back to Jealous, but he shrinks from me, and won't take it. Murmurs of confusion circulate through the crowd, and quickly congeal into outright hostility.

'It is your diamond now, so you give us the money. $6,000. As you agreed,' Dread declares, with an air of finality.

'Look, I don't have any money on me,' I say, and pat my empty pockets. 'I'm not here to buy.' I look over at Ediclozi again, for a cue. He looks ashen, and suddenly much younger than his eighteen years. The diggers are all shouting now. They surround Ediclozi, jostling him. I sense they are about to beat him. I raise my voice.

'Look, I'm really not a *mabhaya*. I have come to see how you are doing here. I heard about the problems you had here, with the police and army, so I came with the MDC MP, Lynette Kore-Karenyi, to see how things are here.'

They look thunderstruck. Not a *mabhaya*? Ediclozi and I are talking at the same time, placating, explaining that I mean no harm. But I can hear some of the men now suggesting that it is risky to let me leave this place alive. That I will tell others, cause trouble for them, inform on them to the police, not their local complicit ones, but the bosses in Harare. That maybe I even work for the police, or the CIO. They have used whites before.

I now realise how stupid I've been. Of course these men don't want any publicity; they don't want outsiders nosing around. They're outlaws, pirates, living this rough, violent life. Somehow, through a series of small, stupid decisions, I've ended up high on this mountain among these desperadoes. Ediclozi's mates were supposed to be here; I was coming with an insider, backed by the local MP. But up here, on top of this mountain, these men are now discussing whether to kill me.

If they kill me, will it draw more attention than if they let me go? That is now their debate. There are two schools of thought. Syndicates led by Dread, Abisha, and Jealous seem to favour killing me, because I will only bring them trouble. Obvious and Madhuku, on the other hand, think that killing a white man might bring even more police attention. No one is physically holding me, but diggers have moved behind me now, cutting off the path back. All digging has now stopped, and the men lean on their shovels and picks, lobbing over debating points. Several start rolling joints. Baboons bark again in the distance, and kestrels wheel on the thermals, and I think of my sons. They will be just getting up in New York. Putting on their school uniforms, their blue-and-yellow-striped ties. Hugo drowsily trying to slick back his bed-head, Thomas full of morning energy ready to wrestle the day to the mat. I think of them waiting for the M5 bus on Riverside Drive, playing tag around the triangular flower bed, doing their time trials to the Joan of Arc statue and back. What was I thinking, coming up here?

They are now discussing whether to hold Ediclozi hostage while I go down to get money, but quickly decide I'll just do a runner, and won't bother to return to bail him out, or worse, I'll return with the police or army. As Ediclozi might, if they did it the other way around, and held me hostage. It's clear that part of the problem is that they can't understand why I've come all the way up here, if not to buy diamonds? I don't want to tell them I'm a writer, or even some sort of human-rights monitor – and risk boosting the murder school of thought among these publicity-averse men. I try reminding them that Lynette is at the bottom of the mountain, waiting for me. But that has no impact on their calculations at all.

Then I wonder if Bennett's writ can possibly stretch this far, into this wild world way off the grid. 'I have been visiting Roy Bennett . . .' I start, and they all pipe down at the mention of his name.

'Pachedu [his nickname – which means 'one-of-us'], how is Pachedu?' call several men.

'I have been visiting him,' I continue, 'in prison.'

In prison? They are aghast. They have no access to current affairs up here, relying on fresh diggers for second-hand news. They have no idea that Roy's been arrested. I launch into a detailed description of how he was picked up, and why. A blow-by-blow account of his court case, his conditions in Mutare jail, and speculation about what may happen next. They are rapt. I feel like an African Scheherazade, trading stories for my life.

They bombard me with questions about Roy's situation, and our relationship begins to change. Some of them sit down on the boulders. I sit too, and start inventing details, embellishing. Pachedu, I tell them, has actually tasked me to come up here to see how they are getting on. And this seems to make sense to them.

Finally, Ediclozi catches my eye and gestures that maybe we should try to leave. I look at my watch. 'Well, we need to go now. I have to get back to Mutare in time for prison visiting hours, so I can take food to Pachedu.'

I unfurl my hand from around the diamond, and offer it back to Dread. There is blood on my palm from gripping the jagged stone so tight. This time he accepts it.

'It's a lovely diamond,' I say. 'Maybe next time.'

'Okay, next time,' he agrees, though we both know there will be no next time. They make no move to stop us from leaving. Many raise their hands in farewell, asking me to take their greetings to Roy. I follow Ediclozi over the top of the rocky parapet into the steep scree field, not bothering with the path this time, just scrambling down in a shower of loose gravel as fast as we can.

Arifin

RUTH PADEL (born London, 1946) is a poet, novelist and travel writer. Her poetry collections include **Darwin – A Life in Poems**, a verse biography of her great-great-grandfather Charles Darwin, which was shortlisted for the 2009 Costa Prize. Her novel **Where the Serpent Lives** (2010) is set in the forests of India, where part of her travel book, **Tigers in Red Weather**, an account of tiger conservation in Asia, also takes place. She is a Fellow of the Zoological Society of London and of the Royal Society of Literature, and is currently Resident Writer at University College London. **www.ruthpadel.com**

Arifin

RUTH PADEL

The rain is lashing glass. I'm looking at it from the porch of a guest house on the outskirts of Pagalaram. Around the open door is a vine of vermilion blossom. The flowers, wide as the Amaryllis lilies that open for my mother every Christmas, nod frantically and their hairy stamens jounce in racing water. Far away over ricefields I can see a mountain, perfectly triangular but blurred. It is like looking at Hokusai's Mount Fuji through molten tissue paper.

I am the only guest here. It is August, I'm on Sumatra to look for tigers, and have been grinding over hole-studded roads on South Sumatra in a car all day, except when the generator fell out of the engine and we waited several hours for another. With Lilik, my translator and guide. I'm trying to plan tomorrow.

Lilik works for a Padang travel company who said he knew all Sumatra perfectly. He grew up behind the walls of a police compound. His father was a Javanese policeman. In the old days, Sumatra was the Island of Gold. Today it's oil; Sumatra is the mainstay of the Indonesian economy and is run from Java. All day, the only villages Lilik approved of have been the ones with tidy white edging stones and fences. He says this means they belong to people from Java.

We have an itinerary and in a couple of days will set off to Mount Kerinci – where human beings and tigers live really close to each other in dense forest – and stay with a Tiger Team which protects humans from tigers and tigers from humans. But I have arranged my first few days on the island around symbolism. My hope, in every tiger range country, is not only to see different types of conservation project and tiger population but also to learn about each country's tiger history and symbolism – what tigers mean to human beings.

Most people in tiger range countries live in cities and don't know what it is like to live with tigers, but even in areas where tigers no longer live they still are thought and talked about. Yesterday I asked a university lecturer in Padang the word for tiger in bahasa Indonesia. '*Harimau*,' she said, 'but in villages they say "Grandmother" instead. They say "Shhh, Granny's near," so the tiger won't hear and be angry. At least, that's what people say they say. I don't really know. I've never been to the villages.'

I want to get closer than this. The Malay world specialises in tiger magic. I have photocopied a chapter from a book about the history of tigers and people here. The Dutch anthropologist who wrote it says there used to be tiger-charmers and were-tigers (like were-wolves) on Mount Dempo; and also a unique carving from the mysterious, megalith-prone culture of first-century AD Sumatra, of two tigers mating. Between the paws of the lower tiger, presumably the tigress, is what looks like a human head.

THIS STATUE STANDS, or it stood seventy years ago, in a village called Besemah on a volcano called Mount Dempo.

Lilik has never heard of a tiger megalith and scouring upland villages for a statue is not his idea of fun. The foreigners he shows round Sumatra want scuba diving and nightlife. But among my photocopied pages is a photo of it taken by a Dutch aviator in 1932. Lilik looks at it suspiciously. 'Your curiosity is very specific.'

'Are we near Mount Dempo?' We should be, we have taken long enough to get here.

'We go, tomorrow.' He has no real idea of where Dempo starts, and has never heard of Besemah. He has no detailed map. We shall just have to start somewhere and ask. He agrees to pick me up at seven and goes off to stay with Javanese friends in Pagalaram. I look at drumming rain and writhing blossom.

Suddenly a willowy boy of about twenty is beside me. He is wearing a T-shirt the same scarlet as the flowers and I feel he has been called out of them. He has streaky shiny hair over a wide forehead, cheeks pitted like corroded stone, bright black eyes and a very smooth top lip with no central groove.

The tiger megalith on Mount Dempo

'Mount Dempo?' I ask. He smiles and waves at the mountain. I show him the photocopied photo. 'Tiger megalith? Do you know it? Tigers? *Harimau*?'

He nods and disappears. Maybe he didn't understand. It's been a long day, with a lot of not understanding in it.

I go indoors and watch a woman cooking rice. Suddenly the boy is back with a blurry pamphlet. In it is the same photo, a larger reproduction.

'You *know* it? You know where it is?'

He nods again, points to himself and Mount Dempo, then puts his hand down as if patting a child on the head. I think he is telling me he grew up on Mount Dempo.

'Tigers?' I say hopefully. 'Real *harimau*? Or people' – I try and mime it and he smiles – 'who turn into *harimau*?'

He has a radiant and confident smile. I suddenly feel hopeful.

'Might you come with us to Dempo tomorrow?'

He nods again. Before seven next morning he is back, in a faded blue T-shirt and floppy hat. The rain has gone.

'Arifin,' he says. We shake hands. Lilik, in a pale apricot shirt with perfectly ironed creases, is not sure he wants Arifin on board but sees I am delighted and agrees to translate.

ARIFIN SAYS HE STUDIES in Benkulu. But he is free, for this one day, to show us Dempo. I say I am interested in finding out about tigers here, and how people feel about them.

There is silence between us as the car bumps along. I stare into early morning mist. The paddy fields are green glass edged with a dim frieze of palm trees.

Besemah turns out to be a district, not a village. Arifin gives instructions to the driver.

'My family,' he says, and Lilik translates as he goes, 'lives in many places on Mount Dempo. My little brother is twelve. He studies in an Islamic school in a high village. Higher up, is the village of the megalith. The village of my father, higher still. My older brother lives lower down on the other side.'

Arifin's track is climbing the slope of the volcano. Green bamboo whiskers trail over little streams. This used to be thick forest: it is now agricultural land and the white flowers of the coffee smell like linden. As we climb, we see misty green gorges and higher peaks beyond, striped with burnt lines where even this secondary forest has been stripped. Far away are even taller mountains, so soft in this early morning light you feel they would arch their backs and purr if you stroked them, and more mountains behind, in a never-ending vista. But not all of them are green. Clearing forest is an industry in Sumatra. For palm oil, for rice, or just on spec. I have seen burning everywhere. Coming in to Padang airfield two days ago I counted twenty-one plumes of smoke from burning forest. The pilot said he often couldn't land for the smoke.

In the upland villages, struggling with poverty, green coffee berries are laid out to dry in the sun and red water liles dot the little ponds. Tiny exquisite goats, white, soft lemon or fawn with trim black socks, play on the woodpiles. Beautiful stippled chickens, white and apricot with long slender bodies, peck around the rutted track. Every shack has a cage hanging from its eave where a songbird perches in sunlight. No shade, I notice sadly. Birdcatching is one of the biggest threats to biodiversity in Indonesia. Everyone wants a bird to sing to them. Many shacks have an empty cage whose dead occupant has not yet been replaced.

'Birdsong makes you happy, more spiritual,' says Lilik when he sees me looking.

As we go higher I realise Dempo is not like Fuji; the symmetry was an illusion. We are climbing a huge ring of mountains curved round a plain, a giant ancient crater from which this active volcano's two current peaks – Dempo itself, about 3,000 metres, and Merapi a hundred metres higher – have emerged like minor warts. There is a lake somewhere, too. But more importantly, I think, somewhere in this crater must be the epicentre of Sumatra's ancient tiger magic.

Some villages have plain names like Big Ditch. Others have grand names like Glory. The megalith village turns out to be called Rimja Sujud – 'Jungle Reverence'. We step out and skirt the coffee berries spread out gleaming green, yellow and brown on orange earth. We walk to the top of the village to meet the head man who is wearing a gold-crusted *blangkon*. However poor you are it is important on Sumatra not to show it. No one is surprised we want to see their megalith. Sixty-six families live here and when the head man escorts us to the tigers we are followed by representatives of them all.

At the far edge of the village is a field edged with banana trees, protected by a feathery fence of dried palm fronds. The statue stands beside the fence, blotched with rings of ochre lichen. The tigers' faces are almost gargoyles, their eyes eroded into pools of shadow. Both are rearing, the tigress to get a good hold on her victim and the tiger to get a good hold on her. Together they are about as long as a small tiger, about seven foot. In 1932, the statue's pedestal was completely sunk in the earth. Now it is clear and we can see the human head is actually a whole baby. Under the tigress's tummy are more human feet.

The head man speaks, gesturing to the tigers.

'The Japanese were here in the War,' translates Lilik. 'They tried to take the megalith away. They cleared away the earth. But it was too heavy to carry. Also too magic. They left it here.'

Another man points to the severed feet and laughs.

'He says this is the result of adultery. Tigers make us keep the law. These tigers have eaten all the mother except her feet. Now they will eat the baby.'

'What about the father?'

All the men laugh. There are no women with us.

'The tiger punishes only woman.'

The head man speaks again.'When this man was boy,' translates Lilik in his precise way, 'the neighbours' village was attacked by a man-eater tiger. But it only ate people who committed adultery. Everyone became very faithful and the tiger went away.'

Arifin smiles and says something to me. I feel he understands what I want to learn. 'He says,' translates Lilik, 'tiger is preserver of the law. These tigers protect Rimja Sujud.'

THERE IS NO REAL JUNGLE near here now, which is why living tigers have disappeared. But reverence for them hangs on. In India and Russia I have met the idea that the tiger is the guardian of the forest. Here, it seems the tiger is protector of the people, too.

I have no idea that in two weeks' time, on Mount Kerinci, I will discover that tigers are very much a living archetype, that the Tiger Team uses tiger magic and tiger reverence to deal with problems between real tigers and people. I will discover the tiger on Sumatra is terrible but, like the Greek Furies, also the enforcer of human law. I will walk on a higher peak than Dempo, which still has its pristine rainforest. There I will be beholden to an invisible preserver of the law. With two members of the Kerinci Tiger Team, I will find tiger footprints laid freshly over mine. A tigress will stand very close to us, unseen, listening, watching, checking us out, and then go by. She will preserve *adat*, forest safety, by keeping herself safe – and also us.

But now I just get back in Lilik's car. We drive up a deeply pitted slushy track. In an hour we pass a village abandoned in the 1970s because of tiger attacks. Was this the adultery village, I wonder. Arifin doesn't know. The car sticks in a rut and we get out. There is dense vegetation either side, long grass, enormous overgrown bushes. Arifin and the driver start putting stones under wheels and I walk on up the track. Round a bend I hear a crashing sound. Something is rushing up to cross the track. Out of the undergrowth thrusts a grey beaky face, a dinosaur, a crocodile – no, an enormous monitor lizard with chest and front legs like a Sumo wrestler.

It stands completely still, staring at me with mad yellow eyes, then turns round and waggles away into the bushes.

I walk down towards the car.

'Look out!' shouts Lilik. Between me and them a thin line of green is moving across the track. I approach cautiously and just have time to see the snake's face before the head disappears in long grass. The upper lip has a pale line as if it has been drinking milk. From hours spent in Benkulu traffic jams studying *Snakes of South East Asia* I think this must be a white-lipped pit viper. It disappears into the long grass, all but the pink tail-tip which lies still, disguised as a blade of dead grass.

We go on up. After hours on the volcano's shoulder we come to open ground and a village on a cliff above a river. Like Rimja Sujud, this village is surrounded by a fence. We go in by a gate beside a large banana tree. Delicate white sheep, splashed and stippled with chocolate, are grazing in the compound, a lure for any predator. The houses are built on sturdy legs with wood piled underneath. I think of pit vipers and monitor lizards as well as tigers. Those woodpiles look very practical.

Arifin's father is a handsome man in a shiny satin shirt and black hat. With him are two men in yellow shirts: a man with a twisted foot and this man's son Rahan. Rahan has a neat moustache and says he survived a tiger's attack when he was clearing land to make the village.

'The jungle was opened twenty years ago,' says Arifin.

Opening the jungle means chopping it down. There are fields all round this village now.

'I was over there early in the morning, under that tree,' says Rahan, pointing to the gate we came in by. 'I was bending over to cut trees. The tiger came behind, put its paws around me and held my chest.'

He raises his T-shirt and shows rows of neat red dots like the line made by a pulled-out thread. 'It clawed my chest and bit my head. I fought with my machete. Then other people came and chased it away.'

'He was two months in hospital,' says Arifin. Rahan takes my hand and rubs my fingers over ridged scars from the tiger's teeth, under his hair.

Upstairs, in the house, I meet Arifin's mother and sisters. They are beautiful and have the same bright eyes, the same wide smile and upper lip. We drink tea and laugh, we talk of families, villages, tigers. Then we say goodbye and descend to a village lower on Dempo, a much richer village where Arifin's older brother lives.

ARIFIN'S OLDER BROTHER has done well. These houses are stone, not wood, and the front room is very pink. Pink carpet, pink lace curtains, pink plush sofas and an empty aquarium with a red velvet crocodile on top. Also a large TV, playing with the sound off. We sit on a sofa under a mobile of luminescent fish. The front door stays open to the street and small goats put their heads in followed by a very old man with a stubbly chin and a plump young man.

The brother's mother-in-law is tiny and wizened, with very snowy hair. Wearing a stripy T-shirt and long orange-and-black satin skirt, she settles on the floor like a cat.

'Her sister was killed by a tiger when she was ten,' says Arifin. 'They were working in the rice field. She remembers flesh spread all around.'

'Are there tigers here now?'

'Many in the hills,' says the young man. 'Many people shoot them.'

'What about people who turn into tigers?'

Lilik translates this very distantly, I suspect, but the young man smiles.

'I know one *masu marai* married to a teacher. He eats like an animal and his eyes stare, like a tiger. He turns into a tiger when he is stressed.'

'*Masu marai?*' I ask Arifin when we leave.

'Men who turn into tigers,' he says. 'They walk with their head down. They have the wisdom of tigers. They have normal children. Food changes them into tigers.'

'But you don't have real tigers in this part of Dempo now. There is no proper jungle.'

'No, but in the villages we have many laws, like you must not wash your saucepans in a running stream. And with all of them we say, if this law is broken, the tiger will be angry. *Harimau marah.*'

We walk between the stone houses on a steep lane to where we left the car.

'There are also tiger-callers,' says Arifin softly.

'What do they do?'

'They are *dukun*.' Lilik, walking between the two of us, looks as if he wishes himself a million miles away. 'A *dukun* uses incense, *kemanyan*, to open the door to the spirits. There is a door you can open. They summon a *harimau roh* – soul tiger – to be your guardian. It will come to your assistance when you call. Sometimes tiger-callers go into a trance. They growl, they are entered by the spirit tiger.'

Lilik reaches the car with relief and opens the door.

'Also,' says Arfin before he gets in, 'many villages have a *pawang harimau*, a tiger shaman, who calls a real tiger, too. But not so often now.'

'How do you know so much about them, Arifin?'

He smiles his bright smile, his mother's smile. We get in the car and return to Pagalaram in silence. He seems to open up only in the open air. Or maybe he doesn't want to betray any secrets.

Real tigers are gone from these parts, I tell myself, but ideas of magical tigers are hanging on here like empty cicada cases when the life has left.

At the door of the guest house I thank Arifin warmly and press money on him. For his studies, I say. For his brother, in the school up the mountain. Wonderful to meet you. So lucky for me. He smiles, we shake hands and I turn to Lilik to make arrangements. When I turn back, Arifin is gone.

I start packing, ready for zoology now. Real forest, real tigers. Outside it starts to rain. My bedroom looks into the jungly back garden, with flowers like orange serrated swords, twining vines, shiny leaves as big as elephant ears. It is like being pressed up close to a wet version of Rousseau's *Tiger Surprised by Lightning*, vegetation Rousseau dreamed up in Paris from the Jardin des Plantes.

Under the tin roof thrumming with rain I glance again at the pages I photocopied from the Dutch anthropologist.

Several clans on Mount Dempo, he notes, trace their ancestry to tigers. In the 1840s, one village was known to be inhabited entirely by people who turned into tigers at night. It must have been noisy up there, I think. Normal tigers are not that keen on each other's company. But maybe were-tigers handle social relationships a little differently.

There is one footnote I have not read before. In the nineteenth century, says the anthropologist, people believed there were ways of knowing who was a tiger in human form. It was useful for women to realise in advance, otherwise they found out only on their wedding night. People who turn into tigers sometimes carry a spotted knife, that's one clue. But the main way to recognise a were-tiger is that his upper lip has no central groove.

The Nun's Tale

WILLIAM DALRYMPLE (born Edinburgh, 1965) is the author of eight works of history and travel, including **City of Djinns**, **White Mughals**, and **The Last Mughal**. 'The Nun's tale' is adapted from his most recent book, **Nine Lives: In Search of the Sacred in Modern India**. Brought up in Scotland, he has lived mainly in Delhi for the past twenty-five years and is a founder of the Jaipur Literature Festival. He is a regular contributor to The New York Review of Books, The New Yorker and The Guardian. **www.williamdalrymple.uk.com**

The Nun's Tale

WILLIAM DALRYMPLE

Two hills of blackly gleaming granite, smooth as glass, rise from a thickly wooded landscape of banana plantations and jagged palmyra palms. It is dawn. Below lies the ancient pilgrimage town of Sravanabelagola, where the crumbling walls of monasteries and temples cluster around a grid of dusty, red-earth roads. The roads converge on a great rectangular tank. The tank is dotted with the spreading leaves and still-closed buds of floating lotus flowers. Already, despite the early hour, the first pilgrims are gathering.

For more than two thousand years, this Karnatakan town has been sacred to the Jains. It was here, in the third century BC, that the first Emperor of India, Chandragupta Maurya, embraced the Jain religion and died through a self-imposed fast to the death, the Emperor's chosen atonement for the killings he had been responsible for in his life of conquest. Twelve hundred years later, in 981 AD, a Jain general commissioned the largest monolithic statue in India, sixty feet high, on the top of the larger of the two hills, Vindhyagiri.

This was an image of another royal Jain hero, Prince Bahubali. The prince had fought a duel with his brother for control of their father's kingdom. But in the very hour of his victory, Bahubali realised the transience of worldly glory. He renounced his kingdom, and embraced, instead, the path of the ascetic. Retreating to the jungle, he stood in meditation for a year, so that the vines of the forest curled around his legs and tied him to the spot. In this state he conquered what he believed to be the real enemies – his ambitions, pride and desires – and so became, according to the Jains, the first human being to achieve spiritual liberation.

The sun has only just risen above the palm trees yet already the line of pilgrims – from a distance, tiny ant-like creatures against the dawn-glistening fused-mercury of the rockface – are climbing the long line of steps that lead up to the stone prince. For the last thousand years this statue, enclosed in its lattice of stone vines, has been the focus of pilgrimage for the Digambara, or Sky Clad Jains.

Digambara monks are probably the most severe of all India's ascetics. They show their total renunciation of the world by travelling through it completely naked, as light as the air, as they conceive it, and as clear as the Indian sky. Sure enough, among the many ordinary lay people slowly mounting the rock-cut steps, are several completely naked men – Digambara monks on their way to do homage. There are also a number of white-clad Digambara nuns, and it is in a temple just short of the summit that I first lay eyes on Prasannamati Mataji.

I had seen the tiny, slender, bare-foot figure of the nun in her white sari bounding up the steps above me as I began my ascent. She climbed quickly, with a pot of water in one hand, and a peacock fan in the other. As she went, she gently wiped each step with the fan in order to make sure she didn't hurt a single living creature on her ascent of the hill: one of the set rules of pilgrimage for a Jain ascetic.

It was only when I got to the temple, just below the summit, that I caught up with her – and saw that Mataji was a surprisingly young and striking woman. She had large, wide-apart eyes, olive skin, and an air of self-contained confidence that expressed itself in an ease with the way she held her body. But there was also something sad and wistful about her expression as she went about her devotions; and this, combined with her unexpected youth and beauty, left one wanting to know more.

Mataji was busy with her prayers when I first entered the temple. After the glimmering half-light outside, the interior was almost completely black. Within, at first almost invisible, were three smooth black marble images of the Jain *Tirthankaras,* or Liberators. Each was sculpted sitting Buddha-like with shaved head and elongated earlobes, locked in the deepest meditation. *Tirthankara* means literally 'Fordmaker', and the Jains believe these figures have shown the way to Nirvana, making a ford through the rivers of suffering, and across the wild oceans of existence and rebirth, so as to create a crossing place between the illusory physical world and final liberation.

To each of these figures in turn, Mataji bowed. According to Jain belief, pilgrims may express their devotion to the *Tirthankaras,* but can expect no rewards for such prayers: the Fordmakers have liberated themselves from the world of men, and so are not present in the statutes, in the way that, say, Hindus believe their deities are incarnate in temple images. The pilgrim can simply learn from their example and use them as a focus for meditation. At its purest, Jainism is almost an atheistic religion, and the images of the *Tirthankaras* represent less a divine presence than a profound divine absence.

From the temple, Mataji headed up the hill to wash the feet of Bahubali. There she silently mouthed her morning prayers at the feet of the statue, her rosary circling in her hand. Then as quickly as she had leapt up the steps, she headed down them again, peacock fan flicking and sweeping each step before her.

THE FOLLOWING DAY I applied for a formal audience with Mataji at the monastery guest house; and the day after that I began to learn what had brought about her air of melancholy.

'We believe that all attachments bring suffering,' she explained, after we had been talking some time. 'This is why we are supposed to give them up. This was why I left my family, and why I gave away my wealth. For many years, I fasted or ate only once a day and like other nuns I often experienced hunger and thirst. I wandered the roads of India barefoot. Every day I suffered the pain of thorns and blisters. All this was part of my effort to shed my last attachments. But I still had one attachment – though of course I didn't think of it in that way.'

'What was that?'

'My friend, Prayogamati,' she replied. 'For twenty years we were inseparable companions, sharing everything. For our safety, we Jain nuns are meant to travel together. It never occurred to me that I was breaking any of our rules. But because of my friendship with her, I formed not just an attachment, but a strong attachment – and that left an opening for suffering. But I only realised this after she died.'

There was a pause, and I had to encourage Mataji to continue: 'In this stage of life we need company,' she said. 'You know: a companion with whom we can share ideas and feelings. After Prayogamati left her body, I felt this terrible loneliness. I feel it to this day. But her time was fixed. When she fell ill with TB, her pain was so great she decided to take *sallekhana*. Even though she was only thirty-six.'

'*Sallekhana*?'

'It's the ritual fast to the death. We Jains regard it as the culmination of our life as ascetics. It is what we all aim for, and work towards as the best route to Nirvana.'

'You are saying she committed suicide?'

'No, no: *sallekhana* is not suicide,' she said emphatically. 'It is quite different. Suicide is a great sin, the result of despair. But *sallekhana* is a triumph over death, an expression of hope.'

'I don't understand,' I said. 'If you starve yourself to death, then surely you are committing suicide?'

'Not at all. We believe that death is not the end, and that life and death are complimentary. So when you embrace *sallekhana* you are embracing a whole new life – it's no more than going through from one room to another.'

'But you are still choosing to end your life.'

'With suicide, death is full of pain and suffering. But *sallekhana* is a beautiful thing. You have God's name on your lips, and if you do it slowly in the prescribed way, there is no pain. At all stages you are guided by an experienced *guruji*. Everything is planned long in advance – when, and how, you give up your food. First you fast one day a week, then you eat only on alternate days. One by one, you give up different types of foodstuffs. Finally you take only water, and then you have that only on alternate days. Eventually, when you are ready, you give up on that, too. Really – it can be so beautiful: the ultimate rejection of all desires, the sacrificing of everything.'

She smiled: 'You have to understand: we feel excited at a new life, full of possibilities.'

'But you could hardly have felt excited when your friend left you like this.'

'No,' she said, her face falling. 'It is hard for those who are left.' She stopped. 'After Prayogamati died, I could not bear it. I wept, even though we are not supposed to. Any sort of emotion is a hindrance to the attainment of Enlightenment. We are meant to cultivate indifference – but still I remember her.' Her voice faltered: 'The attachment is there even now,' she said. 'I can't help it. We lived together for twenty years. How can I forget?'

JAINISM IS ONE of the most ancient living religions of the world, similar to Buddhism in many respects, and emerging from the same classical Indian world of the Ganges basin in the early centuries BC – but the faith of the Jains is slightly more ancient, and much more demanding than Buddhist practice.

Buddhist ascetics shave their heads; Jains pluck their hair out by the roots. Buddhist monks beg for food; Jains have to have their food given to them without asking. All they can do is to go out on *gowkari* – the word used to describe the grazing of a cow – and signal their hunger by curving their right arms over their shoulder. If no food comes before the onset of the night, they go to bed hungry. They are forbidden to handle money. Unlike Buddhism, the Jain religion never spread beyond India, and while once a popular and powerful faith across the subcontinent, today there are only four million Jains left. Outside India, the religion barely exists, and in contrast to Buddhism, it is almost unknown in the West.

The word Jain derives from Jina, meaning spiritual conqueror. The Jinas or *Tirthankaras* – Fordmakers – were a series of twenty-four human teachers who each discovered how to escape the eternal cycle of death and rebirth. Through their heroic austerities they gained omniscient knowledge which revealed to them the reality of the universe, in every dimension. The most recent of those, according to the Jains, was the historical figure of Mahavira – the Great Hero – a prince of Magadha, in modern

Bihar, who during the sixth century BC renounced the world at the age of thirty to become a wandering thinker and ascetic.

Mahavira elaborated to his followers a complex cosmological system that the Jains still expound 2,400 years later. Like other Indian faiths, they believe in an immortal soul and that the sum of one's actions determines the nature of one's future rebirth. However the Jains reject the Hindu idea that the world was created by omnipotent gods, and they mock the pretensions of the Brahmin priests, who believe that ritual purity and temple sacrifices can bring salvation. As a Jain monk explains to a group of Brahmins in one of the Jain scriptures, the most important sacrifice for Jains is one's own body: 'Austerity is my sacrifical fire,' says the monk, 'and my life is the place where the fire is kindled. Mental and physical effort are my ladle for the oblation, and my body is the fuel for the fire, my actions my firewood. I offer up an oblation consisting of my restraint, effort and calm.'

It is a strange and in some ways very harsh religion; but that, explained Prasannamati Mataji, is exactly the point.

AT TEN O'CLOCK each day, Mataji eats her one daily meal. On my third day in Sravanabelagola, I went to her monastery to watch what was as much a ritual as a breakfast.

Mataji, wrapped as ever in her unstitched white cotton sari, was sitting cross-legged on a low wooden stool in the middle of an empty ground-floor room. In front, five Jain laywomen with small buckets of rice and dal were eagerly attending her, with extreme deference. Mataji however sat with eyes lowered, not looking at them, accepting without comment whatever she was offered. There was complete silence: no one spoke; any communication took place by hand signals.

For an hour, Mataji ate slowly, and in total silence. The women waited for her to nod, and then with a long spoon put a titbit of food into her cupped hands. Each morsel she then turned over carefully with the thumb of her right hand, looking for a stray hair, or winged insect, which might have fallen into the strictly vegetarian food, so rendering it impure. If she were to find any living thing, explained one of the laywomen, the rules were clear: she must drop the food on the floor, reject the entire meal, and fast until ten the following morning.

After she had finished her vegetables, one of Mataji's attendants poured a small teaspoon full of ghee onto her rice. When a woman offered a further spoonful of dal, the slightest shake of Mataji's head indicated that she was done. Boiled water was then poured, still warm, from a metal cup into Mataji's hands. She drank. After that, she was finished. Mataji rose, and blessed the women with her peacock fan.

When the silent meal was finished, Mataji led me to the reception room of the monastery guest house. There she sat herself down cross-legged on a wicker mat in front of a low writing desk. At a similar desk at the far end of the room, sat a completely naked man – the *maharaj* of the monastery, silently absorbed in his writing. We nodded to each other, and he returned to his work. He was there to chaperone Mataji during our conversation: it would have been forbidden for her to stay alone in a room with a male who was not her guru.

When she had settled herself, Mataji began to tell me the story of how she had renounced the world.

'I WAS BORN IN RAIPUR in 1972,' she recalled. 'In those days my name was Rekha. My family were wealthy merchants. My father had six brothers and we lived as a joint family, together in the same house. For three generations there had been no girls. I was the first one, and they all loved me. I was considered a pretty little girl, and had unusually fair skin and thick black hair, which I grew very long.

'I was pampered by all of them: in fact my uncles would compete to spoil me. Every desire of mine was fulfilled. Nobody ever beat or disciplined me, even in jest. In fact I do not remember even once my parents raising their voice. It was a very happy childhood.

'When I was about thirteen, I was taken to meet a monk called Dayasagar Maharaj – his name means the Lord of the Ocean of Compassion. He was a former cow herd who had taken *diksha* when he was only ten years old, and now had a deep knowledge of the scriptures. He had come to Raipur to do his *chaturmasa* – the Monsoon break when we Jains are forbidden to walk in case we accidently kill the unseen life that inhabits the puddles. So for three months, the Maharaj was in our town, and every day he used to preach for the children. He told us how to live a peaceful life and how to avoid hurting other living creatures: what we should eat, and how we should strain water to avoid drinking creatures too small to be seen. I was very impressed and started thinking.

'Within a few weeks I decided to give up eating after dark, and gave up eating any plant that grows beneath the earth: onions, potatoes, garlic and all root vegetables. Jain monks are forbidden these as you kill the plant when you uproot it – we eat only plants such as rice which can survive the harvest of their grain. When I also gave up milk and jaggery – two things I loved – as a way of controlling my desires, everyone tried to dissuade me, especially my father. They thought I was too young to embark on this path, and everyone wanted me to be their little doll at home. This was not what I wanted.

'When I was fourteen, I announced I wanted to join the Sangha – the Jain community of which my Maharaj was part. Again my family opposed me, saying I was just a young girl. But when I insisted, they agreed to let me go for a couple of weeks in the school holidays, hoping that I would be put off by the harshness of the Sangha life. They also insisted that some of the family servants should accompany me. But the life of the Sangha, and the teachings I heard there, were a revelation. Once I was settled in, I simply refused to come back. The servants did their best to persuade me, but I was completely adamant, and the servants had to go back on their own. There was a lot of pressure and everyone in my family was very angry. But eventually they gave in.

'When you eat a mango, you have to throw away the stone. The same is true of our life as ascetics. No matter how attached you are to your family, whatever efforts you make, ultimately you have to leave them behind. Wordly pleasures and the happiness of family life are equally temporary. If you close the door, you cannot see; open it a little and all becomes clear. For me, the Sangha was itself like a rebirth, a second life. The gurus taught me how to live in a new way: how to sit as a Jain nun, how to stand, how to talk, how to sleep. Everything was taught anew, as if from the beginning.

'At the end of two years with the Sangha, I finally made up my mind that I would take *diksha*. That November they plucked my hair for the first time: it's the first step, a test of your commitment, because if you can't take the pain of having your hair plucked out you are not going to be ready to take the next step. I had very beautiful long thick hair, and as I was still very young my *guru-ji* wanted to cut it with scissors then shave my head with a razor, so as not to inflict such pain. But I insisted, and said there was no going back now. I was a very obstinate girl: whatever I wanted to do, I did. So they agreed to do what I wished.

'The whole ritual took nearly four hours, and was very painful. I tried not to, but I couldn't help crying. I didn't tell my parents about my decision, as I knew they would try and stop me, but somehow they heard, and came rushing. By the time they arrived, the ceremony was almost over. When they saw me with a bald head, and scars and blood all over my scalp where my hair had once been, my mother screamed, and my father burst into tears. They knew then that I would never turn back from this path. After that, whenever the Sangha would arrive at a village, the Maharaj would show me off: look, he would say, this one is so young, yet so determined, doing what even the old would hesitate to do.

'It was about this time that I met my friend, Prayogamati. One day, our Sangha happened to walk into her village, and as her father was a rich merchant, who lived in a large house, they invited us to stay with them. Prayogamati was the same age as me, fifteen, a beautiful, fragile girl, and she came down every day to our room to talk to us. We quickly became very close, talking late into the night. She was fascinated by my life in the Sangha, and I had never met anyone who seemed to understand me the way she did, someone who shared all my beliefs and ideals. She was about to be engaged to the son of a rich diamond merchant, and the match had been arranged for her, but she was more interested in taking *diksha*. She also knew that her family would not allow her to do this.

'After a week, we left that village, setting off before dawn. That evening, Prayogamati borrowed some money from her mother, saying she wanted to go to a circus. Instead, she took two outfits from her room, and jumped on a bus. Late that night she found us, and asked the Maharaj to accept her. Her family realised what had happened, and begged her to return, but she refused, and our *guru-ji* said it was up to her to decide. From that point we were together for twenty years. We took *diksha* together, and travelled together, and ate together, and spent our monsoon *chaturmasa* together. Soon we became very close.

'Except for the *chaturmasa*, it is forbidden for us to stay long in one place, in case we become attached to it. Some nights we would stay in the house of a rich man, sometimes in a cave, sometimes the jungle. People think of our life as harsh, and of course it is. But going into the unknown without a rupee in our pockets means that differences between rich and poor, educated and illiterate, all vanish, and a common humanity emerges. This wandering life, with no material possessions, unlocks our souls. There is a wonderful sense of lightness, living each day as it comes. No weight, no burden. Journey and destination became one, thought and action become one, until we are moving like a river into detachment.'

'WE LIVED IN THIS MANNER for four years before the time came for Prayogamati and I to take *diksha*. The other *matajis* dressed up my friend and me as brides. We wore identical clothes and jewellery. We even looked alike, so often people confused us. We were taken together in a chariot around thirteen villages near our family *haveli* in Udaipur district. Before us went drummers and trumpeters and men clashing cymbals, and as we passed, we would throw rice and money to the crowds.

'The final day of *diksha* twenty thousand people gathered. We rose very early and walked to the stage where the ceremony was to be held. We said prayers in praise of the *Tirthankaras*, and then we formally asked permission from the Maharaj to take *diksha*. He gave his assent.

'Then came the time for saying farewell to our families. We both tied *rakis* [threads] for the last time on the wrists of our brothers, saying goodbye to them. Then we said goodbye to our parents – we embraced, and wished each other farewell. After this, they were no longer our relatives – to us they were to be just like any other member of society.

'After the farewell, we were led off for the hair plucking ceremony. This time we had to do it ourselves, which was much harder. After it was finished we were given a holy bath in a *shamiana* tent. When we both came out, we were given robes of white cloth. Then we were led back onto the stage, and told our new names. I was no longer Rekha but Prasannamati Mataji. My friend became Prayogamati. Then we were both lectured by our *guru-ji*. He told us clearly what was expected of us: never again to use a vehicle, to take food only once a day, to abstain from emotion, never to hurt any living creature. He told us we must not react to attacks, must not beg, must not cry, must not complain, must not demand, must not feel superiority. And he told us all the different kinds of difficulties we should be prepared to bare: hunger, thirst, cold, heat, mosquitoes. He warned us that none of this was easy.

'Then he gave us our water pot and peacock fan, and we were led off the stage for the last time. That night, we spent on the roof of the house where we were staying. The following morning, we got up before dawn and slipped away. We looked for the signs that led towards Gujarat, and began to walk.'

'EVERYONE HAD WARNED us about the difficulty of this life,' continued Mataji. 'But in reality, we had left everything willingly, so did not miss the world we had left behind. It is the same as when a girl gets married and she has to give up her parents' home: if she does it in exchange for something she really wants, it is not a sad time. Certainly, for both Prayogamati and me it was a very happy period in our lives – perhaps the most happy. Every day we would walk, and discover somewhere new.

'Walking is very important to us Jains. The Buddha was enlightened while sitting under a tree, but our great *Tirthankara*, Mahavira, was enlightened while walking. Living from day to day, much of what I have learnt as a Jain has come from wandering. Sometimes, even my dreams are of wandering.

'It was while walking that Prayogamati began to realise that her health was beginning to fail. It was because of her difficulty in keeping up with me that we first noticed that there was something wrong with her joints. She began to have difficulty in walking, and even more so in sitting or squatting.

'For ten years her condition got worse: by the end, it pained her to move at all. Then one afternoon she was studying in a monastery in Karnataka when she began coughing, and begun to make this retching noise. When she took her hand away from her mouth she found it was covered in blood. After that, there was nothing more for a week, but then she began coughing up blood regularly. Sometimes, it was a small amount – just enough to make her mouth red – at other times she would cough up enough to fill a small teacup.

'I guessed immediately that it was TB, and I took special permission from our *guru-ji* to let her see a doctor. Western medicine is forbidden to us, as so much of it is made using dead animals. But given the seriousness of the situation, our *guru-ji* agreed to let a Western doctor look at her, though he insisted that only herbal medicine could be given to her.

'Prayogamati remained very calm, and for a long time she hoped that she might still recover her health. Even when it became clear that this was something quite serious, she remained composed. It was always me that was worried. She kept assuring me that she was feeling better and that it was nothing serious; but in reality you didn't have to be a doctor to see that her health was rapidly deteriorating.

'Her digestive system became affected, the bloody coughing continued, and after a while, she started showing blood when she went for her ablutions too. Eventually I got permission to take her to a hospital where she had a full blood test. They diagnosed her problem as advanced TB of the digestive system. They said that her chances were not good.

'That same day Prayogamati decided to embrace *sallekhana*. She said she would prefer to give up her body rather than have it taken from her. She wanted to die voluntarily, facing it squarely, rather than have death ambush her and take her away by force. She was determined to be the victor, not the victim. I tried to argue with her, but like me, once she took a decision it was impossible to get her to change.

'Despite her pain and her illness, she set out that day to walk a hundred kilometres to see our guru, who was then in Indore. We got there after a terrible week in which Prayogamati suffered very badly: it was winter – late December – and bitterly cold. But she refused to give up, and when she got to Indore she asked permission to begin embracing *sallekhana*. He asked Prayogamati if she was sure, and she said yes. When he learned that she would anyway probably not have very long to live, he gave his assent.

'Throughout 2004, Prayogamati began gradually reducing her food. One by one, she gave up all the vegetables she used to eat. She began eating nothing at all on several days of the week. For eighteen months she ate less and less. Normally *sallekhana* is very peaceful but for Prayogamati, because of her illness, her end was full of pain.

'My job was to feed her, and look after her, and read the prescribed texts. I was also there to talk to her and give her courage and companionship. I stayed with her twenty-four hours a day. Throughout she tolerated everything, and stayed completely calm – such calmness you can hardly imagine! – I always learned from her, but never more than towards the end. Such a person will not be born again.

'By September 2005 she was bedridden, and I remained continually by her side until the beginning of December. By this stage she was taking only pomegranate juice, milk, rice, dal and sugar. Every day she would eat a little less. She had to summon all her strength to perform the observations that have to be followed. At the end, she was running a fever of 105 degrees, and was covered in sweat. In the afternoon she would feel cold; in the evening she would burn. I asked the doctors, what is the reason for this? They did some tests and said – now she has caught malaria as well.

'The next day the fever was still there. Just after one-thirty I went to take my food, when Prayogamati cried loudly. I rushed to look after her – it was clear her condition was not good at all. There was no one around except a boy at the gate, so I sent him off for the doctor. When I came back, I held her hand and she whispered that she wanted to stop all remaining food. Her suffering was too much for her now. She said that for her death was as welcome as life, that there was a time to live and a time to die. Now, she said, the time has come for me to be liberated from this body.

'Our *guru-ji* gathered the community. By early afternoon all the gurus and *matajis* were there guiding her and sitting together around the bed. Others came to touch her feet. Everyone was there to support Prayogamati, to give her courage. Around 4 p.m., the doctor said he thought she was about to die, but she held on until 9 p.m. It was dark by then, and the lamps were all lit around the room. Her breathing had been very difficult that day, but towards the end it became easier. I held her hand, the monks chanted, and her eyes closed. For a while, even I didn't know she had gone. She just slipped away.

'When I realised she had left, I wept bitterly. We are not supposed to do this, and our *guru-ji* frowned at me. But I couldn't help myself. I had followed all the steps correctly until she passed away, but then everything I had bottled up came pouring out. Her body was still there, but she wasn't in it. It was no longer her.

'The next day, the 15th of December, she was cremated. They burned her at 4 p.m. All the devotees in Indore came: over two thousand people. The following morning, at dawn, I got up and headed off. There was no reason to stay.

'It was the first time as a nun that I had ever walked any-where alone.'

THE FOLLOWING DAY, as I went to say goodbye to Mataji, she told me: 'Prayogamati's time was fixed. She passed on. She's no longer here. All things decay and disappear in time.' Then she fell silent. 'Now my friend has gone,' she said eventually, 'it is easier for me to go too.'

'What do you mean?'

'I have seen over forty *sallekhanas,*' she said. 'After Prayogamati's, I realised it was time I should set out to that end.'

'You mean you are thinking of following…?'

'I am on the path already,' said Mataji. 'I have given up milk and curds, salt and sugar, guava and papaya, leafy vegetables and lady's finger. Each month I give up something new. All I want to do now is to visit a few more holy places before I go. '

'But why?' I asked. 'You are not ill like she was. Isn't it a waste? You're only thirty-eight.'

'I told you before,' she said. '*Sallekhana* is the aim of all Jains. It is the last renouncement. First you give up your home, then your possessions. Finally you give up your body.'

'Do you think you will meet her in another life,' I said. 'Is that it?'

'It is uncertain,' said Mataji. 'Our scriptures are full of people who meet old friends and husbands and wives and teachers from previous lives. But no one can control these things.' Again Mataji paused, and looked out of the window. 'Though we both may have many lives ahead of us, in many worlds,' she said, 'who knows whether we will meet again? And if we do meet, in our new bodies, who is to say that we will recognise each other?'

She looked at me sadly as I got up to go, and said simply: 'These things are not in our hands.'

OLIVER BULLOUGH

The Last Man Alive

OLIVER BULLOUGH (born Hereford, 1977) grew up in Wales, and moved to Russia in 1999. After spells in St Petersburg and Bishkek, he became Reuters correspondent for Chechnya and the Caucasus Mountains. **Let Our Fame Be Great** (Penguin 2010), his first book, was based on his experiences as well as travels in a dozen countries to find communities of highlanders. He is currently researching a book on Russia's demographic collapse, and working as Caucasus Editor for the Institute for War and Peace Reporting.

The Last Man Alive

OLIVER BULLOUGH

I was collecting stories of Stalin's atrocities when I met Mukharbek Zabakov, and I had high hopes of him. Most of the Balkars, Chechens and Karachai I had interviewed had been children when their nations were deported. They could remember details – their dogs, their friends, their cousins dying – but these were just flashes of horror, not the whole grinding truth of it. Zabakov, born 1922 in the mountains of Upper Balkaria, was different. He had been twenty-one on 8 March 1944, when Stalin's security troops swept the mountains clean of his people, and he would remember everything. I was looking forward to it, and had a new notebook all ready.

He wore a grey suit and a trilby. Straight-backed, tall but stocky, he showed no effects from the vodka the four of us drank with lunch. I was the youngest by fifty years and Zabakov was almost a decade older again than the two other men who would tell their tales once he was done. That is the rule in Balkar etiquette. The oldest man says his piece without interruption, even if like Zabakov he looks younger and fitter than the men flanking him. The women stayed silent and brought us salad, kebabbed meat and vodka without us having to ask.

When the food was finished, I moved my plate, put the new notebook on the table, took the cap off a blue ballpoint pen, opened the notebook, wrote his name at the top of the page next to his date of birth, and looked up at him. So, I asked, what did he remember of the deportation?

I always began like that, and it was the only prepared question I ever had. I never knew what these old survivors would tell me until they told it to me, so I didn't know where to focus until I knew what they'd say.

He was not, he said, present during the deportation.

What, I asked, forgetting my etiquette.

He was a prisoner of the Germans, he said.

Oh, I replied, in that case.

I turned to one of the other two men. I was there to hear about the deportation, and had no interest in anything else. Their stories would not be so good as his might have been, but would still include new details I had not heard before. I was about to cross out Zabakov's name and write one of theirs at the top of the page, when I realised he was still speaking. It appeared that he had no intention of stopping just because I was not interested in what he had to say.

He had, you see, been conscripted on 5 May 1942; taught how to stand, march, fire and salute and been sent to the Front. In August, he was already on the Don where the Germans were approaching. The Don was wide, and no one had known where the Germans would cross the river and his unit was waiting in the wrong place.

In one night, the Germans built a bridge, and all the tanks crossed, and his unit was pulled back. They marched on foot, and his commander told him to get food for the unit, so he put his gun down. It was 11 August, and he went to the place where food was supposed to arrive, and waited there, but there was no food. He found a place to lie down, and waited, and then he understood that there would be no food. So he was with a different unit that was nearby and they marched away, and the machine gunner refused to go, so the commander shot him and he had to carry the discs for the gun now, and there were gullies in the steppe, deep gullies, and they arrived at a place where in summer livestock are kept, but no one was there and they only had bread to eat.

Planes were flying and they were hiding and they walked and walked. It was hot, August heat, and the unit's commander remembered he was from a different unit so the commander sent some soldiers to take him back to his own unit, but when he got there, there was no one there. Everyone had retreated. So he walked further, and saw some wounded people walking, then he saw a column of tanks. And he went to ask the tanks where he was, but there was an explosion and he was injured, and the tanks were German, and he was captured, and he was asked if it was far to Stalingrad, then he was sent to the rear. That, he said, is how he became a prisoner of the Germans.

I have spoken to many men who have fought in wars, and have learned that a single experience can be so traumatic that it overshadows everything else in their lives. It can be annoying if you are trying to find out about something else, since the men will only answer your questions once they have described their particular event. I recognised that this was such an experience, and so I decided to just sit it out and wait for him to stop talking. He surely couldn't last too long and once he was finished I could turn to the other two men.

In the mean time, I kept my pen in my hand, but I stopped writing his story word for word. I just jotted down notes, so he would think I was interested.

Mukharbek Zabakov, Kazakhstan, 2008

The notebook: in prison in Shaktinsk... then different camp... people in just underwear... story about a man called Idris who stole a coat... in camp in Gorlovka... Germans separated out the Communists, the officers, the Jews.... No water... hot, thirsty ... they ran when the Germans brought water, and fought, fought their comrades... the Germans laughed.

Sent to Pskov to a camp called Pskhi... got ill... then to Estonia... to Tartu... Latvia... two camps near Riga... selected to work for a local farmer... new camp by sea... all officers dead.

At this point I appear to have begun to wonder if I should not have been taking more thorough notes. At the top of the page, I can see that I scribbled a star with the word 'Interesting' and a circle round it, and I even started transcribing his comments properly for a while.

He said it was not smoking that saved him. All the officers had smoked, and he had traded his cigarettes with them and had got more food. The officers were dumped outside when they died, which was not a problem because it was winter and their bodies froze rather than rotted.

At this point, I may have been concerned about how many spare pages were left in my notebook, because I began to just note down odd words again. There is even a doodle of a frowning face with a dunce's cap in the top corner of one page. I was getting annoyed. I only had this one day, and I wanted to talk to the other two men properly, and his story was going on for a very long time.

The notebook again, with its odd words: 1944 Warsaw... The Germans organised work battalions... battalion only included men from the North Caucasus: Adygeans, Cherkessians, Karachai, Balkars, Kabardians, Ossetians, Chechens,

Ingush, Kumyks, Nogais... worked for farmers in East Prussia... 16 Jan 1945, Germans moved them from there... Russian planes flying... Polish village... 18 Jan 1945, picked up by Red Army along with eight Germans who were taken away and killed... one of them called Klaus.

I have to admit I was bored. My hand ached. He had been talking for more than an hour and a half. I was getting nowhere in my research, and I tried to interrupt him. He took no notice and talked on.

The Red Army put them under guard and sent them back east to the Soviet headquarters, towards home. They had not been home for more than two years. They were marched along a road. It was a wide road but there was snow on it so you could not know what the road was made of; stones or just mud. He walked and walked and then there was another road coming down from the left, and tanks were coming down that road.

He looked up at me, and gestured for a salad bowl. I passed him the bowl and he took out two pieces of dill and placed them carefully on the table.

It was like this, you see, the road came from the side. And the commander of the tank column stopped them. The commander was a Russian. I mean, ethnically Russian and the commander could see they were not and asked who they were. The guards said they were freed prisoners and they were all from the North Caucasus, of many ethnic groups. And the commander asked them to separate out by ethnicity, so they milled about and the Karachai were next to the Balkars in one group, further along were Chechens, and then the Dagestanis in their different groups, and so on. They were about thirty-five Balkars. The tanks were lining up alongside the column of prisoners, and the soldiers grouped the freed prisoners together in a long line, and suddenly the tanks started to shoot.

Br-br-br-br-br. Zabakov made the sound of a machine gun firing, and flinched downwards to his right towards the table.

The snow was so deep and he threw himself into it, and held his head down. And all around he heard prayers. Allah, Allah, Allah, Allah. He did not know if there was one machine gun or more than one, but he knew there was one very nearby because it was so loud. It fired and fired and fired until the belt ended. Then there was silence, then an order. Those of them left alive should stand up. He saw someone near him was standing up, so he stood up too and he could hear crying and moaning all around him. Then the belt in the machine gun was changed and it started to fire again and he threw himself into the snow once more.

Br-br-br-br, and there was the sound of the hot bullets hitting the snow. Pss-pss-pss-pss. Then the order to stand up, so he stood up. Then they changed the belt and fired again and he lay in the snow and waited to die. He waited for a bullet to hit him. And they fired another belt of bullets and he cried out to Allah, Allah, Allah, Allah. And thanks be to Allah, he was not hit.

Silence. Zabakov looked at me.

Then, he said, came another order. Whoever is left alive stand up. They had shot everyone with the machine gun. And he lay there, but he saw someone else was standing so he was not the only one alive and he stood up. And in the white snow there was a black mass of bodies, all lying in the snow, with blood. They who survived walked to the side, and the machine gun passed along the bodies again. And back. Until the belt ended. Then a tank drove over the bodies. There were arms and legs flying like this. And when the tank left, one more man stood up: a Kumyk. They had shot this Kumyk three times and the Kumyk survived the tank going over, and looked around, all shocked, and walked over to them. The Kumyk had worked as a hairdresser in the camp.

Zabakov reached for his glass of water, and drank from it. They were about 270 survivors, he said, from 1,500 people. And the dead surrounded them. They were dressed in all sorts of clothes that they had made, and he had a hat he had paid for with cigarettes. In short, they were dressed well and the soldiers surrounded them and stole their clothes. One soldier took his shoes, and told him to take shoes from the dead people but he did not want to. He was left in his socks. Another soldier took his waistcoat. Another soldier took his hat.

Then they walked in the snow along the road towards Rodomsk, which is in Poland. He walked there and all the houses were intact. There had been no war there. In the morning they went further. They arrived at the headquarters of the division and all these drunk, half-drunk soldiers started to beat them. Any soldier could take him to one side and beat him or kill him. One man was taken aside but the pistol did not work and the man was saved.

They were put in a barn and all the soldiers beat them with sticks. One soldier asked him how he got there, thinking he was Russian, because he had blue eyes, and the soldier tried to kill him but he was stronger and got into the barn. Then he was beaten inside the barn.

His socks had worn out on the bottom and his feet were cold. That was how it was. These things happened. Then they were taken to a special place for people under suspicion and were interrogated. He got given ten years. All of them got ten years.

There were fifteen of them in the courtroom at the one time. That was in Lvov. There were three judges and everything was clean except the prisoners. They were still dirty. Had they been in a prisoner camp? Had they worked for the Germans? Yes and yes. Had he sworn allegiance to the Germans? No. That was why he got only ten years and he was sent to the North, to Molotovsk to build a big factory. A man asked for carpenters, and he had said he was a carpenter although he wasn't, and he didn't have to work as a carpenter really, just carry wood.

The notebook again: sent to Komi... worked there... Far East... could see Sakhalin... many many camps... plasterer... supposed to go to Magadan camps but too cold.... Criminals all together... former soldiers together...Komsomolsk-on-the-Amur... man called Zaitsev ... story about a Japanese spy... killed the people who over-fulfilled the plan, killed people who under-fulfilled the plan...Zaitsev survived... from there to Mylki, worked in forest... 1953.

He heard Stalin had died on 6 March 1953, and he and the other prisoners cried. Honestly, they cried. That is what happened. His father had died in prison, and he was in prison, and his father had done nothing wrong and he had done nothing wrong and they all had to work, and when he heard Stalin died, he cried. There were all nations there, Russians, Ukrainians, everyone, and everyone cried. That was how they were brought up, he said, to honour the leader. They cried for Stalin. Then, he was released.

He sat back and breathed out heavily, looking at me all the time.

'There,' he said. 'You can ask these two about the deportation now. I know that you didn't want to hear that, and that you weren't interested, but I have been waiting more than sixty years to tell that story to someone who would listen, and I've told it now. I wrote to the newspaper and no one cared.

I tried to tell everyone, and no one listened. I am eighty-six years old and I am the last person alive who knows how our own people killed us in the snow like rabbits.'

He reached for his plate. He speared a fatty lump of lamb onto his fork and ate it, then drank some water. It was only his second drink of water in the whole two hours of the story.

'You know now too, and you will tell the world.'

LLOYD JONES

The Penguin and the Tree

LLOYD JONES (born Lower Hutt, New Zealand, 1955) has written a number of novels, including **Biografi**, **The Book of Fame** and **Mister Pip** – which won the Commonwealth Writers Prize in 2008. His most recent novel is **Hand Me Down World**. Based in Wellington, he visited Antarctica in December 2008 as a guest of the New Zealand Antarctic Centre.

The Penguin and the Tree

LLOYD JONES

Until I received an invitation from the New Zealand Antarctic Centre I had never thought of Antarctica as a place that I must visit. As large as Antarctica is, and despite the fact that after Australia it is our next closest neighbour, it has never really exerted presence.

So it was a surprise to hear and feel contact with ground as hard as concrete as the plane touched down on the frozen ice field of the Ross Sea in December 2008.

In a single file of buffoonery we exited the plane. We were mainly returning American scientists and field workers. Bundled up in four layers, heavy boots that were impossible to walk in, head gear, and special sunglasses, I followed hard on the heels of an equally burdened and shuffling figure – Boyd Webb, from Brighton, England, the other invited artist – into a sun-blazing white landscape.

On the plane down I had finished Sara Wheeler's *Terra Incognita,* and that was the end of my reading for the duration of the trip. It made more sense for me to directly experience the place for myself. So I had stocked up weeks before. I had read Ernest Shackleton's *South* and picked up Frank Worsley's *Endurance* for about the tenth time and as with all the other times read with the same mounting sense of awe. *South,* though, pays closer attention to the daily-ness of the men's lives. I made notes on the quirkier details, such as the banjo Shackleton thought to unpack from the *Endurance;* as well as the endless amounts of seal and penguin eaten by the men on Elephant Island (including the special treat of morsels of undigested fish taken from the gullets of the larger penguins cooked in tin cans strung up on bits of wire around the stove); and the surprisingly small selection of books – a copy of Browning, Coleridge's 'Rime of the Ancient Mariner' and a 'portion of *Encyclopedia Britannica'* to settle the usual disputes.

I'll be brief about the next ten days. What we got up to. The tiresome but understandable rules and regulations around individuals leaving Scott Base on their own. Boyd's elephantine snoring which he professed not to know about. Boyd has the extraordinary ability to go from his last utterance to fast asleep the moment his head touches the pillow. It's a great talent and one which I feel will ensure his longevity so long as one day in the future he is not slaughtered in his sleep. At Scott Base, I had to wear the ear muffs issued by the plane crew for the flight from Christchurch. It was hopeless. The only sleep I got was when we slept out at the ice caves below Mt Misery and at Royds, by which time his snoring had become so legendary and feared that he was sent to sleep in a tiny hut above Shackleton's hut while the rest of the party slept on the ice in tents. Boyd, by the way, is the loveliest fellow you could ever hope to meet.

It is eighteen months since I returned from Antarctica to the marvel of green lawns, bitumen, kerbs and cars. I was nearly run over twice on the five minute walk from the Antarctic Centre to the Christchurch domestic airport. Since then the Antarctic experience has been one of slow devolvement of certain highlights. Such as the time Boyd and I stood grinning at the window of the A-frame hut near the ice caves, urging the distant figure on skis bearing wine for the 'artists' to go faster. And in Scott's Hut, the dead penguin laid out on the dissection table. Presumably it will go on waiting. And on visits such as the one enjoyed by Boyd and myself, poets will commemorate the penguin, painters will paint it; and the penguin will continue on, as it were, to be captured over and over.

In Antarctica, everything is preserved for all eternity – mistakes, follies, vanities, even the exhaust fumes of the massive Hercules landing and taking off. The smell of pony shit in the stables outside Scott's hut lingers on more than a century after the last of his Welsh ponies expired; Discovery Hut continues to be marked by a filthy, smoke-grimed degradation and a dangerous level of boredom.

IT WAS ON the stony wastes behind Scott's Hut at Cape Evans that I first encountered a skua, a large grey bird which from afar looked like a very large seagull as it floated on air, its wings still and cut out against the immense sky; then as it came closer I saw its claws, and as its motionless eye looked down I understood that I was its target. I ducked just in time, and then as it circled, and unfussily lined me up a second time, I picked up a stone. As it swept in, I waited until I could stall no longer and lobbed the stone into its flight path and the skua lifted off again. It seemed to hang in the air, on its wing, before it began another sweep at my head. I lobbed up another stone and it lifted off as before. Then another skua arrived, and joined in the attack from a different direction. I must have lobbed twenty or thirty stones in the air before I regained the safety of Scott's Hut from the nesting ground I had unwittingly strayed onto.

This was also the day we made our way to Royds. After unpacking our gear and pitching tents on the ice beneath Shackleton's hut, after forcing down a few biscuits and hot tea, and after Boyd was shown his own splendid, separate accommodation, we followed a path up through scree and around the 'summer pond' to the Adelie penguin nesting colony. From up there we found ourselves on a high coastal point above the frozen sea. In the distance we could see small numbers of Adelie penguins making awkward progress across the ice to the sea. They had another sixty miles of falling over and getting up again before they would strike open water. They were males and either they had crushed the nesting egg in a clumsy moment, or else had abandoned the nest, fed up with waiting for the female to return from the sea with food. We settled down in a hollow amongst the rocks. Boyd handed me the binoculars. I had them trained on several hundred nesting Adelies when the air shifted just above our heads and the skua came to rest about twenty feet beneath our position.

The whole penguin colony immediately erupted. Those Adelies nearest the skua drew up their flippers and bobbed forward, making aggressive gestures with their beaks. The skua raised its wings as if in readiness to fly off, but it didn't move. It seemed to know it could come to no harm and calmly turned its head to look in another direction. Very quickly the protest settled down. And when I next looked the skua had dropped its wings. Another five minutes passed. By now the Adelies had forgotten about the skua. Over the same time, imperceptibly the skua moved itself deeper inside the nesting Adelies.

It happened to be my turn with the binoculars when the skua, with a shoplifter's sense of opportunism, grabbed a chick in its beak. Once more the penguin colony erupted. Their noise added to the horror of the spectacle. The Adelies gazed up as the skua raised its wings and beat lethargically as it tried to gobble the chick in the air. It didn't manage either task very well. The chick was too big or too fluffy and the skua dropped down to an uncontested area just beneath where Boyd and I crouched, and there it coughed up the baby Adelie. The grey fluffy chick wobbled onto its feet. It shook its head. It shook and shook. It was alive. It was alive – in spite of what had happened, and as it tried to move away I felt the onlooker's horrible dread. It had two more seconds of life left. The skua picked it up in its beak and shook it vigorously until the sides of the chick split. Then the skua released it and dove in with its beak and pulled the red stitching out of the chick's insides, and that red, that shocking red against the immensity of the silent white continent is what remains of my ten days in Antarctica.

BACK AT SCOTT BASE I recounted the event to one of the scientists. He was surprised that I had found it upsetting. It was just Nature taking its course. None of this I disagree with, and yet what remains is this undiminished horror whenever I remember the skua coughing up the Adelie chick. What remains, forever I suspect, is the moment between the 'before' and 'after'; it is the chick shaking off the experience. It has a second more left of life. But for the moment it remains gloriously alive, eternally alive.

I've gone back over the notes I made at the time to see if there is anything more I might add. I see I made a note about the thickness and the size of the Adelie eggs. They lay shattered and piled on the ground beneath where Boyd and I had sat in the rocks. The chicks aren't so much born as smash their way out into the world.

There is something else too which may be relevant. This morning it just surfaced in that way of old memories as I lay in the bath.

I am ten years old. My mate has just handed me his slug gun. It's the first time I've held it, or any gun for that matter, and yet I seem to know what to do. I put the stock against my shoulder, aim casually up at a tree, and squeeze the trigger. To my astonishment a bird falls out of the tree. I am appalled.

Forty years later, I am still appalled.

VICTORIA

HISLOP.

Manoli

VICTORIA HISLOP (born Bromley, 1959) went into publishing and advertising after reading English at Oxford University, and then began travel writing. Her first novel, **The Island**, came out of a trip to Crete, inspired by the story of the leper colony of Spinalonga. An international bestseller, it became a Greek TV series. Her second novel, **The Return**, is set in Granada and recalls the Spanish Civil War. Victoria lives in Kent with her husband and two children, and has a house on Crete. **www.victoriahislop.com**

Manoli

VICTORIA HISLOP

I met Manoli Foundoulakis on 20 January 2007, in a hotel in Crete. It was at exactly six o'clock in the evening. His punctuality was only one of the many differences between Manoli and every other Greek I had ever encountered. We met because I had written a novel set on Spinalonga, a small island off Crete, which was a leper colony from 1903 to 1957, and Manoli had been asked to write a foreword to the Greek edition. He was a former leprosy sufferer, and still lived in the village opposite the island.

When I wrote *The Island*, my complete lack of Greek meant that I had not been able to do any research about the people who had lived on Spinalonga. Everything about the island itself, the patients and the doctors came from my imagination as I sat at my desk back in England. Indeed, Manoli was the first European with leprosy that I had ever met. I had always maintained a firm conviction that those who suffered from this disease would be as funny, clever, charming and wise as anyone else. Why would they not? And in Manoli, I saw how close to the truth my instinct had taken me.

When he emerged from the shadows of the hotel foyer to shake my hand, I was shocked. This was not because of the way he looked as, in spite of the very obvious damage that had been done to his face by the disease, Manoli was still a handsome man. It was more the feeling that a character in my novel had come to life.

I was anxious that Manoli might be critical of the assumptions I had made about the lives of people with leprosy. Instead he thanked me for lifting the stigma which had blighted his life for so many years. However, at that first meeting, someone had to translate every sentence we spoke to each other. I decided there and then that I would find time to learn Greek in order to talk to Manoli. I began my lessons in London shortly afterwards and gradually realised my ambition.

Manoli lived in the hills overlooking Spinalonga, in the village of Ano Elounda, where the streets are too narrow for cars and the population is largely made up of beautiful but elderly widows in black. In summer, we used to sit on the steps in the street, beneath his vine, sipping the overpowering raki that he had distilled himself and in winter we sat inside, my back almost melting from the heat of the wood fire that constantly blazed in the hearth.

Whenever I planned a visit to Manoli, I would put a dictionary in my bag and we would talk. His patience was matchless. One evening, when I took the narrow road up to see him, secure in the knowledge that he would be there, because he always was, I forgot both my dictionary and glasses. So Manoli and I shared his thick-lensed spectacles along with the Greek-English dictionary which he kept in his kitchen, and for many hours we 'talked'. It was painstaking but meant that each sentence had to be worth constructing.

Manoli knew I loved to sit on a particular chair with my back to his fire and after a few hours there, I would emerge suffused with the aroma of wood smoke, my stomach full of horta (Greek spinach, for which he knew I had a passion), barbounia, and coffee, which I would make under his careful instruction. He taught me so much. The most obvious lesson was that, in spite of everything he had lived through and suffered, there was no place for self-pity. Unlike so many people, he never talked about himself, never once complained of anything.

Manoli was a very gifted man. He had immense powers of oratory, and when something stirred him, he could deliver a speech that moved everyone around him, mixing intellect and emotion in a way that even the most talented politicians often fail to do. He became chief advisor and consultant on the TV serial made for Greek television from my novel, and his house became a focal point for all actors who wanted to know what it felt like to suffer from this ancient disease. The series was dedicated to him.

He had an exceptional memory too. One afternoon during the last few weeks of his life, I visited him in hospital with a Greek actor, Theodoros Katzafados, who was playing a lead role in the TV drama. Through the filter of his oxygen mask, Manoli began to recite verse after verse from the *Erotokritos*, an epic love poem written in the seventeenth century in Cretan dialect, by Kornaros, Greece's equivalent to Shakespeare. At a certain point, Theodoros joined in and they spoke the lines together but even he, who had held the stage at Epidauros every summer for decades, was amazed at Manoli's delivery and his powers of recall, which held us both spellbound.

Age meant nothing to Manoli. Until a few weeks before his death last spring, he was as sprightly as someone half his age. Sometimes when I was with him, I felt that his walking stick was just a stage prop and that he might break into a dance routine like Fred Astaire. When he went across to Spinalonga to play a role in the scene when the patients are all cured and leaving the island, he left his stick behind and marched through the tunnel holding my arm. It felt to me that I was supported by Manoli, not the other way round. He was determined to show the reality of the cure, and nothing could have demonstrated more eloquently that leprosy had been conquered than the sight of his abandoned walking stick.

His energy characterised everything – from his passionate devotion to his family, to his strong religious faith, to the way in which he expressed his ideas. Unlike so many people with firm opinions, he would speak and listen with the same level of concentration. Whenever people talk of Manoli, they always mention his *psychi* – his 'soul'. I think of this in the way I think of his hands: larger than life, generous, other-worldly. Perhaps both his soul and hands were shaped and moulded by his experience of leprosy. The positive effect he had on those around him was something very out of the ordinary.

The timelessness of the village in which he lived and the calmness with which we always talked made me feel that Manoli had all the time in the world. I felt that he would live forever: there seemed no reason for him not to, after all the physical and emotional assaults that he had survived.

Just before he died, he told me he was ready to go. With his immensely strong faith, I know he was and, moreover, was looking forward to it. On 28 May 2010 he died, peacefully at the age of eighty-seven. For him it was the right time: his punctuality was immaculate to the end.

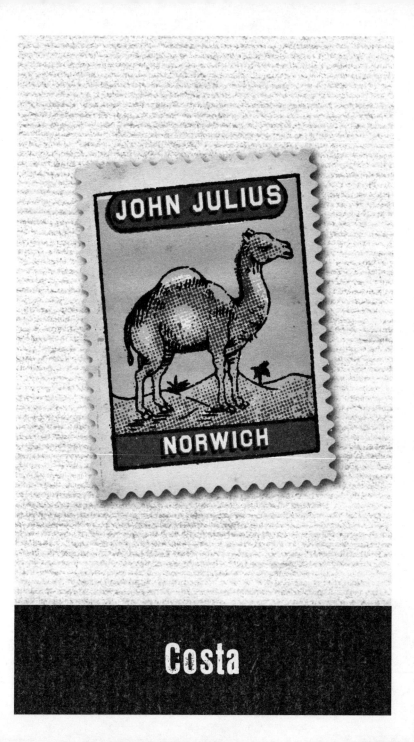

JOHN JULIUS

NORWICH

Costa

JOHN JULIUS NORWICH (born London, 1929), is a historian, travel writer and anthologist.
He has written histories of Norman Sicily, Venice, Byzantium and the Mediterranean, and
presented more than thirty history documentaries for BBC TV. He is also the author of a study
of **Shakespeare's Kings**, and two travel books, **Mount Athos** and **Sahara**. He has recently
completed a **History of the Popes**, and is currently working on a short history of England, as
seen from 100 different locations. His annual **Christmas Cracker** anthology has been going for
41 years. www.johnjuliusnorwich.com

Costa

JOHN JULIUS NORWICH

His real name was Achillopoulos, but he never used it; some of his best friends never even knew it. To everyone, whatever their age or position, he was just plain Costa. He was sixty-ish when I first met him: brown as a walnut, with brilliant green eyes and hair that had gone white overnight when he was twenty. As the years passed, he came to look more and more like Picasso; often indeed, when he went out to dinner in a bistro near Grasse – where he lived when he wasn't in some distant corner of the globe – he would be taken for the great man and obligingly sign menus with a signature indistinguishable from the original.

Brought up in Paris, London and Oxford, Costa spoke French like a native, and his English, apart from a ghost of an accent, was virtually as good. His Greek, he told us, came a poor third, but it sounded perfect to me. He had, after all, transferred from the Free French Army to the Greek as soon as he could. He seemed to be always on the move; there were few countries in the world he hadn't visited, and he was full of hilarious stories about what had happened to him on the road – stories almost invariably against himself. He never had much money, but his Rolleiflex was always with him and in those happy days before mass travel he had little difficulty in selling his photographs to newspapers and magazines.

And so, when in the summer of 1963 Reresby Sitwell and I decided to go to Mount Athos and clearly needed a Greek-speaker to accompany us, Costa was the obvious choice. I had been there the previous year but I had travelled alone, and the journey had been a disaster. It had pelted with rain, my Greek had proved nowhere near good enough, and the donkeys and mules that I had understood to be ubiquitous were virtually non-existent. On the third day, sopping wet and bitterly cold, I had given up in despair.

Costa had immediately accepted our invitation, as I knew he would; and – as I had also confidently expected – he made all the difference. He kept us amused, the monks adored him, and

Costa in the port of Alexandria, 1943

he proved, rather to his surprise, a superb interpreter. 'Then,' he said after a day or two – he began most sentences with that word – 'I am astonished at the excellence of my Greek.'

He was also able, on more than one occasion, to transform our meals. As a result of my previous experience I had perhaps laid it on pretty thick about the Athonite cuisine, for any visit to the Holy Mountain invariably spells gastronomic martyrdom. After that first trip, with the full horror of it still upon me, I had written: *For the first few meals, while courage and self-discipline remain steady, a person of normal digestive sensibility may be able to contemplate – and even in part consume – the interminable platefuls of beans, spasmodically enlivened by a single slice of anchovy or a sliver of briny cheese which, if the monasteries had their way, would stand alone between himself and starvation. But on such a diet the spirit soon flags. Within a day or two those liverish-white lumps, glaring remorselessly up at him from their puddle of stone-cold grease, take on a new expression, hostile and challenging. 'Bet you can't', they seem to say. And they are right.*

Even more than its inexpressible nastiness, it is the uniformity of the Athonite menu that wears one down as the same grim breakfast offering of beans will reappear, congealed, at supper. It doesn't take long to understand and appreciate the old custom of the cenobitic monasteries according to which, as the monks pass out of the refectory, the cooks ask pardon on their knees for the atrociousness of the meal. Nor to understand why, among all the ascetic disciplines of the Mountain, that of almost continuous fasting is so insistently stressed.

Reresby had wisely stuffed his rucksack with a tiny spirit stove and various succulent delicacies from Fortnum & Mason, where he was then employed. But it turned out that

Costa could do more. He would chat up one guestmaster after another, who would then suddenly conjure up a tomato omelette or even a fish. It was also thanks to him that we were quite often, after dinner, presented with a tray bearing generous glasses of the home-brewed monastic hooch, deliciously aromatic and pulverisingly strong.

Dear Costa did however have one failing: he was accident-prone. He had already had one bad fall some years before in the Andes, when he was climbing with George Jellicoe and Robin Fedden, and now, one day as we were walking between monasteries, he trod on a loose pebble – always a danger on Athonite paths – missed his footing and, since the path was unusually narrow and cut into the side of a hill, landed some six or eight feet down the slope. At first he pooh-poohed the accident and plodded on to our destination; but by the next morning he was in agony. He insisted on continuing the journey, but he was bent double and clearly in considerable pain.

At the next monastery – Xenophontos – the monks took pity on him and bore him off to their dispensary (then rare on the Holy Mountain) where one of their number insisted on giving him an epidural injection. The equipment looked far from sterile, and I trembled for him; but the treatment proved an almost miraculous success and the following day he was walking as well as ever. When we returned to London he told his doctor, who was astonished. It was, he said, quite a dangerous procedure; it depended on knowing precisely the right place to put the needle, and was something usually left to specialists. The old monk, it seemed, couldn't have done it better.

APART FROM THAT one little *contretemps*, that second trip of mine to the Mountain was a terrific success; we all enjoyed it enormously, and we learned a lot. I was determined to travel with Costa again; and, three years later, I did.

This time it was he who took the initiative. Early in 1966, my telephone rang. 'Then,' said a voice – it could have been no one else – 'then, there is an expedition leaving soon for the Tibesti Mountains in the Sahara where no one ever goes and where they will make a film. They want two more people so as to have three Land Rovers, which will be safer than two. Then, can you come?' Our fellow-travellers, he explained, would be three ladies of his acquaintance, all of them experienced and passionate *sahariennes*; and they had secured the services of a first-rate guide who knew the desert like the back of his hand.

Now it happened that on the previous day I had typed the final full stop to the first volume of a book that I had been working on for the previous two years; I felt that I deserved a break before starting on the second. Anyway, the temptation was irresistible. Three weeks later we were off. Costa and I flew via Algiers to Djanet in the far south of Algeria, where we met the rest of the party. Then we turned the Land Rovers due east, and headed off into the unknown.

I wrote a book about our adventure and, after some forty-five years, have had to refer to it repeatedly in the pages that follow. The trip was by far the most exciting that I have ever made. Since it lasted some eight weeks, I cannot begin to do it justice in this article – and anyway I am not writing about the Sahara, but about Costa. There was one particular incident, which occurred after about a fortnight when we had reached Auzou in northern Chad, which showed him at his most typical.

When we travel in exotic lands, we nearly all of us run up sooner or later with the problem of the uninhibited onlookers – usually in the form of a group of locals who materialise from nowhere, take up a position a yard or two away and stare and stare, fascinated by one's every action. Even on picnics, this technique can be unnerving enough; but at a night camp, where there are no tents to afford the minimum of privacy and not even any bushes for cover, it can become a serious matter. Never have I known it to assume such formidable proportions as that evening at Auzou. The crowd must have numbered at least forty – forty pairs of staring, unblinking eyes, missing nothing, examining every item we drew from our kitbags, taking in our every move. Never, let me emphasise, was there anything remotely hostile about them. They were perfectly friendly – just very, very curious, and utterly immovable.

Our own reactions varied between agonised embarrassment and stoic fortitude. None of us felt like asking them, in so many words, to go away; without a common language, such a request could only have been exceedingly impolite, and the last thing we wanted was to cause offence. At the same time, there were other needs that were ever more pressing.

After perhaps an hour, one or two of the older spectators had slipped away; but the hard core that remained, consisting almost entirely of children and adolescents, had obviously decided that a long vigil lay ahead, and were digging themselves in for the night. At last Costa took the matter in hand. 'Then,' he said, 'if they are looking for entertainment, that is what we must give them. Then they will be satisfied and go away.' The rest of us were doubtful; but he, by now looking forward hugely to his coming performance, was not to be shaken. Delving into his kitbag, he extracted some colourful garment, twisted it expertly into a funny hat and put it on. Then, trousers rolled up to the knee, he began to dance. And as he danced he sang:

Il y avait dix filles dans un pré,
Toutes les dix à marier;

Il y avait Line, il y avait Chine,
Il y avait Claudine et Martine,
Ha, ha, Cat'rinette et Cat'rina.
Il y avait la belle Suzon,
La duchesse de Montbazon,
Il y avait Célimène
Et il y avait la Dumaine.

Costa was not, perhaps, outstandingly gifted for the dance; his grasp of melody was also at moments uncertain. But he made up amply in verve what he lacked in technique, and he certainly deserved a greater success than he achieved. His audience was baffled. They had not bargained for this. Having no idea how they were meant to respond, they wisely chose not to respond at all.

Visibly shaken, Costa tried again:
Le fils du Roi vint à passer,
Toutes les dix les fit coucher;
Paille à Line, paille à Chine,
Paille à Claudine et Martine,
Ha, ha, Cat'rinette et Cat'rina.
Paille à la belle Suzon,
La duchesse de Montbazon,
Paille à Célimène,
Mais bon lit à la Dumaine.

The line of faces still stared stonily back at him. There was not a word, not a whisper, far less a smile. Now genuinely sad, poor Costa took off his funny hat, unrolled his trousers and returned to the rest of us, shaking his head. '*En effet,*' he murmured, '*c'est un publique très difficile.*'

Then, to our astonishment, we saw that it had worked. Within minutes of the song's end, the entire audience had faded away into the darkness. Just what had prompted them to leave remains a mystery. Perhaps they had enjoyed it all more than their faces had revealed and had accepted it as we had hoped they would, as the grand finale to a memorable evening. Perhaps, on the other hand, they had hated it and been impelled to flee from the dreadful possibility of an encore. My own theory is that by directing his energies so squarely towards them Costa had somehow made them feel involved, saddled with responsibilities they did not understand. The whole thing had suddenly become too complicated. They preferred to go.

EVENTUALLY, WE REACHED our destination – the great volcanic geyserland of Soborom – and started the journey home. On entering the Tibesti ten days before, we had exchanged the Land Rovers for camels, of which we had a string of a dozen or so; they were essential for our food, water and baggage, but – the local saddles being excruciatingly painful – we seldom rode them until evening, when we were too tired to walk any further.

Of all our animals, Costa's was generally the slowest; we had long grown accustomed to hearing his frantic cries of 'Vas-y Alphonse!' or 'Alphonse, NON!', echoing behind us. But one afternoon Alphonse was used by our local guide Abdullahi for an exhibition of galloping, and the excitement went to his head. When, shortly before sunset, we left the mountains and reached the fringes of the Bardai oasis, there was no holding him. He smelt home, greenery and water; and, just as a horse will when approaching its stable, broke once more into a gallop. But a horse has stirrups and a bridle; a camel has neither. Costa, accordingly, took the only course open to him. He fell off – and from the top of a camel it's a long way to the ground.

I had been riding a little ahead and had no idea of what had happened until I got to the camp five minutes later. As I dismounted, Jean – our French guide – ran up, dragging a heavy mattress behind him. '*Viens vite*,' he shouted, '*Costa a eu un accident.*' He dashed to the nearest Land Rover, hurled the mattress in the back, and together we drove as fast as we dared to where Costa lay, conscious but in great pain and quite unable to move. Somehow we got him back to the camp, but then what? Bardai consisted only of a small fort, manned by a handful of the Chad army. It had no doctor, and certainly no X-ray. For all we knew, Costa had broken his back; the slightest wrong movement might snap his spinal cord and paralyse him for life.

The next two days was a time of increasing anxiety for us all. At first we had hoped that Costa might have suffered nothing worse than serious bruising and shock, and that after a couple of days' rest all might be well. But it soon became clear that there was more to it than that: there could be no question of his being able to return in a bumpy Land Rover the thousand-odd miles back to Djanet. He was tortured with pain, unable even to move in bed without assistance. Luckily we had plenty of morphia with us, but we knew that we had to get the patient to hospital as soon as we could. The fort was theoretically in constant radio communication with the regional centre at Faya-Largeau, but by a piece of cruel ill-fortune the electric generator had broken down a few days before and all contact with the outside world had been lost. Costa had by now made up his mind that he was dying – and we were by no means certain that he was not right.

Then, on the morning of the third day after the accident, I was returning from the last of innumerable trips to the fort to see how work on the generator was progressing when I saw a line of camels approaching across the sand. Ahead of them walked a man wearing a curious knee-length khaki tunic and a pale blue *kepi*. As they drew nearer I could also see, in the shade of the *kepi*, a close-cropped reddish beard. This, I realised, was one of the lonely handful of French *méharistes* still patrolling the Sahara. He grinned, and introduced himself: *sergent-en-chef* Jean-François Renn. Did he, I asked, have a radio? Of course he did. Could he send an SOS for us? Of course he could. In five minutes his aerial was set up; one of his local *goumiers* was sitting in the sand, grinding away at a hand generator; and our message was on its way to Faya-Largeau.

Sergeant Renn acted on us like a tonic; we all felt better. But Costa was distinctly worse. He had now developed a hacking cough and a lung infection which we feared – in the primitive conditions in which we were living, without electricity or running water – might easily lead to pneumonia. The reply from Faya-Largeau too was depressing. The doctor would be there on his rounds in about a week. We replied at once: this was an emergency – in a week the patient would probably be dead. Our second appeal worked. A flying doctor and two male nurses were announced to be already on their way and would be at Bardai within the hour.

The long wait was over. Half an hour later the French doctor was at the bedside; Costa was expertly transferred to a stretcher and strapped down; he was slid, with the smoothness of a drawer in a filing cabinet, into a waiting Land Rover; his kitbag was stuffed in after him; and he was gone. We hardly had time to recover our breath before we heard the aeroplane again. It circled twice over our heads to gain height; then disappeared over the mountains to the south.

We missed Costa a lot. It was an immeasurable relief to know that he was in safe hands at last, but the party was not the same without him. His interest in everything, his astonishing knowledge, his sheer enthusiasm had fired us all; now he was gone, we all felt diminished. We were worried too. He had promised to telegraph to us the results of his X-ray; but there was no chance of our hearing anything until we reached Djanet, which could not be for another three or four days at the earliest. Those days were as long as any I have ever spent. The last – which happened to be Easter Sunday – was the worst. Of our twelve hours on the *piste*, six were occupied with repairs after as many different breakdowns. We eventually roared into Djanet – I use the word advisedly, two of our silencers having given up altogether – and made straight for the post office where, sure enough, a telegram was waiting. The news was at least better than we had feared. Three vertebrae had been concertinaed into each other, but nothing had actually been broken. The patient was still lying in a plaster cast, but in ten days' time he hoped to be well enough to return.

Poor Costa – it was only later, when we were all home again, that we learned the full, hair-raising story of his sufferings in Fort-Lamy. Once, in pre-independence days, its hospital had been one of the best in French Africa; and even now he had nothing but praise for the two remaining French doctors and the treatment they gave him. It was not their fault that the supply of anaesthetics was so short that they were obliged to set his spine without any; nor that, while their backs were turned, the drip-feeding apparatus that they had arranged for the patient in the next bed, seriously ill and unconscious, should have been torn away by his family, bursting *en masse* into the ward with much assorted livestock and cramming handfuls of rice into his unresisting mouth. Without an adequate staff of trained nurses such incidents were unavoidable. Untrained nurses seem to have been plentiful enough, but their methods tended to be unorthodox. Over some of these methods, such as the unsolicited and unwanted *petits soins* lavished on the powerless Costa by Georgette, his ward orderly, it is only decent to draw a veil.

Costa recovered; but he was growing older and – possibly as a result of his accident – increasingly bent. For a few more years he continued to travel, but no longer as adventurously as he had in the past; finally he stopped altogether, and settled back with his memories into his little house in the Midi. That was where I last saw him. He was by now virtually crippled, but he greeted us with all his old warmth and talked with his usual gusto throughout our lunch. My last sight of him was standing at his doorway, leaning heavily on his stick but waving cheerfully at us as we drove away.

PHOTO © JOHN GIMLETTE

JOHN GIMLETTE (born London, 1963) began his travels as a teen, setting out across the Soviet Union by train, but was distracted by studying law and became a barrister. He has been writing travel books since 1997, when he won the Shiva Naipaul Memorial Prize for a book on Paraguay, **At the Tomb of the Inflatable Pig**; it was followed by **Theatre of Fish** (about Newfoundland) and **Panther Soup** (on WWII battlefields). His latest book is **Wild Coast** (2011), which describes his travels in Guyana, Surinam and French Guiana. He lives in London. www.johngimlette.com

The Other World

JOHN GIMLETTE

A few years ago, I set off west down the Ridgeway, through North Wessex. After Goring-on-Thames, the beechwoods thinned and fell away. A great, seared savannah unrolled itself ahead of me, and the path was fringed with scabious, yellow rattle, and wild thyme. Not only was the beauty of this countryside startling, but I also experienced the unsettling sensation of being an intruder from the present. Here were forts and funerary complexes that pre-dated the pyramids and shared views with nothing more modern than Roman temples. Further west still, the path becomes almost a ribbon-development of ancient defences; Segsbury, Uffington, Liddington, and Barbury. These places are now all so old that no one really knows who built them, or why.

And that intrigues me. What were the early Britons really like? History is tough on those who didn't record themselves in stone, and assumes they were savages. My great-grandfather and my grandfather had dedicated their lives to excavating hill forts. But all they'd found was pottery and flints. This prehistoric trash only made its owners ever more obscure.

Meanwhile, films and books have always made monkeys of Iron Age men. They're improbably hairy and stooped, and their women are fabulously ugly. They have no pride or humour, and everyone seems to speak with a carnivorous belch. But is that right? Whoever built Uffington shifted thousands of tons of chalk. For that, they'd have needed an army, or at least a miniature economy. That suggests a society, made up in layers. But who would we find if we dug down into their lives? *Who were we?*

There were few clues amongst those still living on the ridge. Although their lives were often intriguing – and occasionally hard – they were, in the end, undeniably modern. I remember one family, living in a hollow of candytuft and hairy hawkbit, sharing their double-decker bus with a small herd of goats. Another lot were out hunting hares, apparently with dingoes.

The Ridgeway, a long walk through the Iron Age world

Down in Letcombe Regis (where the Riot Act was last read out), eleven tractors were parked outside 'The Greyhound', heaped with brawny children. Their fathers were hurling staves at a sort of skull (a game apparently) and then, suddenly, they all mounted their machines and roared away, leaving a heady tang of diesel. The village had inspired *Jude the Obscure* and, the previous week, was busted for 60kg of cannabis.

Even Wantage, where Alfred the Great was born, felt only fleetingly ancient. It was attractive and cheerfully pagan: here, you could still dance your way back to the 1970s, and have your animals blessed at the church. I booked into a pub on the square. 'I think it's going to be one of those nights,' said the barman solemnly.

'What do you mean?' I asked.

'The farmer boys like to come heckling ...'

Alfred's kinsmen, I noticed, were already congregating around his statue.

'At New Year, council covers it with scaffolding,' continued the barman.

'And does that work?'

'Nope, every year, the boys tear it down.'

'To free Alfred?'

'Last year, they even brought spanners ...'

Despite this threat of an Ancient Heckle, I still didn't feel I'd found what I was after. That night, I hardly slept at all. Great, agricultural machines hurtled round the square till dawn, inches from my head.

Nor were the secrets of our forebears written in the landscape. The next morning, I clambered back onto the Downs. It was improbably tranquil except for a twister, moving along the horizon, sucking a tiny thread of straw, helter-skelter, into the clouds. I ambled on, through Betjeman country, into Neolithic Wiltshire. A light plane rose from a field of poppies, and a hobby snatched a linnet from the sky and cracked its neck. Then I passed Silbury Hill, which was created by men using antlers, and is the largest mound in Europe. With such outsized altars and the vast corrugations, it was now harder than ever to shrug off the feeling that I'd never understand the Iron Age world, and that – here – I was the alien. Even the boulders, abandoned by the glaciers, are still referred to as *sarsens* – or foreigners – and they've been here for millions of years.

So, my ancient hunter-gatherer was more obscure than ever. I realised I knew almost nothing about him. He lived in ditches, hunted wild animals and threw his pottery in holes. But what did he and his friends think and do? Did they have laws and hairstyles and wandering hands? Did they dote on their wives, or hide them away? Were they frightened of laughter, or did they tell filthy jokes and light their farts? We'll never know, of course. But, for me, far more dispiriting than ignorance was the easy assumption that man – stripped of his modern trappings – is without personality and character. Something needed to happen, or my Iron Age man would languish forever in caricature.

THAT 'SOMETHING' happened a few months later.

It began when I read a story in the papers about some tribesmen, deep in the forests of eastern India, who'd made a plan to eat their teacher. The tribe was called the Bonda, and was known for its ferocity, and for a way of life unchanged for thousands of years. Here, I decided, were people who could help me. Eight weeks later, Jayne – my wife – and I flew to Bhubaneshwar. There, we hired a guide and a driver, and headed for the hills.

Subrat was thrilled by the tribes of his native Orissa. Their territories began a day's ride beyond the city, and spread over an area twice the size of Scotland. There were sixty-two tribes, mostly animists, mostly resilient to modern life and each isolated by dense teak forests and bewildering languages. Some might have shared a common ancestry with the northern Mongols and Aryans, some might have emerged from the southern Dravidians but the origins of others – like the Bonda – were tantalisingly obscure. 'Perhaps they are Asio-Australoids,' said Subrat. 'Nobody knows how they got here.'

'And what about the teacher?' asked Jayne.

'Ah yes, she was sent by the government ...'

'But why did they want to eat her?'

'Because she had a talent they wanted to acquire ...'

'By eating her?'

'Yes,' said Subrat. 'She was very good at cooking curry.'

'And did they eat her?'

Subrat tutted mischievously. We were sitting in his Ambassador, winding upwards through the Eastern Ghats. Outside, it was ninety, and the forest had thickened all around us. On the dashboard, between Subrat and the driver, the plastic eyes of Lord Jaganath were dilated with panic. He needn't have worried; we'd left the great crush of juggernauts on the coast road, and, up here, the only hazards were monkeys and road gangs of beautiful women. Besides, we were all so tightly packed in with a week's supply of mineral water, bananas, sheets and loo paper that – if we'd bumped into anything – we'd have simply bounced around like a big, mushy ball.

'Cannibalism was always rare in Orissa,' said Subrat.

Human sacrifice, he explained, was different, and had persisted into the 1940s.

'And the teacher?' we prompted.

Subrat grinned. 'She's fine. Back in Bhubaneshwar.'

This was a relief. But what would the tribes make of us?

Subrat shrugged. 'They're friendly. Except the Bonda.'

Most tribes, he explained, had even enjoyed good relations with the British, during the Raj. Of course, there were exceptions. There'd been anger at the banning of infanticide, and the Kondh had reacted badly to the restrictions on human sacrifice. But, otherwise, all went well enough. During World War II, many tribals had even concluded that the passing warplanes were agents of Queen Victoria, flying over from The Other World to check that all was well in the Ganjam Hills.

'Only the Bonda are fierce,' said Subrat. 'You'll see.'

The deeper we got into the hills, the more it felt as if time was tumbling backwards. We passed through the territories of ten tribes in all. The first group we met were the Khutia Kondh. They lived high in the forest, in a pretty village of wattle houses, surrounded by a strong fence. This was to keep out the boars, said Subrat, and the wild elephants. Then we met our first tribesman. Immediately, he scrambled into a tree to get us a pot of frothy, palm liquor. Our second Kondh was a woman, neatly segmented by tattoos. She looked at our white skin, screamed and locked herself in her house. Subrat coaxed her out with a soothing language, and we became wary friends. Her tattoos, she explained, made her less attractive to slavers, and would also convey to the gods of the Afterworld the achievements of her life.

The oxen were not so easily reassured, and refused to plough the turmeric. The ploughmen dropped the reins and came over to us. It was said that their forebears had fed the turmeric on human blood to make it strong and red. They themselves were brawny men with high cheekbones and wide, scaly feet. One had an old British Army musket.

'What do they want?' I asked Subrat.

'Nothing really. Unless you've got any chocolate biscuits ...'

We spent our first night in Baliguda. Subrat warned that we might not like our first hotel but that things would get better after that. He was right. Baliguda itself had a forlorn air and, for want of anything better to do, people drifted in off the street, to study us as we sat in our cell. It had baby-pink walls, and a cement floor. At dusk, the spectators disappeared into a greasy glow of oil-lamps. We spread out our sheets over an archipelago of mattress-stains, and settled down to listen to the drama of a tropical night. At some stage, an enterprising rat got in, and pillaged our bananas. Things could only get better.

As Subrat promised, they did. The hotels in Rayagada and Jeypore, although rather shapeless, could muster magnificent curries and were enthusiastically furnished. One place even had a thick ginger carpet and an enormous fridge that stood in the corner like a van. Air-conditioning and bloodless TV thrillers were also pumped into these rooms but, if we used everything at once, the main fusebox would explode and plunge the hotel deeper into darkness. This happened every night. It was ritually followed by the reassuring sound of waiters, scattered through the building, restoring order and light.

We drove on, deeper into tribal territory. By now, life was thrillingly medieval. Subrat described a remarkable existence. Here, he said, bats could be boiled up, and used as a cure for asthma. He also taught us how to recognise the different tribal women. The Dongria Khond wore clumps of nose-rings and carried tiny sickles in their hair. The Paraja kept their hair bundled up with silvery daggers, and the Langia Saora sliced their ears into long hoops. We agreed that the most beautiful of all were the Dedeye, statuesque women, garlanded in fresh flowers. Their arms and necks were protected from tigers by thick aluminium hoops, and these they'd wear until they died.

Sometimes we visited the tribals in their markets, like Chatikona and Kudili. It was here that we found them at their happiest – sociable, excited and brilliantly jewelled. At dawn, they poured out of the hills, traded their jackfruit and liquor for a few rupees and then – fleetingly solvent – went shopping. After buying salt and dried fish, there was not much change but still plenty to see. Here were druggists and magicians, trap-makers, drummers, barbers and the secretive potters of the Kumbehra tribe. A nursery of acrobats performed around their crippled mother, and – from a rubber tyre – a pedlar hacked out a fresh pair of sandals. By noon, it was all over and, under a scouring sun, the tribals filed back into the forest. They were chattery and exhilarated, and a few a little tipsy. Already, I could feel my hunter-gatherer coming back to life.

More centuries fell away as we got deeper into the hills. The tribes' villages were usually arranged around a large, open space facing a Banyan tree, a block for sacrificing buffalo, or the stones of the earth goddess, Jhankar or Hundi. Inside, the houses were cool, and smelt pleasantly of sandalwood, smoke and herbs. Some of the tribes, like the Khond and the Saora, enjoyed beautifully carved doors but there were few possessions. The Gadhaba showed us the carcass of a bear they'd just killed.

I asked the *naik*, or headman, where they'd found it.

'Here,' he said. 'Here in the village.'

'Had it attacked someone?'

'Yes, so we had to kill it with our arrows.'

'And so now what will you do with it?'

'Sell it. The meat is good.'

Women had a curious place in this ancient world, somewhere between victim and goddess. Often, they were out working in the fields, and only the men remained, looking after the children. Once, however, some Ghadaba girls came in early from the fields to show us their *dhemsha* dance. These stunning, powerful girls well knew their value to the tribe, and boasted of bride-prices worth several years' income. The youngest, aged about thirteen, told Jayne she'd cost her husband a fine cow, and 2,000 rupees (about £30).

'And,' she grinned, 'five pots of liquor.'

In their dance, the girls clamped together, inward-looking and exclusionary. This was their ritual defence against kidnap. Bride-capture, they said, gave suitors an unfair advantage in marriage negotiations. Although their dance was violent and sporadically erupted in fights, it was magnificently effective. By the end, they were drenched, and we were engulfed in a firestorm of dust.

Ghabada girls, dancing away the risk of kidnap

Oddly, it wasn't hard to imagine all this up on the Wessex Downs. The chants, the ash, and the interlocking women. Stripped of technology's trappings, human life can suddenly seem stunningly familiar. I remember thinking how odd it was that, if I'd stopped the clock at any stage in the last ten thousand years, I could still be here, watching the same women and the same dance.

Only possessions changed, and rotted away. In Orissa, these rituals will leave nothing for the archaeologists. Once, we watched some women sacrifice a buffalo. They were Langia Saoras, and, in the middle of the group, the priestess, deep in a trance, called down the ancestral spirits. Despite the intensity of her communication with the Afterlife, a picnic atmosphere prevailed. The older ladies threw off their tunics and lay in the grass, smoking massive teak-leaf cigars. Every morsel of the animal, except its hide and horns, simmered on the fire. Of this extraordinary day, I thought, there will be nothing for future generations, except pottery and bones.

EVENTUALLY, AT THE EXTREME limit of our adventure, we came upon the Bonda themselves. I'll never forget this encounter. The tribe were filing out of the forest, on their way to the market at Onukudeli. I was immediately struck by how small they were, and by their nakedness. This indignity, explained Subrat, was forced upon them by the goddess Sita as a punishment for some long-lost indiscretion. But, as curses go, the Bonda bore it magnificently. The women, barefoot and shaven-headed, were sculpted taut and lean by work. They wore only *ringas*, skimpy kilts of forest fibres, but their bodies rippled with beads and snakes of silver and alloys. The men were more drab but viciously armed with drawn swords and iron-tipped arrows.

'Don't photograph the men,' warned Subrat.

'Sure,' I said, 'but why?'

'Because, if you do, they'll kill you.'

He was quite serious. This reputation of the Bonda men for casual homicide has always intrigued anthropologists. Although entirely indifferent to possessions and devoid of sexual jealousy, they have the capacity for sudden and deadly fury. What they fear most of all is sorcery – and photography is sorcery. Without hesitation, they will kill a photographer and won't deny the crime; to the Bonda man, deceit is worse than murder.

The women were quite different. While the men were impassive, they were confident and coquettish and adored being photographed. They teased Subrat in impenetrable *Remo* but I could tell from their laughter that their jokes were worldly and wicked. These wonderful girls wouldn't marry until they were thirty, by which time the tribe had had the best of their work. Each would then take a husband of about twelve, who, with his brothers, would love her into old age.

'Well, they've got bodies to die for,' said Jayne.

'Sure,' said Subrat absently, 'they've got good food in their villages.'

Ah, yes, food, I thought, and remembered the teacher.

'But food,' said Subrat, 'is a strange subject with the Bonda.'

'Why?' we asked.

'Because they've got whatever they want, yet they still eat rats and insects.'

Soon, it was time for the Bonda to move on. One of the women gave Jayne a heavy metal bangle, not unlike the ones that turn up in Wessex. Meanwhile, one of the men sold me an arrow – for the equivalent of 25p. It's now one of my most prized possessions. The hunter who sold it to me was no higher than my chest but he had the massive forearms of an archer, and regarded me with admirable contempt.

As he padded away, I suddenly thought, There goes Wantage Man. It was, of course, a ridiculous idea. I hadn't found my Iron Age hero at all. Although I had perhaps glimpsed something of his spirit.

Three Tibetans in Ireland

DERVLA MURPHY (born Lismore, County Waterford, 1931) was determined to write, not to marry and to travel to India. She realised two of these ambitions in **Full Tilt**, her first book, which describes her exuberant bicycle ride from Lismore – where she still lives – to India, through Iran and Afghanistan. It has been followed by some twenty further titles, including an acclaimed memoir, **Wheels within Wheels**. Her most recent book is **The Island That Dared**, a series of journeys through Cuba, with her daughter Rachel and her three granddaughters.
www.dervlamurphy.com

Three Tibetans in Ireland

DERVLA MURPHY

O n a cold grey day at the end of March 1964, shortly after my return from the cycle ride to India, I first met a Tibetan in Western surroundings – the foyer of a central London hotel. I had been working for some months in Dharamsala, then an overcrowded and under-funded refugee camp for Tibetan children, and that moving encounter with the Tibetan way of being made me feel slightly apprehensive. How would this young man, Lobsang, only five years out of Tibet and three months out of India, be reacting to our Western ways? But I needn't have worried; by the time our refugee-related business had been concluded I knew he was in no danger of being 'tainted' – he was simply adjusting to his new circumstances to the extent required by good manners.

As we walked through St James's Park my companion explained his background. The second youngest of eight children, he was born in 1943 in Lhasa where his civil servant father practised as an oracle. (Only in retrospect can one fully appreciate the uniqueness of Lobsang's generation of

Tibetans. Born the son of a government oracle, he is now the grandfather of an IT-savvy seven-year-old.) In 1945 he had been orphaned and two years later was adopted by his father's brother, an Incarnate Lama of the Gelugpas, who had founded two monasteries. At one of these – Tubung Churbu, twenty miles west of Lhasa – Lobsang spent his school holidays in a small community of a hundred monks. Although one can't have an informally relaxed relationship with an Incarnate Lama, his Abbot uncle's unspoken affection comforted him. During term-time a warmhearted Lhasa aunt mothered him and three of his brothers.

When the Lhasa Uprising began in March 1959 Lobsang's only sister (a pioneering agronomist) was murdered by the Chinese and he fled to Tubung Churbu; his family was sufficiently prominent for every member to be at risk. The monks were preparing to follow the Dalai Lama to India and two weeks later the Abbot set out with twenty-five young lamas, his sixteen-year-old nephew and a train of sixty mules carrying a library of ancient Sanskrit manuscripts and a famous collection of *t'ankas* – traditional Tibetan Buddhist paintings on silk scrolls. To avoid the Chinese, refugee caravans used perilous passes over high mountains and this comparatively short journey took more than three months. Half the mules were lost through injury.

Lobsang and his friends suffered acutely from loneliness and grief; they already sensed that their exile would be permanent. He described himself as 'caught between two fears'. Would the Chinese successfully pursue them? And what awaited him at journey's end? He spoke only Tibetan and a little Chinese and could not begin to imagine the world beyond the mountains. He was then unaware of the significance of money; always his needs had been provided for yet soon he was to be unsupported.

But not immediately: at Kalimpong Uncle arranged for his nephew to lodge with Sherpa Tenzing of Everest during the monsoon, where he learnt Nepali, Hindi and English. The Abbot continued to Benares where he was soon to hold the chair of Sanskrit Studies at the Hindu University. His *t'anka* collection had survived the journey and a year later formed one of the main attractions at Delhi's International Exhibition of Oriental Art.

In November Tenzing helped Lobsang find a job as house-boy to an expat American family – an unremarkable move by our standards, but in Tibet this youth had been attended by personal servants who wouldn't allow him to put on his own boots. At this stage he found himself being scornfully regarded, in some refugee circles, as too naïve to make the most of his connections. In fact he wished to equip himself with some means of helping the tens of thousands of illiterate Tibetans then drifting about northern India in bewildered misery. After nine months he had saved up enough to leave the Americans and become a voluntary worker at Mrs Bedi's School for Young Lamas. There Joyce Pearce of The Ockenden Venture discerned his capabilities and offered him the opportunity to help settle orphans in European homes, which is what brought him to London.

Before we said goodbye at Waterloo Station, Lobsang had accepted my invitation to spend his summer holiday in Ireland, on the smallest of the three Aran Islands.

IN THE 1960S Inisheer's only roads were narrow dirt tracks, the traffic consisted entirely of donkeys, water was drawn from wells, clothes were homespun, everyone spoke Irish – and there two of my books were written by candlelight. It seemed to me that a Tibetan would find himself at ease on Inisheer, an intuition soon confirmed by Lobsang.

Our two and a half hour steamer journey from Galway, on a cloudless August morning, was Lobsang's longest sea voyage. When we anchored, a fleet of *currachs* – frail little craft of wood-lathe and tarred canvas – immediately surrounded us to ferry passengers and goods ashore. Boat-days were then quite an event for the 280 or so islanders and inevitably Lobsang's arrival provoked uninhibited curiosity. This slightly discomfited me but afterwards it transpired that the refugee had observed a family weeping as they said goodbye to an emigrant daughter and had been more aware of this sad feature of Inisheer life than of his own conspicuousness.

For three weeks we shared a friend's cottage (Daphne was the only outsider living permanently on the island), washing at the well three-quarters of a mile away, cooking over an open turf fire and sleeping on the floor. Lobsang enthusiastically took on many of the daily chores and had soon dug a splendid latrine for use with turf ash. He also volunteered to collect dung to supplement our expensive imported turf but here ethical complications arose; cowpats containing insects were ineligible for burning. Observing this, Daphne and I discreetly abandoned forays to collect barnacles and periwinkles.

After sunset we sat around the glowing hearth and returned to Tibet with Lobsang. He had seen more of his own country than most non-nomadic Tibetans. In 1956 Uncle had taken him on an eighteen months' journey to a sacred mountain in west Tibet. This pilgrimage of a Very High Lama to a Very Sacred Mountain generated a caravan of 100 horses and mules and 300 yaks, carrying camping equipment and stores for sixty monks and servants. West Tibet's barrenness made it necessary to carry so much food – mainly *tsampa* (roasted flour), cheese, dried meat and compressed vegetables, plus emergency fodder for the animals.

At nightfall everyone but the Abbot helped set up camp – excellent training, Lobsang remarked, for him and his pampered young companions (all fledgling lamas). Several flooded rivers had to be forded, the equines swimming through the swift icy water, the yaks being ferried on square, flat-bottomed boats of wood and yak-hide. Excitements were few: a panther killing a dog; hundreds of wild horses galloping across the steppes. Recalling that happy and peaceful journey, Lobsang had to pause occasionally to control his emotions. Already he realised that, even as we spoke, Buddhist Tibet was being changed forever. From him I learned that the sudden violent dispossession prompting a refugee flight is peculiarly traumatic. Apart from the loss of a settled home and traditional occupation, and separation from close friends and familiar places, it is the death of the person one has become in a particular context. Three years after our Inisheer interlude, Lobsang noted: 'Every refugee must be his or her own midwife at the painful process of rebirth.'

BY MAY 1965 I was back in Nepal with the Tibetans, running a children's feeding programme in Pokhara's refugee camp, overlooked by Machhapuchhare. On 12 May, as I walked between ragged cotton tents, occupied by recently arrived nomads from west Tibet, piercing squeaks drew my attention to an object lying on the palm of Ngawang Pema's hand. It was very small, very black and very vocal. Moments later I had exchanged the equivalent of ten-and-sixpence (50 pence in new money) for a twelve-day-old Tibetan bitch to be delivered once she was weaned. I wondered what the astrologists would make of the coincidence that this pup and I had entered Nepal on the same date: 1 May.

Six weeks later Tashi moved in to my mud-floored room in the bazaar and I took time off to help this refugee adjust to her new environment. All afternoon she lay on my lap while I wrote but hours passed before her look of puzzled distress began to fade. Then at last she wagged her tail – a brief and doubtful wag, but this sign of dawning trust enchanted me. A night of unmothered whimpering would have been understandable yet Tashi slept soundly, curled up on my stomach. As she was much too young to be left alone I carried her everywhere, for the next month or so, in a cloth shoulder-bag.

By mid-September Tashi's furry cuddlesomeness had been replaced by a silky strokeability. Her black coat had elegantly symmetrical white and tan markings and her admittedly ridiculous brown feathery tail curled up and over her back. Several schools of thought debated the delicate question of her breed. A local 'expert' pronounced her to be a smooth-haired Tibetan terrier, which was absurd; but Ngawang Pema – hoping to sell the next litter to foreign visitors – agreed with him. An Indian UN official, who himself bred Afghan hounds, defined her as a Miniature Himalayan Sheepdog – a theory reinforced by Ngawang Pema's occupation. Personally I regarded her as a perfectly good Tibetan mongrel or pi-dog. However, anyone besotted enough to go to the immense inconvenience and expense of transporting a dog from Nepal to Ireland must be tempted to pretend, as a face-saving device, that the import belongs to some rare Central Asian breed of enormous snob-value. Therefore the form I filled in on 15 September, to begin the arduous process of obtaining Irish citizenship for Tashi, boldly proclaimed her to be a Miniature Himalayan Sheepdog.

A week previously I had informed the Irish Embassy in Delhi that on 3 December I planned to land in Dublin with a Nepal-born dog. In reply came a parcel of lengthy documents making it plain that Ireland's Department of Agriculture is allergic to alien quadrupeds. One could visualise the thin-lipped bureaucrat who had devised all these regulations to wither any imprudent relationships cultivated by expats. Reading them hardened my determination to 'import a domestic pet of the canine species into the State from a place abroad ... separately confined in a suitable hamper, crate, box or other receptacle which must be nose and paw proof and not contain any hay, straw or peat-moss litter'. Impatiently I completed the preliminary forms and wrote letters to 'the approved quarantine premises' and 'the approved carrying agents' while Tashi lay happily by my feet unaware that during the next few months a lot of people were going to make a very big fuss about a very little dog.

Throughout October and November all my 'reminding' letters to the Irish Embassy in Delhi and the Department of Agriculture in Dublin were ignored. By 26 November Tashi's entry-permit should have been awaiting me in Kathmandu but it wasn't. From there I sent many frantic cables to Delhi and Dublin, Tashi accompanying me every morning to the new 'Indian aid' Telephone and Telegraph office. While I drafted progressively less polite messages the staff eyed my companion derisively and commented on the unusual brand of lunacy revealed by the compulsion to import such an object to Ireland. After four days of impoverishing communications I ended my campaign defiantly; at 3.20 p.m. on 3 December a black-and-tan bitch from Nepal would land at Dublin airport with or without her visa which had been applied for on 15 September.

In Delhi we stayed with friends for a few days while Tashi received and recovered from numerous inoculations. At once she displayed characteristic Tibetan adaptability, both to her new surroundings and her new friends. In a bazaar near the Red Fort I bought the statutory 'nose- and paw-proof' basket which is still in use almost half a century later as a bathroom laundry basket. On the eve of our departure I cunningly took Tashi to Air India's central office and introduced her to the Authorities. Nothing else was necessary; they immediately agreed that it would be superfluous to imprison such a very small passenger between Delhi and London. Moreover, it could easily be arranged to have an empty seat beside mine. And so it came about that Tashi, conceived in western Tibet and born in a nomad's tent at the base of Machhapuchhare, now had the run of a Boeing 707. It's hard to believe that air travel was once so easy-going.

When we stopped at Beirut, Tashi expressed the need for a grassy spot – and promptly disappeared into the darkness of the night. As engine trouble in Bombay had already delayed us by three hours the captain asked the passengers if they would be kind enough to forgive another delay – this time a short one – while Miss Murphy pursued her puppy. At Prague I chained her, lest she might have anti-Communist prejudices.

The scene at Dublin airport was surreal. My final defiant cable had activated a platoon of uniformed officials who were falling over each other in their anxiety to ensure that the infinitesimal Tashi did not break loose and overnight turn the nation rabid. A grotesquely large covered truck stood waiting to transport the mini-basket to the State Quarantine Kennels ten miles away and to my fury I was refused permission to accompany Tashi through the alien cold wetness of an Irish winter night.

Next morning I found that the kennels were exceptionally well run and during her six months' isolation Tashi remained in perfect condition and grew a little more. Although my regular fortnightly visits delighted her she accepted my departures with composure – until at last came the day when she departed too, into breezy green fields and bright June sunshine. The joy she then showed at racing free can have been no greater than my own on seeing that little black body again unfurling its ridiculous brown tail in the wind.

TASHI WAS AGED three and a half when Rinchen Dolma Taring – Amala – came to stay with me in Ireland while writing her autobiography, *Daughter of Tibet*. His Holiness the Dalai Lama had given her four months leave from her job as Director of Mussoorie Children's Homes. Time being so limited, we lived in isolation, working twelve hours a day with only one day off – to celebrate Losar, the Tibetan New Year.

My role was not to ghost Amala's book but to give advice – a much slower process – and I soon realised that a Buddhist's autobiography is a contradiction in terms if the writer is as 'advanced' as Amala. Her spiritual training had encouraged the obliteration of the Self and conventional autobiography requires a certain concentration on that entity. I recall our standing in the kitchen, beside a round table, and my laying a finger on its centre while saying, 'You're supposed to be here, in relation to this book. Everything else must derive its importance from being linked to you.' Amala chuckled, dismissed this primitive notion and went on to write an idiosyncratic volume of layered social and political history.

Amala's father, Tsarong Shap-pe Wangchuk Gyalp, was descended from a famous physician, Yuthok Yonten Gonpo, who, during the reign of King Trinsong Detsen (AD 755–757), studied Sanskrit medicine at Nalanda University in India. Yonten Gonpo's block print biography of 149 leaves, containing some of his drawings and diagrams, was destroyed when the Red Guard attacked Lhasa's Government Medical College. Tsarong Shap-pe married Yangchen Dolma – descended from the Tenth Dalai Lama's family – and Amala was their ninth surviving child. In 1886 her paternal grandfather, Tsipon Tsarong, had been dispatched to the Tibetan-Sikkimese border by the Dalai Lama to negotiate its demarcation with representatives of the Raj.

By 1903 the Raj was feeling extra-twitchy about a Russian take-over of Tibet and the Younghusband Mission set off to put British relations with that country 'on a proper basis'. This alarmed the Abbots of Lhasa's three great monasteries who regarded all outsiders as enemies of Buddhism. They urged the Thirteenth Dalai Lama to instruct Amala's father, the senior lay Cabinet Minister, and his monk equivalent, to hasten to the Sikkimese border (three weeks' ride) and persuade the British to come no further. As a result, the Younghusband Mission became the infamous Younghusband Expedition which on its way to Lhasa in 1904 slaughtered some 500 Tibetan soldiers armed only with obsolete weapons.

Later that year, Tsarong was one of the four Shap-pes (lay cabinet ministers) who signed a Convention with Britain – forbidding Tibet to have relations with any other foreign power. In 1912, when Amala was a toddler, her father and eldest brother – then a twenty-five-year-old government servant – were murdered on the steps of the Potala. Some said Tsarong Shap-pe had made enemies by signing the Convention without consulting the Dalai Lama's government. Others believed that he and his son were distrusted for 'liking foreigners too much' and introducing to the country novelties of ill-omen. When government business took Tsarong to India in 1907 he returned with sensational inventions – sewing machines and cameras.

Amala wrote and talked with honesty, tolerance and humour, describing a society that genuinely cultivated non-violence yet could be very bloody indeed. As the weeks passed I felt as though I had left Ireland, mentally and emotionally, and was living in a world that had survived, almost untouched by the outside, for more than a millennium – and had then been shattered forever a mere decade before Amala sat in my home distilling its essence on paper in her neat, firm handwriting.

Just as the Tibetan language, in 1950, lacked the vocabulary to deal with a mechanised, industrialised, scientific era, so we lack the vocabulary to deal with Old Tibet. In that context, such words as feudalism, serfdom, autonomy, education – even religion – have a misleading resonance. The Lord Buddha is not, conceptually, the 'equivalent' of the Jewish/Christian/Muslim 'God'. And of course 'feudalism' insults the complexity of Tibet's social organisation.

Most Westerners are ill-equipped to comprehend a country in which all legal, social and political systems and institutions were based on the Buddhist dharma which had long ago been modified and adapted to produce that singular phenomenon known as Tibetan Buddhism. Although the pre-Communist way of life was not, as some like to imagine, 'deeply spiritual' – in the sense of being guided by devout, mystical scholar-priests – it was genuinely permeated by abstract spiritual values. Few lamas were 'hypocritical parasites' living off the labour of 'cowed serfs'; only a small minority entered the monasteries for no other motive than to enjoy a life of ease.

Tibet's nobility was based mainly in Lhasa where each of the two hundred or so families had to provide one layman to serve as a government official alongside a monk colleague – the two having equal status and responsibility. In theory, families lacking a male to fulfil this duty forfeited their land, all of which was leased from the state. There was however an escape clause. With His Holiness's permission, a son-in-law could change his forenames, take his wife's family name and save the day. After the assassination of Amala's father and brother, a peasant named Chensal Namgang – a favourite of the Thirteenth Dalai Lama – married one of her older sisters and was ennobled. Subsequently he married another sister and in 1928 he married Amala and fathered her first child. (Most Tibetan marriages were monogamous but polygamy and polyandry were equally acceptable.) In 1929 Jigme Sumtsen Wang-po, Prince of Taring, arrived on the scene: a politically desirable second husband for Amala. Chensal Namgang helped to arrange the marriage of this third wife to her handsome young prince. When my daughter and I stayed with the Tarings in Mussoorie in 1974 they were still very obviously in love.

The upward mobility of Chensal Namgang – son of a smallholder and arrow-maker – was not unusual. Old Tibet was free of European-style class barriers. Rich and poor visited each other's homes and formed friendships if personally inclined to do so. A monk from the humblest background, if suitably gifted, could rise high in his monastery's hierarchy. The families of Dalai Lamas were automatically ennobled; only two of the fourteen came from the hereditary nobility. The same schools served the children of nobles, traders, craftsmen and peasants; an erring young noble might find him or herself being chastised by a peasant prefect. Family servants gave heeded advice about who should marry whom, and other important matters. Each craft – artists, goldsmiths, moulders, masons, boot-makers, tailors, carpenters, weavers, dyers – had its own respected guild. Many craftsmen were richer than some senior noble officials and the guild leaders were always seated above the younger nobles at official Palace occasions.

Even more remarkable was Tibet's cultural history as outlined by Amala – the Buddhist-powered evolution of a pacifist state. Long ago, Tibet's warriors were renowned: brave and ferocious. The Chinese recorded nineteen serious Tibet versus China conflicts between AD 634 and 849 and the Tibetans were almost always the aggressors. At one stage Tibet's army crossed the River Oxus, invaded Samarkand and prompted Harun Al-Rashid, the Caliph of Baghdad, to ally himself with the Chinese.

Buddhism began to put down deep roots after the death in 842 of the anti-Buddhist Kind Lang Dharma. In 1249, when the Sakya Pandita came to power, it was unthinkable that anyone could rule Tibet without the support of a Buddhist sect. The change from militarism to a society influenced by non-violent principles was gradual and sometimes faltering yet there was no fudging on a par with Christianity's conveniently elastic 'just war'. However, Tibet was riven for centuries by sectarian rivalries and inter-monastery jealousies, occasionally leading to brief battles. But those lamentable aberrations were recognised as such at the time; physical violence was no longer taken for granted as a legitimate means of settling disputes. And since the mid-seventeenth century the institution of the Dalai Lama had brought to Tibet an extraordinary degree of social stability, described by the Chinese invaders as 'stagnation'.

Some of Amala's recollections made me wish that I, too, had been born in Tibet in 1910. I would have happily settled for incarnation as a lady's maid if that job required me to ride for twelve days to a country estate, crossing a landscape of incomparable beauty where human beings were scarce and animals plentiful: bears, wolves, bighorn sheep, musk deer, wild yak. On every side roamed huge herds of chiru (a Tibetan antelope), gazelles and wild asses; by the many lakes dwelt an abundance of birds. It delighted Amala that most creatures showed no fear of approaching caravans. Hugh Richardson, a British Trade Consul who lived in Lhasa during the 1940s and was a close friend of the Tsarongs, noted: 'The majority of people make efforts to live as much as possible with nature, not against it.' Because the Chinese live otherwise Tibet's wildlife is by now on the verge of extinction.

To spend four months in the company of only one person, collaborating in the intrinsically intimate task of memoir-writing, is a rare experience. By some mysterious process of osmosis that time of close companionship with Amala changed me – not in any obvious way, but inwardly and permanently. Yet I was never tempted to 'become a Buddhist'. There is a theory – I forget, if I ever knew, who first articulated it – that the Tibetan diaspora, though so heartbreaking for so many, must benefit the rest of the world. I can easily believe that the majority of Tibetan exiles, living out of the limelight and perhaps no longer readily identifiable, are continually enriching the various communities amongst whom they have settled.

On the sad day of Amala's departure, Tashi accompanied us to Cork airport. Her tail dropped as her compatriot disappeared. They had become mutually devoted.

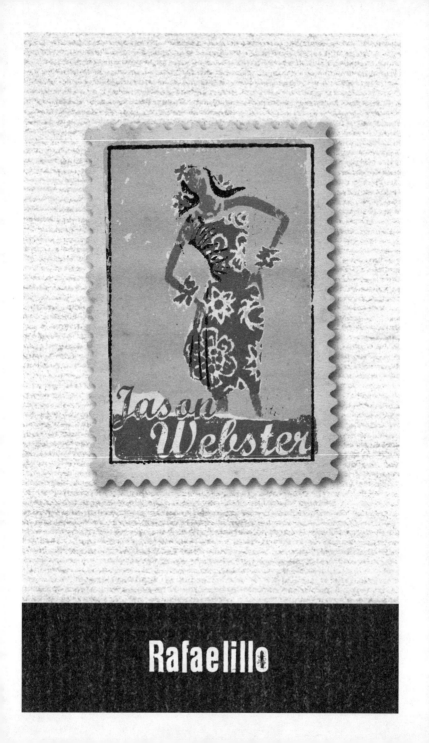

Jason Webster

Rafaelillo

JASON WEBSTER (born Mountain View, California, 1970) is the author of four travel books on Spain, including **Duende**, an account of his experiences searching for the heart of flamenco, and **Sacred Sierra**, about his life on a mountain farm. He is currently writing a series of Max Cámara crime thrillers, set in Valencia, the first of which, **Or The Bull Kills You**, is published in 2011. He lives with his wife, a flamenco dancer, and their two sons, in Valencia. **www.jasonwebster.net**

Rafaelillo

JASON WEBSTER

It wasn't typical bullfighting weather: cold winds were blowing in off the mountains to the north-west and spectators were wrapped in coats and scarves. Not a straw hat in sight. But the people of Castellón were used to it, a small price to pay for the honour of staging the first serious *corridas* of the new season each year. Except that the city's lunar-calculated fiesta had fallen earlier than usual this time, and there was still plenty of force in the tail-end of a harsh winter.

Nonetheless, the bullring was packed. The day before, José Tomás, one of the greatest matadors in the history of *los toros*, had appeared triumphantly here, hauled up onto hired shoulders at the end of the fight and carried through the main gate in celebration of his genius. Today it was the turn of El Juli, José María Manzanares and most importantly Miguel Angel Perera to face six bulls from the Zalduendo farm. If anyone was getting close to José Tomás, they said it was Perera, and every aficionado in the crowd was waiting for the first two matadors to finish so he could come to his own conclusion.

It had been impossible getting a ticket to see José Tomás – the last seats had sold on the black market for thousands of euros.

But for today, at least, I'd managed to find a gap, and the man who would be talking me through the afternoon's slaughter was a retired bullfighter himself – Rafa Ataide, or 'Rafaelillo'.

In his time, Rafaelillo had been a *banderillero* – a specialist with the brightly coloured darts that were thrust with acrobatic skill into the bull's shoulders during the mid-point of the fight. Today, he was an elegant-looking Spanish gentleman, with slicked-back white hair, a cleanly shaven chin and wearing a thick tweed jacket over ochre-coloured corduroy trousers. He smiled politely at the foreigner at his side jotting down comments and observations in a black policeman's notebook.

'Research?'

'I'm writing a novel.'

'About bullfighting?'

'A matador gets killed in it.'

He looked away. 'You'll learn about death here.'

High-pitched whistling cut through the air. A man sitting on the stone seats behind us had stood up and was gesticulating and shouting, joining other spectators in vitriolic protest. Down in the ring, a well-fed horseman was pushing a long spike deep into the bull's neck.

'What's going on?' I shouted to Rafaelillo over the din.

'They want the picadors to stop,' he said. 'If they wound the bull too much it loses its strength to carry on with the fight.'

'So why do this, then?'

No reply. Perhaps some questions wouldn't get answers.

The *banderilleros* strode out, raising their weapons above their heads, provoking the bull. They skipped, then ran at an angle towards the surging beast, deftly planting the spikes into its back before arching themselves to safety and sprinting away. Rafaelillo's attention didn't waver from the men performing what had been his own art form years before.

'Do you miss it?'

'This is my life,' he said. 'That doesn't change when age forces you to retire.'

'Were you ever frightened?' The bulls weigh anything up to 600 kilos, like a small car. And while some scoff from a distance that the odds are stacked in the bullfighters' favour, there was no denying – from here – the animals' lethal force.

'I felt fear all the time,' Rafaelillo said. 'A fear unlike anything other men have felt. You embrace it; it becomes your passion, your lover. You need it.' After a pause he added: 'Fear, yes, always. Cowardice, never.'

The *banderilleros* finished and the final act began – the *tercio de muerte*, or act of death. Perera the matador walked out onto the sand with his red *muleta* cape and sword tucked under his arm. He took off his *montera* cap, saluted the audience, then unrolled the cape and hitched it up with the length of the blade. To the side of him the bull stood panting and bleeding, taking its time.

This was Perera's moment, his chance to perform. The day before José Tomás had had them on their feet, cheering. Would the younger man be able to do the same at this, his first bullfight of the season? A sharp freezing wind blew through us, ruffling the matador's cape. 'That's bad,' Rafaelillo said. 'There's only one thing worse than windy conditions, and that's a *manso* bull, one with no fighting spirit in it.'

I glanced up briefly at the mountains just visible in the distance. Through the dark grey cloud it was possible to make out the peaks turning white with snow.

'Wouldn't an unaggressive bull be easier?' I asked.

'Quite the reverse. A *manso* bull is the hardest to read. Most of the time it's trying to get out of the ring, then suddenly it might lift its horns in a way no one expected...'

He tossed his head to one side, as though skewering an invisible matador standing next to him.

'What you want, what everyone wants, is a truly *bravo* bull, one that takes the fight to the bullfighter, that never gives up and struggles till the very end. That's where the real beauty comes. That's where the art and power is.'

'You make it sound like a sacred act.'

Still looking down at the ring, he pursed his lips. Then without warning he leant over and pulled open my jacket and lifted my jumper up a fraction, then glanced down at my shoes.

'Leather belt, leather boots,' he said. 'I take it you're not a vegetarian.'

'No.'

'I respect vegetarians. I don't agree with them, but I respect them.'

He rubbed long fingers over his chin.

'What I can't abide are those who condemn me as a murderer while eating fillet steak and wearing leather jackets.'

'Perhaps it's the public aspect of this they don't like,' I said. 'Turning it into a spectacle.'

'If you think this is just a spectacle, then you haven't understood anything about bullfighting.'

He turned his attention back to the events on the sand.

I thought of trying another question, but it was clear that Rafaelillo wasn't listening. In the ring, Perera was performing his first moves, his feet planted firmly on the ground, chin pulled in, hips thrust forward. He was tall for a bullfighter, and from his posture and presence appeared to be towering over the bull. The audience had fallen into a concentrated silence, and for a moment the 'fight' became quite gentle, the bull being drawn, as though spellbound, by the red cloth, passing backwards and forwards in front of this man in his glittering suit.

A first, lonely cry of *olé* came from somewhere across the ring. A pause, and it was followed by another, then several more at once. Within seconds the entire crowd was cheering and clapping: a moment of magical force had sprung up, like a jinn, and gripped us. Behind, the whistling man of earlier had stood up again, and was shouting with all his strength.

¡Olé, olé, olé!

I sat motionless, my eyes fixed on the drama below. Perera seemed to have brought the bull quickly and silently under his command.

Then something extraordinary unfolded, something so strange it was like a kiss, an unexpected yet meaningful kiss from a beautiful woman you thought was unattainable. It was as if the division between matador and bull disappeared, as though for a fleeting instant they became one single being, brought together and unified by their struggle: one entity, not separated by their mutual wish to kill each other, but drawn to each other by a kind of tenderness, a passion. It was as if, for a brief time, they were joined through something that felt almost like love. But it was not any kind of love that I had ever sensed or been aware of before, nothing I had ever known. And yet it was there, binding them and making them one.

It came in a flash, one exceptional moment, and was gone. But the entire crowd had felt it as well, and a roar went up. Many were on their feet, clapping, more shouts of *olé* echoing around, while at the other side of the arena the band started up on a *paso doble*.

Rafaelillo turned and looked at me. He could see it in my face: yes, I'd sensed it as well.

'Do you understand now?'

No need to answer.

'It can't be explained. It can only be experienced.'

My gaze returned to the graceful and powerful figure of Perera below.

'This is what they want to take away from us. They are only capable of seeing a man killing a bull in public. Nothing more. And it shocks them, so they want it to be hidden away.'

He swept an arm through the air.

'But this is not an unsung, unheroic death along with millions of others in some industrial abattoir. Here we look death in the face, and the bull looks death in the face, and with that we celebrate life. This is not a sport. Nor is it a spectacle. It is a ritual with ancient roots, involving everyone here – bull, bullfighters and audience.'

Perera was now stretched up onto the balls of his feet, the sword raised high above his head, ready to push down into the bull's back. A few metres in front of him, the bull's horns gleamed a dull white in the overhead lights, sharp and hungry. The final scene: within seconds, one of these two – man or bull – would be dead. The only sound came from the wind rippling through the flags above our heads.

'If you hide from death you run from life,' Rafaelillo said in a low voice. 'Life is not an absence of death. Without death there is no life. That is what bullfighting celebrates.'

I stared down at the sword in Perera's hand, the dark congealing blood, the dry heavy tongue hanging from the bull's mouth. The crisp, ecstatic feeling of just a few moments before still lingered, vivifying the cold evening air.

'That is what makes this sacred.'

The Piece of String

PHOTO © ERANGA TENNEKOON

SHEHAN KARUNATILAKA (born Galle, Sri Lanka, 1975) was raised in Colombo before exile in New Zealand. He has written ads, rock songs and travel stories, but spent the last three years interviewing drunkards and watching Sri Lankan cricket games. The result was a novel about a sportswriter's quest to find a forgotten cricketing genius, **Chinaman: The Legend of Pradeep Mathew**, selected as one of Waterstones top debut novels for 2011.**www.shehanwriter.com**

The Piece of String

SHEHAN KARUNATILAKA

I s this the world's longest staircase? asks Tomas on the way up. Had I the energy I would've replied that it sure felt like it. My companion had dragged me up this mountain kicking and screaming, though after the first hour, my legs had lost the ability to kick. They say only a fool would visit Sri Lanka and not climb Adam's Peak. They also say that only a fool would climb it twice.

Officially, the world's longest staircase is next to the Niesenbach tram tracks in the Swiss Alps. And while it is conceivable that this service stairwell has stories written about it, I doubt they are as numerous and as beguiling as those surrounding Adam's Peak. Known also as Sri Pada and Butterfly Mountain, this cathedral of rock and shrub has attracted pilgrim, explorer, king and holy man for many millennia. Each year the curious and the faithful throng by the thousand to negotiate these jagged steps and greet the sunrise. To watch the mountain's shadow fall upon the clouds and to bow before the footprint at the summit.

We're here to see a man about a piece of string. Not just any piece of string and, according to Tomas, not just any man.

The string in question is a *pirith noola*, an innocuous thread tied around the wrist to ward off evil and offer its wearer protection and strength. Tiger Woods, a lapsed Buddhist, has taken to wearing one, presumably to ward off raunchy text messages from porn stars. He has pledged to wear it for the rest of his life.

Many Sri Lankan Buddhists sport a *pirith noola* as a symbol of piety or as a visual reminder of a solemn vow. You can see one below the batting gloves of '96 World Cup hero, Sanath Jayasuriya or on the wrists of politicians trying to prove their spiritual chops to skeptical constituents. You can pick one up for free at any Buddhist temple around the country. Why we have to climb five hours' worth of stairs to get one is a question Tomas promises to answer once we reach the summit.

A cheerful Scandinavian investment banker in his thirties, Tomas is a frequent visitor to the island his mother hails from. Like many Sri Lankans who haven't grown up here, he sees magic in sights that jaded locals like myself find prosaic. Where I see a piece of string, a pointless climb or an overrated footprint, Tomas sees a mystical quest.

The footprint and its mysteries are shared by four religions. Not unlike how the mountain is shared by four rivers; the Mahaveli, Kalu, Walawe and Kelani. Each using a different path to reach a common destination. Buddhists believe Lord Buddha harnessed the summit's energies to levitate upon it. Hindus see the colossal imprint of Shiva. The Muslims believe it may belong to the first man, Adham, while some Christians claim that St Thomas the Doubter ascended to heaven from here.

I decide to ignore my misgivings and the silly proverb. It is my second visit and though my muscles and joints would beg to differ, I do not feel foolish for being here. My last climb was as a teenager and was less a spiritual quest and more of a box to tick. I raced to the top in under three hours and stifled disappointment that the foot didn't resemble a Hollywood Walk of Fame imprint. The relic was gigantic and adorned with symbolic carvings. In terms of realism, as Dr John Davy described in 1817, it 'bears some coarse resemblance to a human foot'. Unimpressed, I then dozed off during a grey and rainy sunrise.

THIS TIME, FOR PHYSICAL as well as spiritual reasons, I take this ascent slower. I stop to admire the trail of lights weaving across the rock face, chat with pilgrims at the tea shacks along the way, and watch the full moon throwing silver over the evergreens. I gaze at the summit and wonder how many cups of tea before I reach there. That's when Tomas tells me about his last visit. It was December 2004 and he'd just been dumped by his fiancée of eight years. 'I told everyone I was searching for my roots, but that was bullshit. I just wanted to go some place no one knew my face.'

He braved the mountain solo and was smoking a cigarette on a rock, when a man in robes leading an entourage of stray dogs offered him a cup of tea. The man wore thick spectacles and carried his tea in a plastic bag that looked like a water balloon filled with rust. The man poured the liquid into a coconut shell, offered it to my friend and then bummed a smoke.

'I didn't know holy men smoked,' I say, catching my breath.

'That's what I thought,' says Tomas. 'He said it was for a friend.'

The man claimed to have lived in a cave on the mountain since he was thirteen. He said that he had climbed to the top every full moon. He then offered to read Tomas's palm. 'You have lost something that you think you will never find,' said the man. 'But you are wrong.'

The man then pulled a reel of thread from his cloth bag and without warning began muttering in tongues and wrapping the string around Tomas's wrist. When he had finished he smiled at my friend and said something that haunts Tomas to this day: 'You are stronger than you think you are. You will use your strength to help people who have lost more than you.'

Three weeks later, Tomas found himself in the south of Sri Lanka, clinging to a coconut tree, watching refrigerators, bicycles and screaming children engulfed in whirlpools. As the tsunami raged around him, Tomas clung to that tree for twenty-seven minutes staring at the piece of string on his wrist.

SRI PADA HAS ATTRACTED visitors from all corners of history. Moroccan traveler Ibn Batuta writes of pathways filled with giant roses and multi-coloured flowers, a cave spring filled with fishes that no one can catch, and a blessed footprint adorned in gold, ruby and pearl. He also mentions 'chains of faith' that dangle from the edge of the peak, offering intrepid pilgrims a final test of devotion.

In the fifteenth century, Persian poet Ashraff records that these iron chains were placed here by Alexander the Great. The king and his companion, Greek magician Bolina, arrived in Sri Lanka – or Taprobane, as it was known circa 300 BC – to take a break from empire-building.

Today the chains are replaced by steel ladders, railings and steps. While the climb takes me longer than my previous effort, I feel something magnetic and indefinable pulling me towards the summit. It could be my will, though it feels like something far more powerful.

TOMAS SPENT SIX MONTHS after Boxing Day 2004 as a volunteer for the Red Cross, burying corpses, clearing rubble, manning phone lines, arguing with bureaucrats, and playing with silent children. His ex-fiancée called asking him to come home and he politely asked her not to call back.

We see many characters on our way to the top, but none of them resemble the man from Tomas's memory. Tomas extracts a browned morass of thread from his wallet. It resembles hair pulled from a bathtub plughole.

'I've worn this for the past five years,' he says, not without pride. 'I think it's time I got a new one.'

We marvel at old ladies in white negotiating the incline, armed only with walking stick and prayer. There is the great bell at the summit that pilgrims toll to signify how many journeys they have taken. One of these ladies would ring that bell nineteen times and smile at me kindly as I sheepishly rang it twice.

We are followed all the way by one of Sri Pada's many guardians, a brown mongrel dog, who stays three paces behind and stops whenever we do. We meet a Japanese monk who says he climbs twice a week. I look forward to watching him ring the bell several hundred times, but suspect that he may be well past such vanities. He carries a tiny drum, which he taps in rhythm with his footsteps. We ask him if he knows of a bespectacled monk who lives in a cave. He shakes his head.

We meet followers of the sun, who gaze at the descending *poya* moon with pleasure, their camera lenses poised to capture the morning rays.

But mostly it is the pilgrims. Observing customs that date back to 100 BC, when King Valagamba first discovered this mythic footprint. They bathe in the icy streams of Seethagangula, say *pansil* prayers and tie a coin wrapped in white cloth for protection. At Indikatu Pana, some place a threaded needle on a shrub to mark the spot where the Buddha mended a torn robe.

Over the centuries, dynasties of kings have helped clear this trail and raise the temple at the top. We arrive there a few hours before sunrise and visit the shrine to the god Saman, one of the many deities protecting this mount. Tomas is visibly disappointed and I suggest he get a *pirith noola* from the nearby temple.

'It's not the same,' he says. 'If you saw the guy, you'd understand.' People see divinity in strange things. I realise that belief can build mountains. Higher and sturdier than the one we had just conquered.

WE JOIN THE QUEUE to lay flowers at the feet of the foot. This time, I am more respectful. I marvel at the weighty symbols carved upon its face and imagine the original foot relic, said to be buried under the rock and set in jewels.

A brass lamp, set there by King Wickremabahu in the fourteenth century, casts a light that never goes out. We look for some shadow to sit upon. The fluorescent bulbs at the peak, tastelessly kept on throughout the morning, are an aesthetic and spiritual irritation. We opt to settle below the summit and watch as the sky changes colour.

Tomas is silent. December 2004 was a turning point in his life and the *pirith noola* is the thread that links him to his spiritual awakening. I have met too many false prophets in my time and I keep my cynicism to myself. I see divinity in guitar riffs, in camera angles, in a well-told joke or a nicely executed cover drive. I have visited cathedrals, mosques and temples, but God does not speak to me. Even in the holiest of places.

But then the sun emerges and stirs a primal awe in everything around me. Silver gives way to gold. Orange rays obscure the white *poya* glow. The distant sound of chanting melts into the silence and then gradually we begin to see it. The shadow of a pyramid lengthening over the clouds. It sits there for less than forty-five minutes, like a message from God that we are unable to decipher.

Herman Hesse had a transcendental experience at this very spot, gazing upon this revelation of light and shadow. This is where Arthur C. Clarke imagined a portal to the stars. Maybe it's not necessary to decipher a message in order to understand it.

THE DESCENT IS HARD. Paralysis has set into my lower body and I am grappling with the well-trodden path, the rising sun and the whims of gravity. But I am also seeing things that the darkness hid from me. The pitcher plants, the hub-nosed lizards and the pink orchids. The towns in the distance and, somewhere behind the clouds, the ocean.

From the corner of my eye I recognise the dog who followed us on the ascent. A scraggy mutt with a broken tail, he darts off to the side of the trail, where he joins three other dogs in various states of disrepair. Behind them, bearing a cloth bag and a tree branch, is an upright man in his fifties, wearing saffron robes and large spectacles.

Tomas stops in his tracks, clasps his hands and gazes at the man. He holds up his tattered thread and walks towards him. The man smiles as the dogs circle his feet.

Sri Lankans smile for many complex reasons, but usually to disguise confusion. I can see from the eyes behind the thick spectacles, that this man does not have the foggiest idea who my friend is, but recognises a customer when he sees one.

We are led off the track through shrub. The man's name is Chittasena and his English is better than Tomas's Sinhalese. He repeats his story. The cave he lives in was occupied by a great ascetic who died when Chittasena was thirteen. He has been climbing the mountain and looking after its strays ever since.

I am less than convinced. The cave we are led to is a cavern of kitsch. It smells of kerosene and houses a bed, a large alarm clock, a shrine to an unnamed deity and piles of magazines. While it is perfectly acceptable for a holy man to read *Newsweek*, I wonder if the three rat-traps in the corner of his home are in harmony with his beliefs.

Tomas is enthralled as the man shows us how he has diverted a nearby stream to run past his front doorway. The door is adorned with Buddhist symbols and overlooks a river. 'This is where I meditate,' says Chittasena, eyeing me with suspicion.

He speaks in an even tone with long pauses, as if he is listening out for something. I wonder if I am being unduly harsh in my judgements. He offers to read my palm and I decline. 'I'd rather not know my future,' I say.

'You like to travel,' he says. 'But you don't like travelling.'

I ignore him and point at a black eagle soaring below the temple. Two yellow-eared bulbul birds hop from step to step as if observing a vow to abstain from flying. And finally, standing before the cave of a monk I do not fully trust, I see the butterflies.

They fly in waves from all directions to die on this holy mountain. Some say they are angels who leave trails of jasmine leading to the footprint. Some say they are souls flying into the arms of God. I am seized by the sudden urge to follow them. To bear witness to their final sacrifice and to toll the bell a third time.

Tomas gets his fresh *pirith noola*. He tells the man of his tsunami experience and we share cups of tea. There is no bumming of cigarettes. Tomas has long given up and so has our friend, it would appear.

He tells us that he rarely talks to tourists or to the false monks from the Japanese monastery who climb the mountain in designer sneakers.

'This is my last year on the mountain,' he says with a smile. 'It is time for someone else to look after this cave.'

Do I tell Tomas that the man is a charlatan and that he knows less about the universe than we do? Do I tell Tomas that luck saved him from the tsunami and that tragedy awoke his spiritual conscience? That nothing in the world has anything to do with a piece of string?

Of course I don't. Instead I bow reverentially and offer the man my wrist. I think of the shadow of the mountain in the early morning sun, of a lost boy clinging to a coconut tree and gaze at Chittasena lighting the flames of his shrine. Despite myself, I recognise something serene and dignified about the way he carries himself.

I see the look of contentment on Tomas's face and decide that kindness is a far greater force than logic. I offer Chittasena a donation and ask for his blessing.

MANY OF THE WORLD'S holy places are fought over, but Adam's Peak is not one of them. For that I am grateful. It is shared by the rivers, the ravines, the curling trees and the many creatures that stumble to its summit. It tells us that all faiths have more in common than they think. That perhaps all religion could be one.

On the way down I gaze at the *pirith noola* on my wrist and decide that I will hold onto it until it falls off. I accept that the point of the journey is the journey. And that being in a hurry doesn't get you there faster.

Because it doesn't matter what mythology you choose to accept or what the sunrise at the summit chooses to reveal. What matters is that you accept the world for what it is and that you withhold judgement on things you do not understand. What matters is that you surrender to the holy mountain before you. And that you take the journey a step at a time.

SARA WHEELER

The End of the Bolster

SARA WHEELER (born Bristol, 1961) is a traveller, journalist and broadcaster. Her books include **Terra Incognita: Travels in Antarctica**, and **Cherry: A Life of Apsley Cherry-Garrard** (Cherry was one of Captain Scott's sledgers, and the author of the polar classic THE WORST JOURNEY IN THE WORLD). The book she most enjoyed writing, **The Magnetic North: Notes from the Arctic Circle**, was chosen as Book of the Year 2010 by Michael Palin, Will Self, A. N. Wilson and others. This year Jonathan Cape publish **Sara's Access All Areas: Selected Writings 1990-2010** to celebrate her fiftieth birthday.

The End of the Bolster

SARA WHEELER

In 1981, I purchased a return ticket to Warsaw on LOT airlines. I was twenty, with a year of university behind me. Why Poland? I really can't remember, except that the country had been in the papers a lot that year. I had been waitressing throughout the holidays and accrued the absurdly small sum to buy, in addition to the plane ticket, a month-long Polish rail pass.

It was already dark when I arrived in Warsaw, but I had the address of a government accommodation office and managed to get there on a tram. There was throughout the Soviet bloc at that time a scheme which arranged for visitors to stay in people's homes. It was cheap, and I thought it would be a good way of getting to know Poles.

The office had a full-length glass frontage behind which a stuffed eagle moulted kapok. A heavy revolving door scraped through its revolution like an orchestra tuning up. Two gorgons swathed in black behind a Formica desk looked up, briefly. I could see that they found the interruption to their knitting an irritation. A double room, it quickly emerged, was all that was available. I said I'd take it. It was against the rules, snapped

Gorgon One, revealing three gold teeth, for a single person to take a double room. She returned to her knitting with a triumphant clack of needles. I said I was prepared to pay double rates. 'Also illegal,' chipped in Gorgon Two, anxious not to miss out on the opportunity to ruin someone's day. In addition, they alleged there was not one hotel room available in the entire city.

I deployed a range of tactics, including tears. No dice. It was dark, I was in a strange city without a word of Polish.

At that moment the revolving door spluttered to tuneless life once more. All three of us looked up. The crones muttered darkly, no doubt about the damnable inconvenience of a second customer. A tall, blond man with marble-blue eyes and a rucksack sauntered athletically into the room.

'We'll take the double room,' I said to the crones.

She looked at her henchwoman. So it was all true.

The blond man put down his rucksack and held out his hand to shake mine. An elastoplast covered his right thumbnail. I knew from the first syllable that he was Australian. It turned out that he had already been on the road in the Eastern bloc for a month, so when I explained the non-accommodation situation, he found it perfectly normal that we should share a room.

We stayed in a high-rise in the industrial suburbs, guests of a saturnine family who had been instructed not to speak to us. (In those days, Poland was still a fomenting sea of suspicion, and people who rented out rooms were rigorously vetted.) So much for meeting Poles. Once we had settled in to our chilly billet, my new friend took up the cylindrical bolster that lay at the head of the double bed and placed it down the middle. 'No need to worry,' he said. 'This is my half,' and he pointed to the left side of the bed, 'and that's yours.'

The Security Services had been busy that year, doing what they most liked to do – shutting up everyone else, brutally if possible. Millions of Poles naturally reacted with anger, and in March Solidarity activists had coordinated an extraordinary general strike unique in the Eastern bloc. Tension had subsided somewhat, but the economy was a carcrash. Even though every food shop was empty, a queue snaked outside, the people waiting for some tiny rationed bit of something to be doled out from behind the counter. A Solidarity poster on the telegraph poles showed a black skull with a crossed knife and fork under it.

As for Teddy, following in the footsteps of so many of his compatriots, he had taken six months out to have a look at the world. His mother was a Pole who had arrived in Western Australia as a twenty-four-year-old refugee. She had married Teddy's father, a wood-turner from Perth, and they had worked hard and made good. Teddy, who was twenty-four, was the youngest of seven. He turned out to be a fine companion, with a relaxed Antipodean attitude to everything that the Polish system tossed in our path. It seemed natural that we should travel together. Before leaving Warsaw we paid 20p for opera tickets in Teatr Wielki, installing ourselves in the magnificently restored Moniuszko auditorium to listen to a fine coloratura soprano sliding up and down Amina's arias in *La Sonnambula*. Afterwards we sat in bars kippered with smoke, downing tiny glasses of vodka. We left the capital to wander through the mildewed rooms of baroque castles, and tore our jeans climbing to hermitages teetering on Gothic outcrops. We visited Teddy's mother's birthplace, where I took his photograph, and then travelled to the Tatra Mountains, where we swam in Lake Morskie Oko, climbed Mount Koscielec and ate spicy wild boar sausages. We discovered a new world – or so it seemed to us.

By the time we rode the Coal Trunk Line through the steel belt of Upper Silesia, I was struggling to ignore the fact that I really liked him. I kept telling myself that I'd be betraying the whole mature arrangement if anything happened between us. I had somehow absorbed the idea that travelling occurs in a separate moral universe, outside the confines of normal life. I know differently now.

One day, at the end of our second week together, we took an overnight train to Wroclaw. Early in the morning Teddy procured a cup of acorn coffee from a vendor through the train window and brought it to me, waking me by stroking my arm. When I opened my eyes I felt a rush of emotion. Despite all Poland's exotic unfamiliarity, I learnt then that the most foreign country is within.

The end, or beginning, came when we visited Chopin's birthplace, a modest manor in the Mazovian heartland. A group of musicians from the Warsaw Conservatory were giving Chopin piano recitals in the grounds; as we approached they were belting out mazurkas, but when we took our seats a young man began to play the incomparable C-sharp minor Scherzo. The fierce opening octaves uncoiled over forest, glades and the willowed hills behind the fast-flowing Utrata: a perfect setting for the music of an ardent patriot. But Chopin finished the piece at George Sand's summer house in Nohant, France. He was twenty-nine, consumptive, and guilty at his self-imposed exile in Louis-Philippe's France. Folded into the devotion, a betrayal. One forgot all that, though, and one even forgot Poland as the genius of the music took hold. The small amphitheatre of chairs gave onto a glade infused with the butterscotch light of late summer, and the intense final harmonies of the Scherzo – a climax of desire and longing – drifted away over the silver beeches. We sat there in the chequered shadow of the trees, Teddy rested his fingers on the nape of my neck, and that was the end of the bolster.

HUGH THOMSON

Encounter in the Amazon

HUGH THOMSON (born London, 1960) is a writer, film-maker and explorer, specialising in the Andes, where he led an expediton that discovered the Inca site of Cota Coca. He is the author of **The White Rock: An Exploration of the Inca Heartland** and **Cochineal Red: Travels through Ancient Peru**, and **Nanda Devi** – about a Himalayan valley ringed by 20,000 ft peaks. His most recent book is **Tequila Oil**, a memoir about 'getting lost in Mexico'.
www.thewhiterock.co.uk

Encounter in the Amazon

HUGH THOMSON

John Hemming is the epitome of a certain sort of English gentleman – courteous, retiring and extremely modest. Now seventy-five, he was the Director of the Royal Geographical Society for over two decades. He has written definitive histories of both the conquest of the Incas and the tribes of the Amazon. But beneath the reserved exterior of this scholarly explorer lies a life of unusual adventure and risk-taking that began with the most remarkable story. For as a young man, in 1961, he lost his closest friend, Richard Mason, who became the last Englishman to be killed by an undiscovered tribe in the Amazon.

I first met John thirty years ago when I was planning my own expedition to Peru to look for Inca ruins. He lived then, as he still does, in a quiet Kensington square. It was characteristically gracious of him to advise me, as at that stage I had very little experience. He led me down the dark hall of his house and into a study lined with books about South America, with shafts of light from high windows. In a curious way, that moment of entering his study with him felt like the first step in the process of discovery. He told me part of the story then, and over the years I have filled in other sections, but it was only recently that we discussed at length not only the tragic events of the 1961 expedition but his later quest to find the perpetrators.

The expedition had begun so well. It was Richard Mason who suggested to John that they take a team to an unmapped part of the Amazon. They had been room-mates at Oxford and had already developed a taste for exploration: Richard had crossed South America by Land Rover, while John had managed to get a berth on a freighter to Peru. They recruited a third member, the unlikely figure of Kit Lambert, an old schoolfriend of Richard's who was later to be The Who's manager, and set off.

At first the three young men, all in their twenties, felt they were living a wonderful adventure. By night they slept in hammocks; by day they mapped the beautiful and uncharted country along the Iriri River, having fun naming the lakes and hills after their girlfriends, just as a blameless river had been called after Theodore Roosevelt's son Kermit when the ex-president led an expedition to the Amazon in 1913.

Their technique for getting through the jungle was simple. One of them would lead the path-cutting team of wood-cutters. Aiming at a distant tree as a sightline, the leader would crash and hack his way forward through the undergrowth, while two men widened the trail behind and the others followed. John remembers it vividly: 'Sometimes we shot game – wild turkeys or tapirs – but generally we ate little and lost weight. We became pale from rarely seeing the sun, and were covered in bites and scratches. The compensation for all this effort was the beauty of virgin rainforest and the knowledge that no Westerner had ever trodden there before.

'Richard was a wonderful leader. His Portuguese was poor, but his hard work and optimism commanded respect and inspired the men even when the going was toughest.'

Yet progress proved slower than expected. Their stocks of food started to run down and John was dispatched to Rio de Janeiro to get more supplies and drop them back by parachute.

'I had no money. To get to Rio, I had to barter a bottle of whisky with a pilot, and then hitchhike my way from the airport into the city – where I found myself in the midst of an attempted coup. The whole air force had been grounded. Somehow I managed to get an air-sea rescue team to help us and found myself flying back across the jungle in an enormous seaplane to be dropped off with the new supplies. Then we ran into a lightning storm. It was a surreal experience, seeing the lightning surround us and illuminate the jungle canopy by night.

'In the middle of the storm, the co-pilot came back into the cargo-hold to tell me that they had picked up bad news on the radio. While I'd been away, the expedition had been attacked and someone had been killed. At that point they didn't know who.'

Only on landing did John discover what had happened. Richard Mason had been alone and going back down a trail they had previously cut. After months of exploring what the expedition had been told was uninhabited jungle, they had long stopped worrying about Indian attacks. But that is what seemed to have taken place. The others had come across his body carefully laid out on the path, surrounded by forty arrows and seventeen heavy clubs. A bag of sugar was spilled nearby, untouched – as was a lighter. Nothing had been taken.

John found Kit Lambert in a complete and understandable state of shock. In today's culture, Kit would have been more of a candidate for *I'm A Celebrity Get Me Out Of Here* than an actual expedition to the jungle. In later life he led a flamboyant and camp rock'n'roll lifestyle with The Who.

The two men's immediate concern was that there might be a further attack, so they hurried with the rest of their team to the relative safety of the one air-strip they could reach, Cachimbo, 'as isolated in the jungle as a small island in the South Atlantic'.

THE BRAZILIAN AUTHORITIES flew in some medics and a platoon of 'jungle troops' – who looked like they would have been more at home in the nightclubs of Rio. John asked if the body could be cremated. He was told that first there would have to be an examination to make sure that he hadn't been killed by other members of the expedition; they all had to return to the scene of the death.

For John, it was a terrible journey: 'We walked sombrely back along that familiar trail, sleeping at an old camp site. I remember it all as dreamlike, with the landmarks along the trail seeming unreal and the once-cheerful camp gloomy and strangely sinister. The medics embalmed Richard's body and we carried it out, wrapped in canvas and slung under a pole, for eventual burial in the British cemetery in Rio de Janeiro.'

While, like Kit, John was still in deep shock, he tried as best he could to rationalise his friend's death. As Kit and he agreed, at least it had been almost instantaneous – it could as easily have been a crash in one of the fast cars that Richard was so fond of driving. And then John did something which some might find surprising. He decided to leave a gift of machetes for the unknown attackers, hoping that they would conclude that the white men were well-intentioned. This was in the tradition of earlier Amazon explorers like Colonel Rondon.

The question that haunted John was how the attackers had come across Richard in supposedly uninhabited jungle: had they seen the smoke flares lit by the team for several days to guide John's plane when it made its expected parachute drop – and were they from an unreported village nearby or a long range hunting party from tribes known to be living in the far distance?

For many years it remained an unresolved mystery, though by carrying one of the jungle arrows back to an academic in Oxford ('I felt very conspicuous on the train'), John was able to get an identification for the tribal group who had committed the murder. It belonged to the Panará, at that time uncontacted by the outside world, and feared as savage and violent by neighbouring Brazilian tribes who called them 'The Men With Heads Cut Round' because of their pudding bowl haircuts.

In the decades that followed, John continued working in other areas of the Amazon and became a well-known expert on its history. It was not until forty years later that he finally came face to face with the tribe.

'I ASSUMED THAT all the Panará involved in Richard's death would by now be dead, and that their descendants would have forgotten that distant ambush. They had suffered too many calamities of their own since then. Within two years of their first face-to-face encounter with the outside world in

1973, their numbers had fallen from 600 to 80. They were then forced off their tribal land by gold prospectors and cattle-ranchers. The Brazilian Government's Indian Service had restricted access to them as a result. But when by chance we were able to reach the new Panará village when visiting another tribe nearby, I found that they did remember that first contact with a white man.'

With great good luck, one of the three people in the world who could speak the Panará language, anthropologist Elizabeth Ewart, was at the village when he arrived, so could translate. She told the tribe that John was a friend of the man they had killed and they became worried and apprehensive. Their leaders revealed that it had indeed been a long distance hunting party veering far from their usual path in search of Brazil nuts who had come across Richard in the jungle – or rather had come across the path the expedition had been cutting which, as John says, must have seemed like a motorway. They had waited beside it until they heard the 'swish' that Richard's jeans made from far down the path as he approached. One man said that the hunters had called out 'Come here' to Richard, and when he had not understood, they had killed him.

'I learnt,' said John, 'that doing so has always been the Panará way. Their word for "stranger" – for any non-Panará – is the same as for "enemy". It was also an old Panará tradition for every member of a party that killed someone to leave his weapons beside the body.'

None of the original killers were still alive, but one old woman revealed to John that she was the widow of the recently deceased Chief Sokriti, who had been among the hunting party. She was able to give more details: that the hunters had removed Richard's revolver – for signalling in case he got lost – but, not knowing what it was, had tried to smash it. They also clubbed something 'shiny and mirror-like' – his cigarette lighter, which the others later found near his body.

JOHN ASKED ABOUT the machetes he had left there and found that, as he had hoped, they had been accepted as peace tokens. To his surprise, given that Amazon Indians are not given to niceties of gratitude or sympathy, one man – a 'gentle giant called Teseya' – told him: 'We killed your friend in the old days when we did not know white men. We did not know that there are good white men and bad white men.' He named the good white men who had helped the tribe to return to part of its lands. 'You are a good white man. You may come back.' John took this as a form of apology, even remorse, for the ambush forty years before.

On leaving the Panará, John again flew over the Iriri River country that he had seen all those years before, much of it now looking like a lunar landscape from the damage left by cattle-ranchers and soya farmers. By ironic coincidence the Panará have ended up living in precisely that area where Richard Mason was killed – then a part of their distant hunting ground, but now one of the last bits of forest left to them. However, as John has pointed out in his recent book, *Tree of Rivers: The Story of the Amazon*, there are some optimistic gleams of light through the undergrowth. Since the 1960s the population of Amazon Indians has quadrupled, and there is now more respect for them in Brazil as the natural custodians of the planet's most important lung. Many Indians that have had contact with outside society, after seeing how the West lives, have chosen to go back to their own way of life. And even today, there are still at least thirty Indian tribes in Brazil who are known only because they have been seen from the air, and have never been contacted.

John still bears no bitterness to the Panará over the death of his friend: 'We were trespassers in their forests after all. The Brazilian Government's Indian Service have a saying for expeditions like ours: "Die if you must, but never kill". I do wish, though, that they had given Richard the time to convince them, even by sign language, of his good intentions, as I'm sure he would have.'

John Hemming's latest book is *Tree of Rivers: The Story of the Amazon.* It describes the struggles that have taken place in order to use, protect and understand the Amazon, and recalls the adventures and misadventures of the explorers, missionaries, indigenous Indians, naturalists, rubber barons, scientists, anthropologists, archaeologists, political extremists, prospectors and others who have been in its thrall.

RORY MACLEAN

Love in a Hot Climate

RORY MACLEAN (born Vancouver, Canada, 1954) is a writer, broadcaster and blogger. He is the author of eight books, including **Stalin's Nose** (Berlin to Moscow in a Trabant), **Under the Dragon** (on Burma), **Magic Bus** (reliving the hippy trail to India) and, most recently, **Gift of Time**, in which he comes home to travel with his mother on her final journey. He has visited Burma often over the past twenty years, moved by his encounters with the people: 'not least with the young woman named Ni Ni whose story seemed to encapsulate the tragedy of that beautiful, betrayed land'. www.rorymaclean.com

Love in a Hot Climate

RORY MACLEAN

n front, behind. In front, behind. She recalled his hands, so large that they had held her as a nest holds a bird. In front, behind. She felt his touch, his lips on her neck and thigh against hip, and let her head roll back in surrender. The gesture had excited him, making her laugh like the bulbuls that hid in the green groves of peepul trees. She felt foolish, always laughing at the wrong time. In front, behind. He had cupped her, clutched her, then found her again. Twist into upright. His urgency had scared her yet still she traced an ear and knotted a finger into a thick curl of fair hair. She felt the white heat blaze out of him. His broad limbs wrapped her to him, pulled her body onto his own. In front, behind. Leave the end. Lay in a new strand. He rose inside her, so deep that she thought she might burst, weaving himself into her flesh, coming with a sudden violence that made her want to cry out loud. In front, and behind the next stake. He fell silent yet held her with no less intensity, his pale skin folding around her own burnished brown.

Through the fevered February afternoons it had been that single moment of stillness which had touched her, knitting their fingers together as she now wove her baskets, her small copper hand contained within his palm. In front, behind. She had believed herself to be safe in his arms, as secure as she had felt with her father. The two men of her life – her lover and her father – had protected her. Now both were gone. Ni Ni finished the weave, working the bamboo in pairs, picking up the right-hand stake as she moved around the border, and tried to remember; what did it mean to love the right way?

IT HAD BEGUN with theft, and ended in ruin.

Ni Ni had grown up alone with her father in two small rooms that opened onto Rangoon's leafy Prome Road. She was an only child because her mother, who had never loved her husband properly, had run off with the refrigeration manager of the Diamond Ice Factory. The manager's cold demeanour had made Ni Ni and the other children shiver. It was his icy feet, they had whispered, which cooled the bottles of Lemon Sparkling and Vimto which no one could afford. But he had been a bolder man than Ni Ni's father, with better prospects. He had also come home at night to sleep, an important consideration for any young wife. The desertion had condemned her father to an existence on the periphery of life, for it had left him not tied to any woman's heart. Yet he continued to try to provide for his daughter. She may have worn *longyis* of plain cotton, not Mandalay silk, and sometimes found no *ngapi* fish paste on the table, but they seldom went hungry. Ni Ni wanted for nothing, except perhaps for less sensitive hands.

Ni Ni ran a small beauty stall from their second room selling lotions, balms and *tayaw* shampoo. Her hands had earned her a reputation for preparing the neighbourhood's finest *thanakha*, the mildly astringent paste used by Burmese women as combination cosmetic, conditioner and sunscreen. She would have preferred to go to school – pupils at Dagon State High School No. 1 wore a smart uniform with a badge on the pocket – but her father didn't make enough money to pay for the books, let alone the desk and teaching levy. So instead she helped to earn their living by laying her fingertips on her customer's cheeks. She leaned forward, willing from them confessions and complaints, then prescribed the ideal consistency of *thanakha*. Her sensitive touch could also advise them on a change of diet, even tell if they had eaten meat or made love last night. In a tea shop she could pick up a coffee cup and know if it had last been held by a man or a woman. Sometimes though the sensations became too painful and she could not bear even the lightest touch. The breath of air from a falling feather might send shivers to the ends of her fingers. A cooking fire's warmth would scald her. She dropped things. Then she would withdraw, her young laughter disguising adult tears, and wish away her paper-thin skin. She longed to have hard hands like her father.

Every evening Ni Ni's father rode his battered Triumph bicycle into the fiery Rangoon dusk. He worked nights in a central hotel for foreigners near the Sule Pagoda, massaging tired tourist bodies. The hotel collected his fee, paying him only a small retainer, but he was allowed to keep his tips. So sometimes at dawn Ni Ni awoke to the vision of a pound coin or a five euro note, tokens that her father had been given during the night. Over breakfast *mohinga* he told her about the far away places from where the money had come, not with resentment for those who could afford to travel or with a craving to see other countries himself, but out of simple curiosity.

'They are all yours,' he told her with pride. 'So when you marry you can be free to love your husband in the right way.'

'I will always stay here with you,' she assured him in childish devotion, then cheered away poverty's imprisonment. 'The right way is just to care for each other.'

The notes and coins were tucked into the matted walls and Ni Ni's father curled up beneath them, their sleeping room not being long enough for him to lie out straight. She and her father possessed only the two rooms and two *thin-bya* sleeping mats, a rice pot and betel box, her beauty stall and the bicycle. In a world so large they were content with their peaceful corner of it. Desire did not blind them, like the pickpocket who sees only the monk's pockets.

Ni Ni was thirteen years old when the bicycle vanished. Her father had left it leaning against the gate for no more than a minute. He had woken her with a crisp 1,000 yen note and returned to find his cycle gone. None of the neighbours had caught sight of the thief, not their friend Law San who owned the Chinese noodle stall or even the hawk-eyed gossip May May Gyi. Only Ko Aye, who ran a makeshift barber shop under the banyan tree, claimed to have seen an unfamiliar khaki lorry pass by, although nobody paid much attention to his observations. He had lost an eye back in 1962 and for more than forty years had confused running children with pariah dogs, ear lobes with tufts of knotted hair.

All that morning and half the hot afternoon Ni Ni watched her father standing beside the Prome Road looking left and right then left again. He glared at every cyclist who clattered past him. His suspicions were aroused by any newly painted machine. He chased after a man who had turned to ride off in the opposite direction. Ni Ni had been taught that the human abode meant trial and trouble. She understood that the theft, though unfortunate, was not a tragedy. Yet the disappearance of the bicycle made her fingertips tingle, as if she could feel her father's Triumph being ridden far away.

The bicycle is man's purest invention; an ingenious arrangement of metal and rubber that liberates the body from the dusty plod to ride on a cushion of air, at speed or with leisure, stopping on a whim, travelling for free. Its design is simple and its maintenance inexpensive. Yet for all the ease and economy the bicycle possesses a greater quality. It offers the possibility of escape.

Without his Triumph, Ni Ni's father had to walk to work. He could not afford the bus fare and needed to leave home two hours earlier to reach the hotel. At the end of his shift he returned long after Ni Ni had risen, ground the day's supply of *thanakha* and opened the shop. Foreign coins no longer jingled in his purse. Tourists grew dissatisfied with his tired hands. Instead of sharing the world with his daughter he slumped, weary and grey, onto his sleeping mat. Ni Ni stroked his brow but the noises of the day – the droning of doves, the throaty hawk of Law San, the call of boiled-bean vendors – began to disturb his sleep. He tossed and turned through the long afternoons. She traded her favourite silver dollar for a small chicken but not even aromatic *hkauk-hswe*, served in coconut milk, could lift his spirits.

SOME TEN DAYS LATER, Ni Ni's father spotted his bicycle, stacked with half a dozen other machines against the wall of a local barracks. The officer at the camp gate offered to arrange its return, but for this kindness he asked for more money than Ni Ni's father earned in a month. The soldier's greed kindled Ni Ni's father's discontent and, at the end of that summer when he lost his job, he found the courage to join one of the city's rare public demonstrations. In central Rangoon students made speeches calling for democracy, for an end to one-party rule and for freedom for political prisoners. Monks carried their alms bowls upside down, to show their support for the protesters. Then Ni Ni learnt that armoured cars had driven into the heart of the crowd. Soldiers had stepped down from the vehicles, taken up position and opened fire. Machine guns had cut savage swathes through the mass of unarmed civilians. Hundreds had fallen as they ran. The monks who stood their ground were bayoneted. A scattering of lost sandals littered the gory pavement, and Ni Ni's father vanished forever.

WITHOUT HER FATHER'S INCOME Ni Ni could not pay the rent. She was cast out of their rooms, saving only her dowry of foreign coins in a cotton purse. Without her beauty stall she could not practise her craft. Without money she had to take the first job she found. She worked at a large building site, teaching herself to bear the splinters and sprains, to endure the chafe of masonry, and soon the rough labour began to scour the sensitivity off her fingertips. It was there that she caught the eye of the building's English architect. He asked her out to dinner. Ni Ni had never before been to a restaurant, apart from Law San's noodle stall, and she ate with caution. After the meal sitting in the dark in his car he asked her where she lived. When she would not answer him, he took her home like a take-away meal.

The architect knew that Ni Ni was young, very young, and wondered at himself for a moment. He was hard-working, loved by his parents, from Berkshire. At home he bought flowers for his grandmother and made donations to good causes. His designs favoured open-plan architecture, not the hierarchical structures which set in stone the tentacles of power. He was not at home, but he reasoned that he could still do good. I can help this one, he told himself. I can give her a home, a bed and a start in life. It's almost an act of charity, he lied. He took her with gentleness, handling her as a caged bird, whispering soft vows, until the heat and frustration swelled up inside him and he tore deeply into her flesh, making her bite her tongue so as not to cry.

When Ni Ni moved into the architect's villa, all she brought with her was the purse of coins and her few worn clothes, which Louis stripped off her that evening. They tumbled on the shreds, ripping the seams of the threadbare cloth, then while the flush of their copulation was still on her, he dressed her in a new silk blouse and a Chinese silk *longyi*. Its rich salmon-pink complimented her high colour.

'It costs nothing,' he said as she gazed at the unfamiliar reflection in the full-length mirror.

In Burma physical contact is an intimate matter. Men and women do not touch in public. For the next few months Ni Ni's life hung between innocence and barbarism, caring and abuse, East and West. Her actions further dispossessed her from her society. To compensate for the loss she convinced herself that she was tied to the Englishman, that his convenient liaison was love. He did nothing to dissuade her. But when the building was finished and his transfer to the firm's Singapore office arranged, he did not ask her, a fourteen-year-old orphan, to come with him.

'Ni Ni, you are young,' he told her on their last morning together in bed. 'Your whole life is in front of you,' he added, turning his unease into platitudes.

Ni Ni slipped out from under the sheet, her lightness leaving no impression on the mattress to show that she had ever lain beside him, and crossed the room to the wardrobe. She opened a lower drawer, burrowed under her fine new clothes and found the bag of coins. Ni Ni knelt beside the bed and emptied out the money onto the pillow. There were silver quarters, a few Swiss francs and a single Canadian ten dollar bill. She arranged her funds with care, sorting them according to colour and size, not by value or nationality. She explained that her father had saved them for her, every day for five years. The architect sat up in bed, pulled the orderly display towards him, and roared with laughter.

'About sixty dollars,' he calculated. 'Five years, you say? My poor Ni Ni.' He shook his head. 'And where is your father now?'

PROSTITUTION DOES NOT exist in Burma, at least it cannot be mentioned in the press. The Burmese kings had a history of taking numerous wives, and religious sites always offered the service of 'pagoda servants' to pilgrims. Neither custom still exists today, officially. The girls on the steps of pagodas sell flowers and candles, religious requisites, not physical comforts. The royal *zenana* has been replaced by the executive escort agency. But both traditions remain part of the culture and, as the result of the smallest misfortune, a woman can become trapped.

A FRIEND FROM the building site promised to find Ni Ni work in Thailand as a dishwasher. The wage offered was double that which she could earn in Rangoon. He paid for her bus ticket to the border, where she was met by a Thai driver. There were five other women in his car: two Burmese, two Shan girls with milky-white complexions and a single, silent Chinese. On the road to Bangkok the driver paid a uniformed man at a checkpoint. In the brothel Ni Ni was given a number and told to sit in a windowed showroom. She toyed with the hem of her blouse when bypassers stopped to stare at her. The first man who took her in the *hong bud boree sut*, 'the room to unveil virgins', paid the owner 120 baht – less then five dollars – and tipped her the same amount. During that month she was sold as a virgin to four more clients. She was allowed to keep her tips. They were the largest that she received over the next four years.

The friend had been an agent. The debt which enslaved Ni Ni was his fee, plus her transport, clothes and protection money, compounded by 100 per cent interest. She was required to wear high heels and a mini-skirt instead of her silk *longyi*. In lieu of money she received red plastic chips; one for every client. Each morning she counted them twice to calculate the amount to be subtracted from her debt. She kept the chips under the cement bunk where she was forced to prostitute herself.

The cubicle measuring six feet square was her home. Here Ni Ni slept and worked, twelve hours a day, seven days a week. Only two days a month were allowed off, during her period. The clients were mostly Asian, although Westerners paid for her too, flying in from Frankfurt and Brussels on 'Sexbomber' package holidays. She served five or six men each weekday. On weekends she often had as many as thirty customers.

The demand for new faces dictated that every few months she be moved to a different hotel. Once in a cubicle she thought that she heard the sea, though it could have been a passing *tuk-tuk*. The frequent displacement left her no time to get to know the other girls or even to consider escape, especially as none of them ever knew where they were incarcerated. In these grimy grey neon-lit rooms the years crept upon her, ageing Ni Ni's firm young body. Men began to choose her less often, and those who did were less particular. One client put a gun to her head when she asked him to wear a condom. It wasn't because she was afraid of pregnancy – she had often paid the owner's wife to give her Depo-Provera injections – or even because he was filthy. It was simply that he frightened her. In life there is a path of fear and a path of love, and Ni Ni had been unable to follow the latter one alone. The owner threatened her with a beating if she ever came out of the room before her client again.

Ni Ni's hands touched and stroked and satisfied the men but she felt nothing, sensed nothing through the empty years. Only once or twice in an Englishman's clumsy, hurried embrace did she remember the architect. But he never came to rescue her. Then with luck the Thai Crime Suppression Division – in co-operation with the Commission for the Protection of Children's' Rights – raided her hotel in an operation stage-managed for the world's press. The girls were arrested and interrogated for the cameras and Ni Ni, along with the other Burmese nationals, was sent to the penal reform institution in Pakkret and then deported. In Rangoon a doctor tested her blood. There were tablets and injections to be taken every day. The girls were told that they could go home as soon as their parents came to collect them. Some families were too poor to travel to the capital. No one came to claim Ni Ni.

In front, behind. In front, behind. She worked the bamboo in pairs, picked up the right-hand weaver, moved it around the border. In the absence of any Burmese government help, a foreign charity established a sheltered workshop to reintegrate former prostitutes into society. There in the peaceful studio she trained to be a basket-maker, picking up the right-hand stakes, weaving the frayed strands of her life back into order. Her small sensitive fingers produced the workshop's finest, most detailed work. The other women, who had chosen instead to learn to become secretaries or tailors, teased her, for the Burmese word *hpa* translates as both basket and whore. But Ni Ni worked on unbothered, even volunteering to draw other vulnerable girls into the training programme, so that they too might have a choice, so that they need never be trapped. In front, behind. Shape the form, trim off the ends. In the last summer of her short life Ni Ni had discovered that there were three things which most matter. First, how well did she love?

'With both my hands,' Ni Ni said, not lifting her eyes from the weaving but laughing at herself for an instant.

Second, how fully did she live?

'As best I could,' she could only reply.

Third, how much did she learn to let go?

'Not enough,' Ni Ni confessed. 'Not enough.'

There is an old story of a poor woman who came to Buddha weeping. 'O Enlightened One,' she cried, 'my only daughter has died. Is there no way to bring her back to me?'

Lord Buddha looked at her with compassion and replied, 'If you bring me a basket from a house where neither parent nor child, relative or servant has ever died, I shall bring your daughter back to life.' The woman searched for many months, travelled to many villages and towns, and when she returned Buddha asked her, 'My daughter, have you found the container?'

The woman shook her head and said, 'No, I have not. The people tell me that the living are few, but the dead are many.'

JASPER WINN

A Confederacy of Ghosts

JASPER WINN (born Kent, 1959) grew up in West Cork, Ireland, which remains his home. He left school at age ten and rode horses, learnt to play guitar and to work with leather; all skills perhaps better suited to earlier times. But it was an upbringing that has shaped a lifetime of almost constant travel and writing. He lived and journeyed for eight months with nomadic Berbers, canoed the length of the Danube, and has ridden horses across more than twenty countries in five continents. His first book, **Paddle** (2011), is an account of kayaking alone the whole way around Ireland. **www.jasperwinn.com**

A Confederacy of Ghosts

JASPER WINN

The trip started out as comedy, or at least farce. The scene was a small town called San Miguel de Allende, in northern Mexico, the time the turn of the millennium. The country's itinerant pyrotechnicians were in high demand and early in the morning of New Year's Eve, a team of men drive a battered van into town and set to work in San Miguel's main plaza, constructing a tower of canes. This they tie together with string, strong enough for them to climb up and erect another storey above, and then to climb that to tie on a third. When they have finished, the tower is perhaps eight metres high, tapered to a point and with many arms sticking out. The men continue working all through siesta, wiring Catherine wheels, Roman candles, strings of fire-crackers and many sizes of rocket to the struts. By late afternoon they are lacing a web of home-made fuse wire between the fireworks. Finally the fuse is run across the paving stones to a small stage set up in one corner of the plaza.

It feels good to be here, in rural Mexico, on the edge of the sierra and I have a notion of literally riding out to meet the new millennium – travelling alone and on horseback up into the hills. I'll rent a horse for a few days and take off. Riding alone will allow space to reflect – to remember people, hear forgotten voices, meet strangers – all at a gentle trot.

There is one problem. I had imagined it would be easy to arrange a cowboy-lite adventure in San Miguel, but it is proving hard to find a horse. The man with the most ideas is the shoe-shine who, from his wooden throne on the edge of the plaza gardens, directs me to a dude ranch doing horse trips, and an American woman who had *buenos caballos*. Both are a long walk away and both are wasted journeys. The former will rent a horse, but only at an hourly rate; the tough blonde *yanqui* horsewoman won't trust a stranger with her horses at any price. After several hours of scuffing through dust I find myself back at the plaza needing a boot-shine; maybe that had been the plan all along. Dusk has fallen by the time he has conjured up a mirror shine with the last snap of his cloth.

All evening a large but muted crowd has gathered in the plaza while a mariachi band toot and strum on stage. Most are too poor to do much beyond waiting for the fireworks, their mood one of mild curiosity, as if the millennium's turning was an episode in the political season, like an election, and of equally little import. As midnight approaches, an official in a dark suit, the mayor perhaps, begins talking long and stridently. Then he lights the fuse and sparks and little flames sizzle across the cobbles to the tower and follow paths up and down the pyramid.

Immediately the Catherine wheels and Roman candles erupt into great swirls of flame and fluorescent colour and with them the tower begins to sag. A firework has burned through a supporting leg and the whole edifice sinks from the vertical, transforming itself into a missile launcher that sends rockets firing in a screeching blaze just over the heads of the crowd and straight into the leaves of the shade trees. From there a large flock of black birds rises panicking from their roosts into the flak and smoke above the crowd, where they proceed to spatter everyone with a hail storm of watery bird shit.

It is the strangest scene but one that the locals take in their stride and not long after midnight the plaza empties. I too begin walking back to my hotel but on the way come across two policemen riding horses down a side street. They are more cowboys than cops, with their ten-gallon hats, holstered pistols and chest-pocket badges, and are on patrol, clearing drunks, checking up on things.

They stop when I hail, and seem friendly, so I raise the question of renting a horse – in fact, of renting one of their horses. *Si, quizás* came the response – maybe we could let you have a horse for a few days. Come see us tomorrow.

SO ON THE FIRST DAY of the new millennium I head out to the San Miguel police stables – a ramshackle line of stalls, a bunkhouse and a tethering circle on barren ground on the edge of town. Raul and Luis, my police friends, are lying on camp-beds in the uncomfortable chill of a winter siesta in the mountains. Raul rouses himself, takes some ropes and catches up two horses, and asks me to choose between a small tough-looking grey and a strong chestnut gelding.

I choose the big and raw-boned chestnut, who looks a hammer-headed cuss with his ears back but, I figure, will be a good partner for a few days' travel into the hills and back again. The fee is a little over a hundred dollars, with an ancient rawhide and wood saddle, a curb bridle and a braided halter thrown in. The horse is to be back – right here – by sundown on the fourth day.

I ready to leave, tying on minimum kit for travelling and sleeping out in the winter sierras: a length of rope, a nosebag, a water-skin, a small ditty-bag of coffee and biscuits, a thick woollen *serape* as poncho and blanket. Raul offers advice. Asks if there's a gun, a revolver, in amongst that kit. No? Says that most people would carry a gun riding out to the hills. And to reach those hills? Go on a straight line to San Luis and then beyond. Raul isn't sure. '*Alambre* – wire. A lot of this country is fenced nowadays. You might have problems.' A shrug. 'Well, you'll find out.'

THE SHOD HOOVES of the horse clink on the cobbles riding into San Miguel. The horse has no name, so becomes Horse. It's cold. My long coat is pulled tight. Hat brim down. From one hand dangles the lead-weighted rawhide whip. In the plaza the shoe-shine raises a hand.

Then riding out of town again on the far side. Narrow streets. Then gaps in the houses. And yards growing in size till they become gardens and, further out, fields. And the houses become farms. Then the fields become scrub and cacti. And along both sides of the road are wire fences, with an overgrown stock trail squeezed between them and the tarmac. The horse's shuffle gait scuffs up dust, and a bottle shatters at his kick, amid all the rubbish thrown from passing vehicles. But mostly the sound is the growing roar of a truck or pick-up far behind or up front, getting closer, then in sight, and suddenly abreast, often a blaring of horn, or a shout, sometimes jeers, and then the noise receding. Silence again. Far ahead the town of Rodriquez.

Along the road, at regular intervals, are small shrines with crosses, dried flowers or small headstones, marking crash deaths. For one long stretch, half an hour of jog trot, a fire has burnt through the vegetation on both sides of the road leaving the bottles and beer cans and rocks and crosses standing out against ash and charcoal.

Rodriquez is a one-truck town with a mission church, and a row of shack-shops selling sturdy work clothing and flimsy festival dress, soft drinks and snack foods. A chance to fill the nosebag with grain for Horse. I buy cheese, hard bread and a quart bottle of rum. A mile beyond the edge of town there's a simple bar, a corrugated and adobe two-roomed hut with a plank nailed across two thin tree trunks outside as counter. There's a hitching rail. A woman and four children stand in the doorway. They all move back into the room, out of sight, as I tie up Horse and loosen the cinch. Inside, eyes adjusting to the dark, I make out a feed store calendar, a crate of bottles, a rusty fridge, small boxes of cheap sweets. All the people have pulled back into the room behind this bar-room and closed the door. The sounds of whispering, a woman's voice raised. A small girl maybe eight years old, bundled up in second-hand American clothes, is pushed out and edges up behind the counter. Dark eyes wide and unblinking.

Hola, niña. ¿Que tal? No response.

Dame una cerveza. She silently opens the fridge door, takes out a bottle, puts it unopened on the counter, takes the note and gives back a handful of change. Then she goes back into the room.

I drink the beer outside, watching the trucks and jeeps passing. Then I swing up and ride off, still penned in by highway on one side and fence on the other. Towards evening, I turn onto a smaller road. The fences are now rickety; reused barbed wire strung between twisted branches, armfuls of thorns as stockades, hedges of cacti. Sometimes there's no fencing at all, the land so poor that there's little to keep in or out. I pass a couple walking on the road, a man and woman, walking one after the other, both carrying small bundles. The tipping of the hat brim, a raised hand, a called greeting gets no response. The man looks up briefly, in a sideways glance at the horse; the woman keeps her eyes down.

With dusk there are more figures in the landscape, struggling from the fields back to this dust road and then along it. Some are herding a few goats, carrying tools. There are bright patches of irrigated fruit trees. Maize stubble. Worked land. Small rough houses and shacks at the end of paths. I'm looking for a place to tether the horse and sleep but this landscape is too busy. One cabin, though, is surrounded by signs of small prosperity: old machinery, a maize stack bigger than the rest, animals. A lined-faced, powerful man comes across the yard, gesturing. I swing off the horse to a suspicious, cold greeting, but the horse is unsaddled and tied to a tree and given an armful of maize stalks.

I'm shown to an almost empty room where I lay the *serape* across the bare iron bedstead. In the cabin next door there's a seat by a fire of burning thorn branches and a tin plate of beans, and water. I pull out the bottle of rum and hand it across. The man talks little. His wife more. She has a long story of the first time she waded the Rio Grande to work in the States and the money she'd made. She shows a photo of herself, smiling, in a Californian kitchen. Then a far shorter account of her second crossing, being caught, returned to Mexico. And now here she is.

In the morning I offer a few notes, a fair price. The man's expression shows both surprise and resignation at the amount; it might have been less, it might have been nothing, it might have been so much more. As I'm saddling up in the bitter cold before light, the woman brings out a hot flat bread and a mug of bitter coffee. The man – Miguel – points across the fields in the direction of San Luis. 'There is only one way nowadays,' he says, 'but when I was a boy you could ride this country straight in any direction you wanted to go. Now, *señor*, all the land is wired.'

TO A STRANGER there seem many more ways than just one. Riding across country there are innumerable small fields, thorn hedges and stands of cacti and cane. Tracks peter out, or stop at walls or locked gates, or lead to dusty cabins either empty of people or with small children and elderly women pulling back into the dark and closing the door. Those men and younger women not away working in the cities, or in the States, are in the fields bent over hoes, wrapped in old, ragged clothing against the chill.

Asked directly, a man straightens himself from the earth and elaborates a route of minute details, each rock and twisted tree and distorted cactus and dried-out *arroyo* a landmark. But only the larger scale of the sierra on the horizon makes sense as Horse jogs on. And the crosses and shrines, even here where there is no road, still marking untimely deaths. A rattlesnake bite? Falls from horses? The sudden stab of a knife? There is no way of knowing. Most are old-looking. Rusty if metal. Eroded or tumbled down if stone. A tin can with pieces of wire spilling out may once have been filled with the stalks of paper flowers.

Some crosses have empty tequila or rum or beer bottles laid beside them.

A track twists direction, down from the badlands into a valley, funnelled by more fences. A distant roar. Then an acrid smell on the breeze. The track becomes a dirt road, then badly paved, then busier, then T-junctions with the six-lane Highway 57 from Mexico City to the border. There is no escape. Impassable fences and walls line the land. Following another stock trail, parallel to the road, deposits me amid drifts of rubbish, auto repairs and tyre shops. Angry guard dogs run out, snarling and snapping at Horse's heels. Trucks and trailers rumble by. Cowboy pick-ups filled with sombreros, and moustaches, playing mariachi fanfares on their horns.

We come to a truck stop on the edge of San Luis where tens of cargo lorries are parked up beside lines of bars and *cantinas* and fast food stands with *tacos*, caldrons of beans, brains on toast, ice-box bottled beer. Horse, tied to a post, breathes in the diesel fumes and dust while I sit on a bar stool with truck drivers and bus pilots – Mexico's new cowboy drovers. Confident men talking about rodeos, and America and women and their families.

It's a chance to buy food. A tin of fish, bread and cheese. A few apples. I stuff them into a bag hung from the saddle and, as I pull away onto a side road, the silence slowly descends. I stop to negotiate with a *campesino* in a field for a bundle of corn straw, and tie it behind the saddle.

I sleep out tonight, when caught by darkness, barely hidden in a stand of trees, unsettled by the roads and trucks and the fences and thinking about the downcast eyes, and the refusal of greetings. Horse is tied close, browsing through the straw, his body heat and the sounds of his stomach rumblings and breathing crossing the few yards of cold darkness and silence to my rough bed.

I MAKE ANOTHER dawn start. There's no reason to linger so I roll up the blanket and chew stale bread and hard cheese whilst saddling up, walk the first few miles beside the horse to get warm. Then, mounted again, I ride down into a dry river bed and climb the crest of a hill to reach a valley and in its shelter a *hacienda*. A house with the grandeur of a château, its windows are shuttered; it has walled gardens, a stable courtyard, a bull ring and a church. It is run down but not abandoned. Through the church doors there's a glimpse of a black-shrouded woman kneeling in prayer. And riding out from the gates of the courtyard is a *vaquero* on a strong cow-pony, his ancient big-horned saddle with ornately tooled leather wings to deflect thorns and cactus spines.

Our eyes are on the same level and he looks straight, from under his hat brim, over his moustache, taking me in. He says he will show me the way to the sierra, but as we ride there is no talk. Whistling up two dogs, spinning the pony – *Venga, charro* – he leads the way past the house, up a track, into a maze of tracks amongst head-high cacti. After half an hour we come to a break in a fence – a tangle of sticks and wire – that is the only way through in many miles. The *vaquero* points out a track leading straight towards jagged peaks and deep gorges on the skyline. Turning, he rides away and back, the dogs at his heels.

Before darkness, Horse is picking his way up the dry stony bed of an *arroyo*. There are big boulders, bars of loose gravel, the soaring sides of a wide canyon. Then a sandy flat in an ox-bow bend. Tethering Horse means tying the rope around a piece of fall wood and burying it in the fine sand. I give him a nose-bag of corn, lay out the saddle and the blankets, collect firewood and make a blaze. I toast bread and melt cheese and open the tin of fish; brew coffee and cut it half and half with rum. Then I settle down fully dressed, wrapped in the *serape* and the coat, with the saddle for a pillow.

Later I wake suddenly. A noise. There's ice on the outside of the blanket. Horse has moved closer to me and the fire, a shadowy black bulk. His presence is a comfortable familiarity, the slight sound of his hooves grinding the sand down under him as he shifts weight, intensifying the silence. Emphasising the sudden yipping call from further up the *arroyo*. And the answering call from much closer, higher up amongst the rocks. Coyotes, first calling shyly, then drawn out yelps and singing back and forth, as they move towards each other. It's been a hard, uncomfortable, discomfiting ride to get here, this far out, through a countryside that doesn't like strangers. Not knowing what would make it worthwhile. It's turned out to be this: a night of sierra wilderness – nature and the wild.

THE RETURN on the fourth morning starts off on a straight line from the sierra across country to San Miguel. First the open country, following the dried water courses running south. Then the badly built walls and slack wire fences, again. Untwisting the wire to make a passage through. Then big open land, a rich man's land, wired around with seven strands on concrete posts running clear across the route as far as the skyline on both sides. A heavy locked gate containing emptiness. A whole morning's ride off course to round the edge of the property, where it meets the road. Back on the verge, Horse jogging along, easy-going, kicking up the dust and dried grasses and beer cans.

I ride into the plaza in San Miguel in time to get Horse back to Raul before sundown. Dust-covered, trail-weary, wanting a beer. From the sidewalk a tall man steps out, wearing jeans, well-polished boots, casual shirt, a cowboy hat – though he's not a cowboy. He takes in Horse, the blanket and bags on the saddle and the long coat and hat, and addresses me in English.

'You're not from here, no? You've been out riding? I have horses out in the country here, I like to ride out for a few days sometimes. I like to ride this country. How did you find it?'

'It went well enough.' I tell him how I hired the horse from the *policía*, rode out to the sierra past Arroyo de Medina, slept out three nights. Tell him it was a good trip, though too much of the land was fenced and I was forced along the roads and highways.

'Sure,' he says. 'Most of the land is fenced now for cattle ... the owners don't want people riding their land ... they leave the gates open, maybe, or they steal the cattle ... the old story. And along the roads can be bad. Some bad people there. The sierra, too. Some people aren't too friendly, some are unfriendly.'

I tell him that nobody was too friendly – and I didn't quite understand it. Normally when you're riding, people like you for being on a horse, and doing the same thing as they are – you're out in the same weather, dressed like them, need the same things – shelter, fodder for the horse, a drink. But I didn't get that feeling. Didn't feel welcome.

'Well, you know the reason,' he explains. 'It's because you're thinking like you're a cowboy, a *vaquero*, and people are going to like that. But here a man on a horse, a man alone on a horse just riding across country, a man they don't know – isn't going to be a good thing. That's our history. Revolutions and outlaws and strangers on horses with guns. And a lot of the poorest people out there are *indíginas*, Indians. They still have memories, older memories, of men on horses. Spaniards, *criollos*, masters. You saw how they are, they don't want to talk to you, they don't look in your eye, no? For them you are like meeting a ghost. From the past, the bad past. For those people you were a ghost on a horse.'

Where we stood I could see the black scorch marks and exploded cardboard tatters and smell gunpowder from the millennium tower. The twenty-first century is underway. It's time to hand back the horse.

AMINATTA FORNA

The Beggar King

AMINATTA FORNA (born Glasgow, 1964) is an author and television documentary maker. She has published two novels, **Ancestor Stones** and **The Memory of Love**. Her memoir, **The Devil that Danced on the Water**, recalled her dissident father and one of her countries, Sierra Leone. She lives in London with her husband, Simon, and Maude, a wall-eyed lurcher. **www.aminattaforna.com**

The Beggar King

AMINATTA FORNA

In the year 2000 I returned to Sierra Leone, the country of my childhood. It had been nine years since my last visit. The war had endured for the same length of time and would endure for two more years. I had gone home in search of my family, and truths concealed for a quarter of a century, for a book that I was writing. In the six weeks I spent in the wreckage of the land I still called home I saw up close the final verdict of an oppression that had begun in my childhood years by a population who had nothing left to lose.

War had torn through the country like a tornado. Freetown had been invaded by different rebel forces twice: in 1997 and in 1999. The first time my mother managed to escape, first by sea and then by air. My sister waited under the cold lights of the Stansted airport arrivals hall for her plane to land. She stepped from the plane in the same dress she had been wearing the day she had fled the house, her luggage a single handbag lent by a friend who sheltered her before she found passage on a refugee ship bound for Guinea. My sister phoned me later to say she had arrived safely, adding that she had seen a childhood friend at the airport, his clothes stained with dried blood.

Just over a year later the government declared the war over and my mother returned to Freetown. She wanted, she told us, to be home by Christmas. The second invasion was far bloodier, more enduring than the last; this time there was no way out. The people were caught between the mountains and the sea, like rats in a barrel. The last of the expats had left two years before, so no foreign government was inclined to send a ship.

WHEN I SET OUT myself for Freetown, in 2000, with my husband, Simon, we left from Heathrow amid a plane full of tourists to the Gambia. There we waited for two days before an ageing West Coast Airlines plane, piloted by Russians, took us on to Freetown. It was the only airline prepared to land in Sierra Leone and was doing most of its business taking people out of the country. Flying in, we felt like reverse-refugees. From the air I stared out of the window and wondered how it would be to crash into the mangrove swamps below. (Three years later the very same plane went down taking with it everyone on board.)

Nothing in Freetown was as I remembered it. The people stumbled through the streets like the survivors of an earthquake, with glazed expressions and awkward gait. They grasped at strangers and familiar faces alike, as if waiting for the earth to open up and swallow them again, like convalescents wandering their hospital grounds. Yet, the bars and nightclubs heaved, and after hours people dodged the curfew patrols – though the soldiers were under orders to shoot on sight – for the chance to forget for one or two hours longer.

WHEN THE TIME came to return, we rose before first light to reach Hastings airport, where it was claimed that a plane would arrive to take us the first leg of the journey out of Freetown. That was how it went. A rumour would start and people would pursue it until it turned out to be false.

Outside the locked gates of the airport we found a crowd. Those in front gripped the bars of the gate and peered through them to the empty tarmac of the runway, upon which an unseasonal rain had created pools of water. The airport hut was dark, nothing moved. Nobody turned when we arrived. They stood facing the runway, like worshippers facing the dawn, as though focusing their collective energy upon the airport building, willing the plane to come. Behind them was piled vast quantities of luggage, enough for a lifetime.

We sat on our suitcases in front of a low wall and waited. I didn't believe a plane was coming to get us, but I said nothing, partly out of some kind of superstition, partly because I was ashamed at how desperate I had become to leave the place.

Around eight a street performer appeared and began his routine. Nobody watched except me. I recognised him and became excited. Here was someone from the past. He used to perform at a club by the beach where my family spent our Sundays. I had been perhaps his greatest admirer, so much so that my father, in a fit of parental indulgence, had hired him to perform at a birthday party. I even knew his name: Musa. There in front of the airport he performed a routine that must have been as elaborate as it was joyless. He was over sixty, yet he flipped this way and that, stood on his hands to pour water from one glass to another; quite literally he bent over backwards to entertain. He never smiled.

When he was done I went over, gave him some money and prodded at his memory. He smiled as he answered my questions and accepted my gift: 'Thank you, Ma. May God bless.' He claimed to remember me too, but he was lying. It was there in the way he nodded: too fast, too readily. And the fact that he never looked at me.

THE CROWD WAS GROWING. We began to fear being overtaken by numbers so rose and joined the crush at the gate. A woman next to me wept silently, her head bowed as the tears poured out of her. Sierra Leone had been a country where public tears never failed to attract the sympathy of strangers but nobody put out a hand to comfort her. I'm afraid to say I behaved no differently. Among so many sad souls, what was one more? The minutes passed. The young woman wept on.

Then at the rear of the crowd, came a man's voice, calling loudly: 'So, here you are. What are you doing here?' People kept their faces averted, locked in the act of willing the plane to land. 'Come home,' he boomed. 'Come home with me.' I am guessing at what he said, because at first I wasn't listening to the words and nor had I turned to look at him. But somebody nearby tittered and this caught my attention.

'Please, I beg you.' I turned around and saw a young man: slim, dressed in a plain white cotton robe with a white embroidered round hat. He looked as though he was on his way to the mosque. He was strikingly handsome: bright-eyed and burnished of skin, with dimples in his cheeks.

'Don't leave me. Don't go away. Whatever I have done we can make better. I will change. I can become a different man.' Now he had caught our attention. People craned their necks to see who he was talking to, murmured and whispered.

The handsome young man racked it up a notch: 'If you get on the plane you'll be taken away from me forever. If you go to America, you'll never come back. Take me with you.' He was addressing the weeping woman, speaking his words to her back. By now people were openly curious. The young man continued: 'That other woman means nothing to me.' And as an afterthought: 'Well, not a great deal.'

A burst of laughter from the crowd. Suddenly we realised we were watching a street performer, who had picked as his victim the weeping girl. He shook his head and continued: 'But the other three, they meant very little. And as for the rest, nothing at all!'

The crowd hooted. The young man had us laughing, but it seemed unfair to pick on this unhappy young woman. Her head was bowed, her shoulders continued to shake. With the back of her hand she wiped away her tears. The street performer dropped to his knees and spread his arms: 'See how I beg you. Look at me. I won't move until you give me just one glance.'

Everyone looked at the girl, whose back remained turned. I looked at her too. Then I saw the shaking of her shoulders no longer came from sadness, but from laughter. She was helplessly crying and laughing as one. Slowly she lifted her head, turned and faced the young man. Her face was soaked with tears, but she smiled.

We went wild.

Footsteps, a shout: the manager of the airport building. He was angry, on the brink of rage. He gestured threateningly at the young man, who leapt to his feet, took his hat from his head and passed it into the crowd. Delayed by a locked gate and hampered by an impossibly large bunch of keys, the manager swore, raised his fist and proceeded to give vigorous chase as the young man danced through the crowd. We closed around him and at the same time passed his hat from hand to hand, stuffing it with money.

When he had made his way to the edge of the crowd the young man made a run for it. Soon enough the manager broke free of us too. Now they were out in the open. The manager charged. The young man skipped out of range. Somebody held out his hat. The young man darted sideways to receive it. The manager lumbered after him, an ox in pursuit of a cat. Rage had the better of him. He screamed at the young man and at us, too. He would not tolerate beggars outside the airport building. The young man, by now standing atop a low wall shouted: 'I am a beggar, true. But am I not the King of Beggars?' It was all very Errol Flynn.

There was much cheering and clapping. The Beggar King bowed, leapt from the wall and was gone. We followed the manager into the airport building. He was angry with us, but processed our papers all the same. Sheepishly we followed his orders to the letter. An hour later a plane landed. We boarded it and left, some among us forever.

As for me, I have been back to Freetown many times since and I often see street performers, have come to recognise many of them by face or the nature of their routine. I have even seen Musa again, contorting his body into impossible shapes for the amusement of the new arrivals who came in the wake of war: the UN soldiers, the armies of aid workers and consultants, the profiteers. But I have never again seen the Beggar King.

Some years after the war I came across these lines from Bertolt Brecht: 'And is there singing in the darkness? Yes, there is singing in the darkness.'

And sometimes, just sometimes – there is laughter too.

Ian Thomson

The Fall and Rise of
a Rome Patient

IAN THOMSON (born London, 1961) is a writer and journalist. He is the author of **Primo Levi: a Biography** (which won the W.H. Heinemann Award), **Bonjour Blanc: A Journey Through Haiti**, and **The Dead Yard: Tales of Modern Jamaica** (which won the Ondaatje Prize and Dolman Travel Award in 2010). He is currently working on a history combined with family memoir, **Darkness in Tallinn: World War II in Europe's Forgotten City 1939–44**. He lives in London with his wife and children. The photo above was taken in 1984 during his convalescence in Rome.

The Fall and Rise of a Rome Patient

IAN THOMSON

One day in the autumn of 1984, after an unexplained fall, I woke up in a hospital in Rome acutely head-injured and disorientated. 'I'm afraid you've had an emergency brain operation.' A blurred but familiar face came into focus as the English woman who shared my flat near the railway station. I protested, 'But why me?' Then the face dissolved and I was out again.

I was found sprawled on the kitchen floor of 195 Via Salaria with my breathing irregular and speech slurred. In Hitchcock manner the phone was dangling off the hook. The police suspected an intruder, yet nothing it seems had been stolen. I was twenty-three and newly arrived in Rome to work as a journalist and teach. The city struck me then as beautiful with the autumn light at dusk turning a dried-blood red. I was in a relationship with my flatmate, Gilly, and beautiful things were promised for the falling year.

At the time of the accident, bizarrely, I had been on the phone to the Italian novelist Italo Calvino, whom I hoped to interview. I believe I was the only person in the flat that afternoon. The phone rang and I answered it. Then something hit me hard and the room spun so fast that I seemed to hit myself on the back of the head with the floor. Time passed after that in a blur of pain. By the time Gilly discovered me later that evening, handprints of blood had covered the walls and congealed on the floor where I lay in a stupor. I was bleeding profusely from my left ear, and my speech had become garbled or, in neuro-speak, aphasic. Later, Calvino told me *un tonfo* (a thud) had sounded at my end before the line went dead. At the time he thought it was a faulty connection.

TODAY I CAN TAKE STOCK of what happened twenty-five years ago in Italy. On the anniversary of the injury, 17 October 2010, I returned to Rome in order to meet the surgeon who had operated on me and saved my life. Since then I have learned much about the nature of my injury, as well as the fevers, frets and disorders that afflict our most precious and mysterious organ: the brain. Twenty-five years is no mean portion of a human life, however, and my memory of the events is consequently hazy at times.

After neurosurgery I regained consciousness amid a tang of ammonia mingled with carbolic and slops. I was outside a latrine on the sixth floor of San Giovanni Hospital. A sign at the end of the corridor announced: TRAUMATOLOGIA CRANICA ('traumatised crania' – head injury unit). Like a bedlamite I had been strapped to some sort of a wheeled iron bed. Other patients were recuperating with me on trolleys in the corridor for want of space. Presently a group of nuns – Sisters of Mercy in coifs and black habits – swished past, each bearing a carafe of white wine. Was I in paradise? The carafes turned out to contain urine samples.

Nuns were often to be seen in San Giovanni Hospital, adjacent to the baroque basilica of the same name. Along with priests and social workers they acted as paramedics owing to a nationwide shortage of trained lay nurses. Soon enough a couple of nuns came to provide me with a basin into which I emptied the previous day's meal. I blasphemed in shock as a catheter was disconnected from under my sheets: 'Madonna!' Why had I blasphemed in Italian? (The pop star Madonna was then all the rage in Rome, but I cared nothing for her or her music.)

The operation for an acute epidural haematoma – a build-up of blood between the skull and the brain's outer membrane – had lasted two hours. During that time my flatmate was kept in the dark about my chances of survival. Instead she was told to remove her shoes lest her restless pacing up and down disturb the patients out in the corridor. Wretchedly for me, my parents were away in China and other family members were nowhere to be found. I was alone in a foreign city with no clear direction home. Surgery had left me with a cavity in the back of the skull where the haematoma had been evacuated. It was the size of a healthy tangerine as is usual for a craniotomy, or surgical removal of a section of skull.

Prior to the operation it seems some temporary brain damage had occurred as I made lewd advances (so I was later told) to a nurse in the hospital lift. Dimly I recall attempts at fumbling or lunging. Disinhibited sexual behaviour is a consequence of brain injury; as well as lewd, my movements had become uncoordinated and my pupils non-reactive as I drifted into unconsciousness.

For two weeks I lay in the hospital's neurosurgical unit with attendant memory loss and a degree of intellectual and physical impairment. My head hurt like hell and my right arm had gone blue where the Sisters of Mercy ministered their morphine jabs. Lying in the public ward, unable to do anything, I was nevertheless filled with relief at having pulled through. Each day I was visited for therapy by my surgeon, the quaintly named Professor Milza (Professor Spleen), and a group of trainee doctors. 'And how is our Englishman today?' Tests for hand-eye coordination involved a spatula pressed against the tongue and noting pupil dilation with a pencil-torch. Tests for mental alertness met with less success. With every incorrect answer I gave to my times tables in Italian (in fact there were no correct ones as maths is hard enough for me even in English), the doctors cast each other nervous glances and moved on to the days of the week instead. Here I encountered few difficulties as my spoken Italian had by now become unaccountably fluent. 'Very impressive,' Professor Milza raised an eyebrow. 'It's hardly the Berlitz method, but a blow to the head can certainly work wonders.'

In the men's ward with me were motorcycle crash survivors and victims of brain tumours and physical assault. As nuns and other paramedics were rarely to be found on duty at night, visitors were allowed to sleep in the wards. After midnight my flatmate was prevailed on to run all sorts of errands from procuring pain-killers to raising the alarm whenever an incontinent lost a catheter. 'Signorina, signorina!' the men beseeched her. Cries for help came in particular from the patient they called Luigi 'Sure Thing', a huge and porcine man whose habit was to break wind quite loudly after lights out. For such a visual phenomenon, Luigi had a small voice and quiet manner. Every day three women relatives of his would visit from Naples, all of them dressed in black and the oldest with a faint soupçon of a moustache. In a parody of the Adoration they would prostrate themselves before Professor Milza and even offer him foodstuffs. It was as though they divined a power in him of life over death. But Luigi was not long for this world. One awful day screens went up around his bed, and we never saw him again.

From the solitude of my sickbed I took in the incredible sights and sounds around me. Food was usually a stew of fish and rice submerged in oleo-margarine, or else half-boiled lumps of pork gristle, soft and tallowy, which we patients resignedly referred to as *grasso di rinoceronte* (rhino-fat). On a good day we might find a few currants peeping from the pudding. One evening we were eating the pudding as usual in respectful silence as though a coffin were in the room, when a patient yelled out loud: 'Oh what is it? I not taking fucking this stuff!'

We all lowered our spoons. Mustah, a young Tunisian, was not right in the head after someone had assaulted him with a hammer. A great scar like a railway track ran jagged across his right temple. In his post-traumatic delirium he believed his mother and sister had been replicated by duplicates who looked exactly like his real relatives. '*Ho paura di nessuno!*' (I'm not afraid of anyone!) he would yell at the nuns in broken Italian. Was Mustah suffering from Capgras delusion, a florid neurological syndrome caused by damage to parts of the brain which specialise in face and object recognition? Dr V.S.Ramachandran, in his influential book *Phantoms in the Brain*, suggests that Capgras is most commonly the result of traumatic brain injury.

In response to brain injury, neurons may reorganise and re-map themselves in the most peculiar ways, altering the circuitry which was laid down in foetal life. Abnormal remapping in the wake of tumours, strokes, epilepsy, head injuries and other causes of brain trauma can give rise to absorbing neurological puzzles. Lord Nelson had experienced the most compelling phantom limb pain after the loss of his right arm in 1797 at Santa Cruz de Tenerife. The sensation that his fingers were digging into his non-existent palm led him to believe in the existence of the spirit after death. (If an arm can exist after it has been removed, why then should not an entire person survive annihilation of the body?) In terms of modern scientific revelation, the sea lord's neural connections were trying to make sense of the pain of the injury, only the wiring had gone awry.

As my brain began to adjust to the blow and the cells made new connections, I marvelled at my sickbed fluency in Italian. True, I had been trying to learn Italian prior to surgery, but that hardly explained my untutored brilliance in a language I previously spoke poorly if not at all. Though quirks of language are not uncommon following brain injury, speech restitution in neurological patients is still not fully understood. We still have no clear idea how the brain itself even works.

A WEEK INTO my stay, and the men's ward had become so stuffy after the air-conditioning broke down that a nurse suggested I sleep on the roof. A makeshift bed was set up for me on the terrace overlooking San Giovanni basilica and its stone statues of Christ and John the Baptist. A frozen late October light hung over the church with wisps of mist off the statues. Disquietingly, the terrace had been hemmed in with high mesh wire to prevent suicidal patients from jumping off, a not uncommon occurrence. One day I saw a group of patients in pyjamas running like mad towards the Egyptian obelisk in the middle of Piazza San Giovanni. Perhaps they were making a break for freedom; a handful hopped on board a public bus. Their hare-brained escapade cheered me.

A few days later Professor Milza informed me that I was 'clinically recovered' and it was time for me to leave. Having regained much of my physical self-confidence I walked out of the hospital on the arm of my flatmate and hailed a taxi, bearded and no doubt unrecognisable. A week later, wonderfully, it was snowing in Rome – the first snowfall in ten years. Flakes were falling over St Peter's like down from a pillow fight. I was convalescing steadily in my flat on Via Salaria when, wedged behind a cupboard, I found an X-ray of the previous occupant showing a fractured skull. The co-incidence seemed extraordinary: had he too suffered a blow to the head? That night I dreamed that an intruder had hit me on the head just to watch the life run out of me. In a fright I took the next plane home to London. It was New Year 1985; a black January.

A quarter of a century has now passed since the surgeons of San Giovanni contemplated the fall and rise of their Rome patient. Since then I have often dwelled on the circumstances of my injury and relived it too in dreams. For twenty-five years in fact I have wanted to thank Professor Milza belatedly for restoring me to life; but first I felt I needed to return to the scene of the accident.

VIA SALARIA IS a wide airy street of nineteenth century tenement blocks near Termini railway station. At all hours the station mills with hustlers and migrants from the Philippines and Africa. Had my assailant come from here; or had I fainted and lethally banged my head? On the brass plate outside 195 Via Salaria, to my surprise, was the surname 'Belluci': twenty-five years earlier, Remo Belluci and his wife Raffaella had been the caretakers here. Were they still in business? I pushed the bell, and heard it ring inside far off. A wary-sounding voice answered: 'Who is it?' I explained my presence; yes, said the voice eventually, this is Raffaella. She remembered me all right; she remembered the night the ambulance came.

I walked in past the porter's lodge to a familiar-looking inner courtyard with washing hung out to dry and green-shuttered windows. Raffaella was waiting for me outside an apartment stairway. 'Nothing's changed much since you left,' she said; she looked more careworn than I remembered, her hair dyed a smudged blonde. Solicitously she held the door wide, and I went in past her to a dim interior with an old-fashioned lift cage. A smell of frying hung on the stairs. We took the lift up to flat number 18, four flights up, where I used to live.

I HAVE ONLY 'islands of memory' of what happened that autumn day in 1984, no consistency. At about 3 p.m. on the afternoon of 17 October Italo Calvino telephoned, and soon afterwards came the 'thud'. And then what? A sensation of dizziness took hold as I tried to sit for a while on the marble steps on the landing outside the flat, my vision blurred and a taste of copper rising salty in the mouth. At a certain moment I must have tried to orientate myself back indoors, leaving the handprints of blood on the walls and floor as I did so. During semi-lucid intervals I remember the most excruciating headache.

Gilly's call for help had been relayed via the police emergency number 113. Owing to rush-hour traffic it took an age for the ambulance to arrive. When it arrived, the orderlies apparently had difficulty fitting me in the back as one of the doors had jammed. As they struggled with the door, Signor

Belluci the caretaker made an appearance and, pointing to the casualty on the stretcher, exclaimed: 'He's overdosed! That's why he's gone all yellow.' His face above me flashed a spectral white and blue from the ambulance beacon.

My flatmate rode with me in the ambulance. At the Policlinico near Termini station they wheeled me in for neurological assessment, but the hospital lacked the technological know-how for conclusive diagnosis. Time was running out fast. At a subsequent hospital, the Nuova Clinica Latina, a prototype computer scanner with the user-friendly acronym of PET (positron emission tomography) took rapid cross-sectional images of my brain. These showed hyper-dense bleeding within the brain cavity, contusions at the brain-bone interface and a fracture in the lower left rear region of the skull. The fracture indicated the presence of a high-speed impact of some sort.

Plainly I was a neurosurgical emergency yet precious hours had been lost in trying to locate a suitable hospital. The last my flatmate saw of me before surgery was as a group of white-coated orderlies rushed me down the corridor at San Giovanni to the operating theatre. '*Stai ferma!*' they shouted at the terrified girl. 'Stay right where you are!' Eight hours were to elapse between the proximate time of the injury and the operation. The prognosis then was: '*Coma oppure morte sicuro*'. Coma if not certain death.

RAFFAELLA UNLOCKED the door to my old flat, and I followed her in to a small pleasant hallway. The smells I knew so well from long ago – a compact of old carpet dust and camphor – hit me forcibly and it was as though I had never been away. The phone was still in its place up on the wall by the front door and the kitchen's blue majolica tiles had not changed.

The current occupant was away, yet the flat showed no sign of occupancy since I had left it. There was something mournful about the place – sad and lone. I thought of the unexplained mystery of the X-ray.

Raffaella said, pointing at the front door: 'I know what people say: a burglar came in and hit you.'

'That's what the police thought – I mean they didn't rule out the possibility of third-party involvement. What about you?'

'Who knows?' Raffaella answered with a shrug. 'There are too many things that could have happened.'

I nodded but said nothing. In the hall by the phone I noticed a low, marble-topped table with sharp-looking edges. Had I fainted and banged my head against that? I do remember drinking a quantity of wine that lunchtime; fully half of traumatic brain injuries involve alcohol: perhaps the wine had done for me? Next door, at number 17, Signora Romaldini might have remembered something, said Raffaela, but she was in no fit state following recent diagnosis of a brain tumour. Disappointed, I walked off into the autumn night, not much the wiser, the sky above Via Salaria stained red from the harvest moon.

PIER GUILIO MILZA was forty-seven when he operated on me in 1984, a little younger than I am today. Time had moved on fast yet I felt humbled to meet him again. Extending a hand, he said: 'I remember you very well.' Thrilled, I made him a gift of a bottle of Talisker malt whisky and (poignantly for me) a copy of my biography of the Italian writer and chemist Primo Levi. 'I couldn't have written this if you hadn't saved my life,' I said, meaning it.

With his brown eyes attentive behind half-moon spectacles, Professor Milza struck me as a man of old-fashioned courtesies.

He had retired from San Giovanni eight years ago, in 2002; we met at his private consultancy off the Via Appia Nuova. The walls were hung with diagrams of the optic nerve and of the brain in cross-section like a pink cauliflower. Noting my interest, Professor Milza said the brain accounts for just two per cent of our body weight, 'yet its electro-chemistry works so hard that it burns up a fifth of the food we eat.' As he spoke, morning sunlight filtered through slatted metal blinds.

Such was the severity of my injury, the professor reminded me, that it ruptured the transverse sinus vein at the base of my skull. This vein receives blood from all zones of the brain, and its rupture can cause an insidiously slow build-up of venous blood in the brain cavity. In lucid intervals the subject may act and feel as if nothing potentially fatal had occurred. In 2009 the actress Natasha Richardson died of a seemingly mild head injury after a fall in Canada while skiing. At first she appeared unhurt, but then she developed a headache and was subsequently brain-dead on arrival at the hospital. 'You were very lucky,' Professor Milza said to me, adding: 'It was a very close brush with mortality.' Forty per cent of acute epidural haematoma cases are expected to die. At twenty-three, though, one is unprepared for so terminal a judgement. I had my life before me; death seemed an impossibility.

For all the suffering it causes, some neural damage remains darkly hilarious. In 1931, in a famous case, a London plumber named Willy Anderson was seen to attend his adored mother's funeral only to start giggling as the gravediggers lowered her coffin. Eventually he staggered off among the gravestones audibly guffawing. Later that evening he died of severe subarachnoid haemorrhage. At the time his behaviour was thought to be inexplicable (as well as highly inappropriate). Yet mind science has moved on immeasurably since then;

brain damage that sets us giggling inappropriately is now known to be located in the hypothalamus area.

Death by laughter might have resulted when I was interviewed for a job in London two years after my injury, in 1986. By then I had had a cranial plate fitted to protect my neural circuitry. ('You are missing some bone and therefore less thick-skulled than before,' Professor Milza had told me, charmingly.) Once more, surgery had left me without hair, exposing a scar. Melvyn Bragg was reading the previous candidate's application when he looked up. 'Good God! What have you done to your head?' Needless to say I did not get the job.

With the hindsight of twenty-five years, I still do not know for sure if I was hit on the head in Rome, but I believed it then. I remember a week later thinking that I could never be the same person again, as a head injury is an injury for life. After writing this article, and made anxious by Professor Milza's talk of lingering brain impairment, I went for a check-up at the National Hospital for Neurology and Neurosurgery in Queen Square, London. My head was glued with electrodes as rolls of chart paper registered my firing brain cells. The frequency readings for the alpha rhythms were good; in medical terms at least I appeared to be 'neurologically intact' and I needed further surgery like a hole in the head.

Chris Stewart

Cures for Serpents

CHRIS STEWART (born Horsham, 1951) is the author of **Driving Over Lemons**, the story of how he bought El Valero, a peasant farm in a remote Andalucian valley. It has been a bestseller in both the UK and Spain, along with its sequels, **A Parrot in the Pepper Tree**, **The Almond Blossom Appreciation Society**, and a sea-going prequel, **Three Ways to Capsize a Boat**. In an earlier life, Chris was the original drummer in Genesis. He still lives at El Valero, with his wife Ana, and from time to time their student daughter, Chlöe. **www.drivingoverlemons.co.uk**

Cures for Serpents

CHRIS STEWART

igh in the Alpujarras, a four hour walk uphill from our farm, through the wildest of mountain scenery, lies a village which is blessed by the presence of a *curandera*. Which is to say something between a faith healer and a barefoot doctor.

As a nation dons the cloak of modern urban existence, such people and their ancient gifts tend to vanish, but in the Spanish countryside today the tradition is very much alive. If anything there has been a resurgence in recent decades, now that they can practise without persecution. In Franco's time, *curanderos* were frequently beaten and jailed by the Guardia Civil at the instigation of his henchman, the Church – who, typically, felt that the monopoly on miracles should be theirs alone.

Now our local *curandera* was on my mind because I had just heard a story about a London journalist who had been on holiday in her village. The poor man suffered from eczema, and, hearing about the *curandera* and her particular gift for curing skin diseases, was intrigued enough to pay her a visit. Within three days she had cured his eczema, simply by stroking the affected part. Fascinated and impressed, and of course enormously relieved, he wrote the episode up in his column. This came to the notice of a man who was unfortunate enough to have shingles in, of all places, his eye. The doctors had told him that there was nothing they could do and he might as well get used to the idea of losing the eye. He made some enquiries and came to the Alpujarras, where, after three sessions with the *curandera*, the shingles simply disappeared.

Of course, there are plenty of stories like this but they are not necessarily about healers in your own backyard – and it was the backyard aspect of the story that got me thinking. For I myself had been suffering from a skin complaint, albeit – unlike the journalist and his follower – neither shingles nor eczema. No. My complaint was of an altogether more delicate nature – and afflicted that part of my person of which we do not speak.

To put the matter bluntly, I had a horribly inflamed dick.

LIKE ALL THE BEST medical conditions, mine had a good and chequered history. It began back in the mists of time, almost a quarter of a century ago, when I was fortunate enough to enjoy the favours of a lady, whose name conveniently escapes me. During the course of a relationship that pertained more to the nether abdomen than to the heart, she inadvertently left me with a painful little something to remember her by.

She and I were far from the only people in history to whom this has happened, and I bear her no ill will. And the painful little something was of the sort that comes and goes; indeed, the doctor said that it would appear and disappear with ever less frequency until it vanished altogether. This it proceeded to do until then suddenly, many years later, the whole thing flared up again, like a long-dormant volcano, causing acute tenderness and a nasty swelling, that not only put paid to any notions of amorousness but made it remarkably difficult to walk.

I mentioned the problem one morning to my neighbour, who suggested that I might have 'fallen prey to a wind-blown particle'. He then proceeded to show me a most villainous-looking infection on his ankle that had, apparently, blossomed from a tiny microbe blown there by the wind. The theory didn't seem entirely plausible but, given my rural and monogamous state, it was as good as any other. So off I went, with my bandy-legged gait, to the local clinic. There, the doctor studied the affected area with little enthusiasm and sent me home with a *pomada* – a cream – that I was to slap on three times a day. Not that it was certain to do me much good, he added discouragingly.

Having bought this stuff, I set to studying the list of *efectos secundarios* on the packet. 'Skin irritation,' it began. Well, I was used to that, though it did seem out of the frying pan into the fire. 'Loss of appetite...' It didn't say what sort of appetite but at my age you need all the appetite you can get. 'Nervousness... depression... chronic depression...' On and on it went.

It seemed manifestly unwise to apply this preparation to my person – particularly the more sensitive parts of it – so Ana, my wife, consulted her herbal tomes and suggested the alternative of a saline solution. This seemed innocuous enough, though you need a very strong solution. Seawater at 3.5 percent is not good enough, and even the 7 percent brine that you keep your olives in – the solution at which an egg floats to the surface – is not enough to deal with the maleficent microbes that can make life such a misery. No, to get those microbes scurrying for the hatches the solution must be no less than a ferocious 15 percent.

For some days, morning and night, I applied this bestial solution to my person, and there was enough of a tang in it to make me feel that it was actually doing some good. But when I began to develop a sort of crystalline crust, not unlike the caramelised sugar on a toffee apple, it seemed wise to call a halt.

Next out of the natural medicine chest was an essential oil made from grapefruit pips. I applied this stuff daily, drop by drop, from the tiny bottle – but as a certain piquancy in the affected part started to become apparent, I belatedly consulted the label. Under no circumstances, it noted, should the product be applied neat. 20:1 with almond oil or suchlike was the recommended dilution. By this time, the grapefruit seed oil had virtually flayed the flesh from my poor bone.

Finally, Ana came up with gentian violet. 'It says here,' she announced, after another read of the herbal, 'that it's a gentle, uninvasive and surefire cure. I think we've got some gentian violet.' Which we did, though it was rather more than ten years past its sell-by date. 'Doesn't matter,' pronounced the wife. 'It's hardly going to go off, is it?'

What you do with gentian violet is drop a few drops in some water in a mug, and then hang the affected part in it for a bit. It has a gentle antibacterial action, though if the truth be told, it didn't seem to do much good, beyond dyeing my dick a spectacular, deep and more or less indelible purple.

IT WAS AT THIS MOMENT of despair that I came across the journalist's account of his trip. It was clearly my last and best hope. I shillied and I shallied, and dithered a little, and then, after a few more days of bandy-legged agony, lunged for the telephone and rang the *curandera*.

'Speak,' she commanded. (This is what you say on the telephone in Spain.)

'Hello,' I said. 'Would you be the *curandera*?'

'Yes, that's me.'

'Well, I have a bit of a problem, and I was wondering if you might not be able to help me…'

'I'll do what I can. What is this problem?'

'It's a skin complaint…'

'That's what I do.'

'Yes, but… you see, well, it's on… I mean… what I'm saying is that…'

I had not rehearsed this as I ought to have done. I was digging a hole for myself and getting in deeper.

'You mean it's a penis, perhaps?'

'Well, in a sense, yes… it is a penis… er, do you do penises?'

'*Claro* – no problem. Can you come tomorrow?'

AS IT HAPPENED, it was Christmas Eve the following day, but that was okay. This was a ball I wanted to get rolling. And after a great deal of thought, I decided to go on foot. Of course I could have taken the car and saved myself a lot of time. But it didn't feel right; it wouldn't have been portentous enough for an expedition of this nature. The *curandera* had told me that it wasn't necessary to be a believer, nor go to church, in order to benefit from her ministrations, but even so, I felt that any element of spirituality that I could enlist on my behalf could only help. And the very act of walking has a certain spiritual dimension – more than driving the car at any rate.

And so, thus determined, I gathered the dogs, and, with hope in my heart and my complaint hanging heavily upon me, set off up the mountain. I decided to take the dogs along because although spirituality is not exactly their thing, they do manifest joy and transmit it to their human companions… and joy is a commodity of which one ought to take all one can possibly get.

As for the journey, well, placing one bandy leg in front of the other, time after thousands of times, and puffing and panting fit to burst my heart and lungs, I made headway through bright golden gorse and blue clouds of rosemary alive with diligent bees. I felt the elation that clambering amid mountains and raging rivers induces, and a tentative exuberance, at the thought that I might soon be rid of my burdensome ailment... and just a hint of apprehension. It was a complicated pot to keep on the boil.

Little by little I left the sounds of the valley below, the roaring of the rivers swollen with winter rains, the sounds of cocks crowing and dogs barking. By the time I got to the *aljibe*, the stone vaulted cistern that stands on the ridge between our valley and the next, there was nothing but the moaning of the wind in the broom. This is a sound of sinister portent, one that touches the darkest chords of our collective being.

I felt like a character in a Dennis Wheatley novel, the hapless protagonist in an imminent battle between the forces of good and evil. And things didn't improve as I entered the village and made my way, as instructed, past the spring, left at the end of the alley and down to the last house on the left. I stood collecting myself for a minute before the green wooden door. From inside came the sound of children's laughter. That didn't seem right; the last thing I needed now was children laughing... this was no laughing matter.

I thought for a minute of doing a bunk, calling the whole beastly thing off. I stood there vacillating, rocking back and forth, but then took heart and knocked hard on the door. The voices fell silent; then a cry: 'It'll be your man.' The door opened and a woman peered out, dressed in floral housecoat and carpet slippers. She had an interesting and intelligent face and kindly eyes. 'Hello,' she said. 'Can I help you?'

'Er... I hope so... I'm the person with the... you know, I rang you yesterday...'

'Ah yes – you're Cristóbal. Don't mind all these people. Come inside.'

The door opened directly onto a small room, in the middle of which sat an incredibly aged woman in a straight-backed chair. 'This is América,' said the *curandera*, indicating the old lady, 'and this is Carmen.' Beside América stood a young hairdresser, making some adjustment to the few sparse strands of blue-grey hair that remained on the old lady's wrinkled head. The tableau was completed by a motley assortment of babies and children, scampering or crawling about the room, while a teenage boy sat in an armchair and glowered morosely at everybody.

At my entrance, the show seemed to have come to a stop: the scissors hovered motionless in the air while the hairdresser considered me with a bemused smile; the babies dribbled; the teenager offered me a sneer of dankest disdain; América looked me up and down with an expression of utter bafflement and increasing distaste, until all of a sudden, she staggered half to her feet, opened her lipless old mouth and vomited copiously onto the cold tile floor. Everybody screamed. I was hustled urgently through a door into a parlour.

The door slammed behind me. I stood there alone, listening to the clattering of mops and buckets, the shrill cries of admonition to the children, the pitiful croaking of the now hysterical América, and the general pandemonium.

The parlour was a whitewashed room – even the canes and beams were whitewashed – and I stood hesitantly next to a large TV until the *curandera* came in, pulling the door half-closed behind her. 'Poor old thing,' she said. 'She's ninety-five years old, you know.'

'I… I hope it wasn't my fault,' I ventured idiotically.

'What? The vomiting? Heavens no! She does that all the time.'

She put her hands in the pockets of her housecoat and gazed at me in silence. I shifted my weight from one foot to the other and squinted back. After a bit she said: 'You're the one that wrote the book, aren't you?'

'Er… yes.'

'You live down there at El Valero, don't you? I know all about you. I liked the book, too.'

'Thank you.'

'Right, what seems to be the problem?' she asked with a flap of her housecoat.

'It's my… er…' and I indicated my crotch.

'Alright then,' she said. 'Out with the *culebrina* and let's have a look.' (A *culebrina* is a little serpent.)

This was it. I fumbled with the buttons of my fly, then bent over and reached in, gingerly coaxing the timid little creature from its lair for inspection. The *curandera* peered at it, aghast. It was not looking its best.

'It's a nice colour,' she observed after a bit. 'Don't you worry… we'll fix it up in no time.' And so saying, she sprinkled some talcum powder on the affected part, and set to rubbing it with a gentle circular motion.

This was far from unpleasant… in fact it was really rather nice. I strove to think about something disagreeable in order to discourage any untoward tumescence. But try as I might, the thoughts wouldn't come. It was too nice a day: there was a beautiful low winter sun; I had enjoyed a long walk accompanied by joyful dogs to a lovely Alpujarran village; my penis was being rhythmically rubbed; and soon I would be walking back to a blazing fire and a Christmas supper. I could feel blood creeping ominously about my body, looking for some empty space to fill, some erectile tissue perhaps, to make turgid... and turgid was the last thing I needed right now.

The *curandera* meanwhile was still rubbing. So I struggled to think of something boring instead. This of course is a tried and tested sexual technique; instead of meditating on say the beauty and sinuousness of bodies, or silk knickers, music and wine – lines of enquiry that can easily bring things to too abrupt a head – one considers, for example, the Spanish predilection for acronyms, or the lamentable decline in whale stocks, or the curious relationship between a liquid's viscosity and its meniscus.

There are plenty of such things but it's sometimes hard to fish them out when you need one. However, there was a silver crucifix on top of the telly, and this put me in mind of the mines of Potosí in Bolivia. Now there are few topics better conceived to banish impure thoughts than the horrific treatment imposed by the conquistadores on the indigenous populations of South America. My coursing blood was instantly stilled.

'Can we talk?' I suggested, thinking to lower the tension by means of some banal conversation.

'Of course we can. What do you want to talk about?' The *curandera* applied a little more talc.

'You said that I don't have to be a believer to benefit...'

'No, no, not at all. It makes no difference. I've treated all sorts, all the local boys – and they're not believers, I can tell you. The doctor sends them straight to me nowadays; he knows there's nothing he can do.'

She went on to tell me how she first realised she had the gift of healing. At the age of nineteen she had felt compelled to stroke the skin of a village baby that was suffering from a painful skin complaint: 'I don't know why; I just had this urge, so I asked the mother if I could hold the poor thing. I picked it up and stroked it where it was sore, and it stopped screaming.

I went back every day for a week, and by the end of the week it was healed... I've been doing it ever since, about forty years now it must be. People bring me all sorts of things to cure...' She paused. 'And I've seen an awful lot of penises. There, that ought to be done now; you can put it away.'

I buttoned up thankfully while the *curandera* returned the talcum powder to its drawer.

'How does it feel now?' she asked.

'Well I'd be lying if I said it was better, but that was very soothing, and I think it's less painful.' And I meant it.

'Come again tomorrow morning, but not too early.'

'It won't be that early; it took me four whole hours to walk here...'

'Walk? You didn't walk all the way from down there!'

'I did indeed.'

'What on earth for? Why not drive like any sane person?'

'Well I like walking, and... I thought it might be more appropriate for a thing of this nature, more... spiritual?'

'I've never heard such nonsense. Heavens no, bring the car tomorrow; it'll save you a lot of time.'

ON CHRISTMAS DAY I took the car. I wanted to be home for lunch, for one thing, and it meant I could take some gifts – home-made apricot jam, a sack of oranges and a bag of aubergines. The *curandera*'s village is too high for orange trees, and that year we had late aubergines.

After the third treatment, the inflammation had almost disappeared, and I asked how much I owed.

'Come and see me one more time in a week and we'll check that it's all over,' she said. 'And as for the money, you don't owe me a thing. I don't do cures for money.'

'But... but,' I spluttered. 'Nobody does anything without money. Have you never taken money, then?'

'I've never really thought about it, but it's a gift, and it wouldn't seem right to accept money for it.'

I looked around the little room. The *curandera* was far from being a wealthy woman. She had told me that she took whatever work she could get: cooking, cleaning, grape and olive harvesting and suchlike.

A WEEK LATER, the day of the final check-up, I rose in the very best of spirits: a cool winter sun was pouring from a cloudless sky, and there wasn't the slightest twinge of unpleasantness from my trousers. On such a day the only way to go was to walk, and I rocketed up the hill like a jack rabbit. Gone now the bandy-leggedness, no more the hoots of pain from the penis. There was a skip in my step this time as I entered the village, where I found the *curandera* sitting on a bench in the sunshine with three or four village women, passing the time of day.

After a last brief session with the talcum powder, we agreed that my ailment was good and gone, and sat in the kitchen for a while exchanging aubergine recipes. I gave her some olive oil from the farm, a box of home-made quince jelly and another sack of oranges.

On the way home, the dogs skipped about in the scrub, visible only by their tails held high – and if I'd had a tail myself, I think I'd have wagged it right off. We were all feeling that good. And as we breasted the rise where the long descent into our valley begins, I stopped for a bit to admire the lowering rays of sunshine making shadows in the folds of the sierras. The gentlest evening breeze rose from the bowl of the valley. It was the time and place, I reckoned, for a leak.

I looked about me and sought out a plant that would benefit from a warm watering with nitrogen-rich, pathogen-free pee. A tiny, perfectly formed juniper bush presented itself and I gleefully soused the little plant, while a million billion infinitesimal particles rose from the valley on the wind, bathing us in an invisible cloud... But what did I care? There was always the *curandera* up the river.

MICHAEL JACOBS

On the Way to Timbuktu

MICHAEL JACOBS was born in Genova, Italy (1952) to an Italian mother and an Anglo-Irish father. He has lived largely from his writings on art, travel and the Hispanic world. His many books include **The Good and Simple Life**, **Between Hopes and Memories**, **The Factory of Light**, **Ghost Train through the Andes**, and **Andes**. His next book, provisionally entitled **The Robber of Memories**, will be an account of a journey along Colombia's Magdalena River. A regular broadcaster on Spanish radio, he divides his time between London and a small village in the Andalucían interior.

On the Way to Timbuktu

MICHAEL JACOBS

was on my way to Timbuktu. I was meant to be writing a book promoting the legacy of Islamic Spain, but new enthusiasms were constantly leading me astray. My latest obsession was with the fate of the Spanish *Moriscos*, Christianised Muslims who had fallen between two cultures, and had ended up expelled to Africa, feeling more alien than ever. I wanted to know more about what had happened to them on the other side of the Mediterranean.

At first I had intended going only as far as Morocco. But, while staying in Granada, I had met a man from Timbuktu called Ismael Diadié Haïdara. He was of distant Spanish Muslim origin, and would later be in charge of the Timbuktu's major library of manuscripts from al-Andalus. He persuaded me that I would find in this desert town the ultimate destination to which my ever broader researches seemed to be leading. He also promised to be there himself should I ever decide to visit his birthplace. He wanted me to stay in his family palace.

Instinct and an implicit trust in others have so often guided my steps as a traveller. After my brief encounter with Ismael, I decided unhesitatingly to take up his invitation, and to set off as soon as I could to Timbuktu. I was drawn by the idea of its being the furthest outpost in Africa where Spain's exiled Muslims had settled. And I genuinely sensed that something of great consequence would result from the journey.

In the meantime I realised that a visit to Timbuktu was no longer as easy or safe as I had imagined. The town, so famously remote that nineteenth century explorers had competed for the honour of being the first westerner to get there, was becoming once again cut off from the outside world. It was the spring of 1992, and the nomadic Tuaregs were still at war with the Mali government. A combination of army blockades and severe drought had made the town almost unreachable by road and river. Aid workers and missionaries had already evacuated the place, and barely any other foreigners were left. The unlit streets were said to be dangerous after six in the evening, and the desert surroundings had become lawless at all times. A Swiss consular official, on a recent visit to a community fifty miles away, had been kidnapped and killed.

UNDETERRED IN MY DESIRE to visit Timbuktu, I realised that my only option was to trust my luck to Air Mali, whose tiny fleet of ancient planes had been reduced by half following the crash a few weeks earlier of one of them. The surviving plane, as far as I could gather, ran a once-weekly service that connected the country's four major towns along the Niger valley. The problem was that there was no way of reserving this flight from abroad, nor indeed any certainty that the service would run at all.

I flew from London to Mali's capital of Bamako, unsure if I would be able to travel on any further. But an English friend staying at Bamako was waiting for me late at night at the airport to say that there was a plane leaving for Timbuktu shortly after dawn, and that she had managed to reserve for me one of the last available tickets.

I had time for just a few hours' sleep before setting off again. My tiredness was soon dissipated by a sense of mounting exhilaration. I had never been anywhere in Africa other than Morocco, and I was absorbed at first by everything, beginning with the dawn taxi ride back to the airport, through the city's outer fringe of tall, dusty trees, alongside gaudily painted shacks and peeling billboards, into a flat expanse of scrubland illuminated by an intensifying pink glow.

The ticket that was handed over to me, in a terminal more like a bus station than an airport, was a poorly printed scrap of discoloured paper. Yet it had the name Timbuktu on it, which persuaded me that this most notoriously elusive of places was almost within my grasp. We were due to arrive at Timbuktu at midday, after a stop at Mopti, an important commercial hub on the Niger. My worries about last-minute hitches gradually disappeared after the plane had begun its near imperceptible ascent, to fly at a low altitude over shanty settlements, a stony wasteland, mud hut communities, baobab trees, until the horizon was transformed into a crumpled band of orange, my first glimpse of the Sahara. I was euphoric.

The few other tourists on the plane did not noticeably share my excitement. These were mostly Japanese pensioners, whose reasons for travelling to Timbuktu were as perplexing to me as their expressionless faces. The remaining foreigner was a sweating and disgruntled-looking New Yorker coming to the end of a 'six-country tour of West Africa'. He travelled, he confessed, largely to notch up countries (he had been to seventy-nine so far), and to record on video all that he saw.

Africa, for him, was a lazy and unhygienic continent where everyone was conspiring to rob him, rip him off, and confront him with bureaucratic obstacles.

On touching down at Mopti, we were told that even those continuing to Timbuktu were obliged to get off the plane and pass through customs and security control. The American cursed loudly, and was still moaning as we walked in the now blinding sunlight towards a concrete block, eventually to be let out again onto the runway. A handful of new passengers had preceded us there, and were standing waiting outside the plane while a couple of unhurried technicians tightened some of its bolts.

AMONG THE NEWCOMERS was a man who immediately cornered my attention. He was a white-haired but youthful-looking Westerner dressed in khaki. He had a bronzed bald forehead, a broad face and smile, and a manner that transmitted curiosity and enthusiasm for all that was going on around him. I was intrigued too by his way of drawing everyone into conversation, and keeping people amused and spellbound, even the hawkers now infiltrating the runway with goods ranging from cassettes to a stuffed monkey's head. I timidly shuffled my way closer until eventually I was able to read the label on his hand luggage. Large, hand-written letters spelt out a name at which I stared for a while in disbelief.

The crew had already returned to the plane, and the passengers were forming a disorderly queue in preparation for imminent boarding. I realised this might be my last opportunity to talk to the man in khaki, to make absolutely sure he was the person I presumed he was, *the* Kapuscinski – Ryszard Kapuscinski, the Polish reporter whose novelistic eye for detail, and deep sympathy for the downtrodden, had made him memorably begin his book about the emperor Haile Selassie with a description of the servant whose only job is to clear up the urine left by the imperial dog. I eventually plucked up the courage to speak to him.

Encountering authors you admire, if only as photos on a dust jacket, can be deeply disillusioning. Yet the warm, charismatic, and modest-seeming man in front of me lived up exactly to the image I had formed of him from his writings. He appeared genuinely surprised and pleased to be recognised. And he wanted to know all about me, and why I was travelling to Timbuktu. He himself was researching the book later to be titled *The Shadow of the Sun*, a work about his lifetime of African journeys, his current one being planned as one of the last. He had only secured his plane ticket to Timbuktu after bribing the manager at Mopti airport.

He spoke to me at first in poor English, switched for a while to Spanish, and ended up speaking a far from perfect French. His linguistic limitations were surprising for a foreign correspondent who had spent long periods in Africa and Latin America. But they clearly did not impede his extraordinary ability to communicate, and to make others feel empathy with him. In a matter of minutes I was convinced a great bond was developing between us.

We had at least one thing in common: neither of us had been before to the Sahara. When we got onto the plane he sat down at the window seat directly in front of mine, and kept on turning round to exchange with me his thoughts and emotions. The two of us became like excited children as the plane headed into a sandy emptiness later characterised by Kapuscinski in terms of mysterious geometrical patterns serving as clues to some ultimately indecipherable mystery.

Suddenly the Niger was once again below us, with its fishing boats and moored rafts, its fringe of reeds and cultivated fields, its banks laid out with rows of drying fish and clothes. The plane swerved violently towards the nearby Timbuktu, inciting dozens of ant-like figures on the ground to start running to meet us at the airport. 'C'est magnifique!' shouted Kapuscinski, giving me his final verdict on the scenery as he tore himself for a moment from the window.

I was hoping to see him again once we were in Timbuktu, but he explained that he was only going to stay in the town for little more than two hours. He would catch the same plane as it headed on to Gao and then back again to Bamako by evening. He needed to be in Liberia the next day. But he asked me if I had any plans for visiting Warsaw in the near future. He scribbled down his address there just in case.

We did not have the chance to say goodbye. I lost him within minutes of arriving at Timbuktu's tiny and chaotic airport, where I was delayed at customs by a soldier pumping me with questions and searching through my luggage. I was half-anticipating being met afterwards by Ismael Diadié Haïdara, but was confronted instead by a mass of waving arms, desperate to catch my eyes, offering me Tuareg rings and bracelets, attempting to grab me by the hand. In the far distance, lit up by the midday sun, a large van drove off, stirring up a cloud of dust that obscured everything. I thought I saw some Japanese faces, I thought I spotted Kapuscinski. Then I found myself staring into nothingness.

THE REST OF THE DAY was spent in a trance-like state. Timbuktu has so often disappointed travellers, who have expected more for their troubles than scarred adobe walls spreading out formlessly into the desert. Yet I was seduced by the town the moment I left the airport to enter its sandy labyrinth. Ismael may not have been there to meet me (he was rumoured to be still in Spain), but I was able to stay all the same in his rambling adobe home, looked after by his tall, beautiful wife and a bewildering array of brothers and cousins. I was greeted by the news that I had arrived at Timbuktu on a very special day, and that nights of music and dancing lay ahead. A peace treaty had just been signed with the Tuaregs.

Not all my days in Timbuktu would have the intensity of the first, and, as the town's heady exoticism became increasingly familiar, I ended up playing heated games of Scrabble on pirate Tuareg sets. Nonetheless the trip proved profoundly influential, if not in the way that Ismael had led me to expect. Instead of uncovering dazzling enclaves of the Hispano-Moorish past, I discovered the pleasures of living in a traditional isolated community, which encouraged me three years later to settle in a quiet Spanish village. At the same time I was inspired to undertake a series of ever more ambitious journeys, driven by a growing belief that the traveller's life is as full of strange and marvellous coincidences as the pages of *Don Quixote*.

For a long time afterwards I kept on thinking back to my encounter with Kapuscinski. I wanted to tell everyone about it, but failed at first to find anyone who was aware of Kapuscinski's importance, not even a well-read Scottish couple whom I ran into on my return to Bamako, and who told me they had shared a train compartment with him all the way from Nigeria to Mali. They said how friendly and helpful he had been, and that he made a living as a journalist. They had no idea that he was one of the greatest reporters of his generation.

I held on for ages to the scrap of paper on which Kapuscinski had written his address, intending one day to visit him there, or at least send him a letter. But these intentions were lost to other projects, and the address, stored in my wallet, became so creased and worn as to be illegible. In the meantime his fame continued to grow, until he was tipped for the Nobel Prize for literature.

The news of his early death reached me at the start of a journey in the Andes and I read the subsequent revelations about his life: about his notorious womanising, his close ties to the Polish Communist Party, and his later fears that these would be exposed. I learnt that he took great liberties with the truth, that he claimed to be an eyewitness when he was not, and that Haile Selassie's dog never pissed on the shoes of courtesans. None of this really mattered. He would always remain for me the compassionate, wonder-struck observer whom I had met for little more than an hour, on the way to a place that did not seem quite real.

TIFFANY MURRAY

Big Yellow Taxi

TIFFANY MURRAY (born Rustington, West Sussex, 1970) studied at New York University and the University of East Anglia and currently teaches creative writing at the University of Wales. She is the author of two novels – **Diamond Star Halo** (2010) and **Happy Accidents** (2005) – both of which were shortlisted for the Bollinger Everyman Wodehouse Prize. She has been called 'the glam rock Dodie Smith' and lives in Wales and Portugal. **www.tiffanymurray.com**

Big Yellow Taxi

TIFFANY MURRAY

When I first saw one it was driving over Queensboro Bridge, the iron cradle of the bridge throwing shadows; Manhattan in the distance. I was eight. I knew what a 'big yellow taxi' was because my mother played Joni Mitchell as she cooked. I didn't know that what I was seeing was a bridge called Queensboro – the bridges I knew had the names Kerne and Severn – and I didn't know that somehow, nothing in my life would be the same again.

My childhood was spent in landlocked countryside in Wales, in England, and in woodland gardens that breached both borders. If there was a remote house on an isolated pocket of boggy ground, my mother plumped for it. When I first saw that yellow cab on a small TV screen we were renting a house on an ancient estate – an English, feudal type, with a landowner. The estate was the flat top of a hill with one looping road that either ran up or back down, depending on point of view. It was a single country lane with a mission of monks at one end and a cattle-grid at the other. While the monks travelled the world, I rode my Raleigh bike around and around the looping lane until I was dizzy: that was my thrill. The estate was ruled by a gamekeeper who had a habit of stringing up quarry on the fences that lined this only road and hence every journey we made. If we lost cats they would eventually appear in his garish line-up. My mother would accelerate on the ride to school, 'Don't look, just don't look,' she'd say. I'd press my nose up against the back seat window and wail, 'Jenny! Tramp! Meissen!'

Even so, the gamekeeper's daughter was my best (and only) friend. Because of this my bedroom smelled of gristle. This is no reflection on Annie, we simply both believed that we were Robin Hood and after school meant running off into the bracken with our knives to check the snares we'd set in the woods. It was grisly. Our habit was to cut the tail off any poor creature that had the unfortunate luck to be caught in a child's badly set wire. I remember being particularly confused at what to do with a hedgehog: no tail, you see. Annie had gifted me deer legs, cut off at the knee (or whatever the deer equivalent for a knee is) and my bedroom was littered with these and the tails of grey squirrel, stoat, weasel, polecat, and fox, at various points of decay. I was a feral only child.

Perhaps it's no surprise that I turned to the imaginary worlds I found in books. But as I knew that I couldn't truly go to Never Never Land or Wonderland, and Ratty's Riverbank seemed as damp as our house, I turned to American TV. It was the time in Britain when US comedy was shown late at night, and it was smart and funny. I had laissez-faire parents who believed a child was quite capable of looking after itself; I also had parents who were kind, and though down on their luck, generous. That Christmas they gave me a tiny colour TV with one button that controlled *everything*. My father fixed it up in my bedroom, with the obligatory coat hanger aerial, and my love for the appendages of small woodland creatures waned: my mother got out the bin liners and cleared my room.

This TV gave me *Rhoda*; it gave me *Soap* and *WKRP in Cincinnati*. Finally it gave me my favourite: *Taxi*, the show with the opening credits where a yellow cab rumbles across Queensboro Bridge to the sound of that mournful flute. I was transfixed by the adventures of the Sunshine Cab Company. I fell in love with the Reverend Jim Ignatowski (Christopher Lloyd), I was soothed by Alex Rieger (Judd Hirsch) and I lost bladder control over Latka Gravas (the great Andy Kaufmann). I laughed and cringed at Louie De Palma (Danny DeVito) and I marvelled at Elaine's perpetually bouncy hair. Like the Empire State, the Chrysler Building and Miss Liberty herself there is so much that a NYC yellow cab symbolises, but for me at eight years old – transported from a damp bedroom on a feudal estate – it was simply a colourful car that could take me somewhere magical and funny; like Chitty Chitty Bang Bang could.

Soon, yellow cabs were popping up everywhere. Late one night sometime between Christmas and New Year, I watched *Midnight Cowboy* and I thrilled at the moment Ratso Rizzo bashes his fist on a NYC cab and yells, 'Hey, I'm walking here!' I cried my eyes out that Christmas and *Midnight Cowboy* became my favourite film. It was then that I started to collect pictures. I would tear pages from magazines and Blu-tack them to my walls next to the gymkhana rosettes that always said '3rd'. 'Bloody hell, Tiff, can't you get another obsession?' Mum asked as she gazed at my wall of yellow cabs crowding out the pony rosettes.

I couldn't. I was a feral and obsessive child.

I FIRST TRAVELLED to New York when I was eleven. I went on my own but stayed with a friend of my mother's in early

1980s SoHo. Unfortunately this friend picked me up from the airport, but I do remember my first glance at a long line of yellow cabs: the classic Checker cabs and the new Chevrolet Caprice and Ford Crown Victoria models roared in the morning air; my stomach flipped. My dreams had literally become reality. I wanted to play the mournful flute; I wanted the Reverend Jim to drive me over the Queensboro Bridge.

I spent my first few days in Manhattan walking around SoHo, watching steam rise from grills and manhole covers as cabs speeded past. My first trip in one was uptown. I remember floating up the Westside Highway, I remember the generous bounce of the seats, the thrill of being thrown about, almost crashing into the bullet-proof partition with the full force of a yellow cab that wants to get there. I remember the little payment hatch and the scratched perspex. And the smell; I remember the smell. You could say it was hot-dogs, incense: maybe the Little Tree that dangled from the rearview mirror, or the lingering scent of old West Side ladies draped in fur. I'd hate to think it was the stuff Travis Bickle had to wipe off his seats after a Saturday shift.

My mother's friend soon moved me to the West Village to stay with her stepchildren. They were rather wild. I bought a Dracula cape and a pirate hat and a green spiral earring. I thought I was a New York City punk. Of course, I was an eleven-year-old country girl. One night these stepchildren took me to the Mudd Club. A man said, 'Hey baby, let's hit the floor,' so I went upstairs to sleep. These stepchildren sat in Washington Square Park in the afternoons, and while they smoked I skipped about the fountain watching the grey and black squirrels. I remember standing under the Arch in Washington Square and staring up Fifth Avenue in awe. 42nd street was magical then, dangerous certainly, but not a Disney store.

I watched the streets for Ratso Rizzo, because to me he was as real as Smike from *Nicholas Nickleby*.

I flew home a day before my school entrance exam. My maths was awful but I scraped in on the power of my story: about a New York yellow cab and a poor little lost boy called Rizzo.

THE INTERVENING YEARS did nothing to stem my obsession: *Taxi Driver* set me off again and that was it: yellow cab, yellow cab. *Once Upon a Time in America* reignited my love for Manhattan and later, Jim Jarmusch's *Night on Earth* had me telling the Unemployment Office in Ross-on-Wye that I wanted to be an immigrant and a New York cabbie. I couldn't drive; I still can't.

I did, though, end up living in Manhattan. I couldn't help it. I lived there for eight years. There are many yellow cab memories: a boy kissed me – unexpectedly – in one; each time I took one from JFK or Newark, I would watch Manhattan rise before me and I'd grin. My best cab memory is a night the New York Yankees won the World Series. I sat in the back of a cab driving up Eighth Avenue while cars honked horns and flashed lights. I wound down the window and stuck my head out, and there was Queen Latifah, head and torso sticking out of a limo's sunroof in the next lane. 'The Yankees won, man!' she yelled at me and laughed. My yellow cab accelerated with that V8 roar that can only roll forward; I waved goodbye; the fare ticked.

It was a New York moment.

I was in Manhattan during the era of the Ford Crown Victorian, and, at the end of the 1990s, there was the strange sight of a Toyota people-carrier (a yellow cab people-carrier!). I was told to 'buckle up' by Whoopi Goldberg on recorded loop, and the cabs – a little like Giuliani's city – became too shiny for me. None of these vehicles compared to the black-and-yellow Checker cabs I'd first seen on my TV in Ye Olde England (although, when I could find them on the streets, I'd yell for them). Perhaps during my time in New York I was chasing something that was fading, something that wasn't necessarily there. The last Checker cab was decommissioned in July 1999. It had almost one million miles on its milometer. I left Manhattan the same year.

It's simple math, as the Americans say. The yellow cab I first saw on American TV when I was eight years old represented everything I couldn't grasp at the time; freedom, adventure, opportunity, power; it truly was everything that my life up on that hill wasn't. I didn't dream about London or Paris or anywhere in Europe in the same way. It is a coming-of-age cliché, but my obsession with the yellow cabs of New York City became my escape. The opening line of *The Godfather* is, 'I believe in America,' and I think that up in my damp bedroom that's how I felt, in spite of all the sentiment and contradiction that this statement holds. To me America, and specifically Manhattan, was a gloriously bright (and yellow) world somewhere magical, and every child believes in magic.

Of course the lasting irony is that now, in my nearing middle age, I'm back on a rural hill. There are no missionary monks here, there is no gamekeeper; this is Forestry Commission land. I still don't drive, but there are *two* roads that lead up to my hill. There is some evolution then, but I miss New York City and those yellow cabs with all my heart.

ROBIN
RHT
HANBURY-
TENISON

The Orchid Lady

ROBIN HANBURY-TENISON (born London, 1936) is a writer and explorer. He made the longest river journey in the world – alone – from the mouth of the Orinoco 10,000 km to the River Plate, and has led over thirty expeditions, including the massive Royal Geographical Society expedition to the heart of Borneo, which sparked global concern for tropical rainforests. He was one of the founders of Survival International, and remains its President, working since 1969 for the rights of indigenous people. He is the author of over twenty books, notably **The Great Explorers** and **The Oxford Book of Explorers**.

The Orchid Lady

ROBIN HANBURY-TENISON

When I was twenty-eight years old, in 1964, I was persuaded by Sebastian Snow to join him in an attempt to be the first people to bisect South America by river. Sebastian was famous as the first man to have gone the whole length of the Amazon from source to mouth; and six years before my friend Richard Mason and I had become the first people to cross the South American continent at its widest point from east to west.

Sebastian and I decided to do the journey from north to south, travelling in a small boat from the mouth of the Orinoco to the River Plate. We acquired enough sponsorship to buy a thirteen-foot Avon Red Cat and two 18hp motors, tried the boat out on the lake on my farm on Bodmin Moor and shipped it out to Venezuela. Two collapsible rubber petrol containers, each holding fifty gallons when full, took up most of the floor space, leaving precious little room for us and our meagre equipment. We perched on each side and bounced through the waves as we set off up the wide Orinoco. After a thousand miles we passed into Brazil and joined the Rio Negro, having navigated the Casiquiare Canal, an extraordinary phenomenon of a river which runs over the watershed between the vast basins of the Orinoco and the Amazon. The Brazilian border consisted of a smart little military post with a row of whitewashed thatched huts. The commandant barely glanced at our passports, invited us to stay and regaled us with his only 78 record: Harry James' Orchestra playing 'Sleepy Lagoon'. We found out much later that we had entered Brazil completely illegally, since strict permits were required to drive, let alone import, a boat. When it came to leaving the country and crossing into Paraguay, I had to try and do so at night pretending to be a patch of floating weed. But that all lay far ahead.

Sebastian, who was always eccentric, had begun to behave even more irrationally than usual. I thought at first that this might have been because he had managed to acquire a dose of clap during the week he had been in Venezuela ahead of me, a week in which he had run through a fair part of the expedition funds on riotous living. The doctor in Puerto Ordaz, whom we visited the day before setting off, prescribed massive doses of penicillin, which I had to inject nightly into Sebastian's bottom. Our first chore on making camp was to boil our sole syringe and needle. However, his symptoms began to worsen to include an almost complete loss of balance, which was not a good thing when spending all day in a small open boat. He also had a tendency to drop vital pieces of equipment overboard. I was beginning to worry about him.

A hundred miles downstream on the Rio Negro, we came to our first rapids at Uapés and, beside them, the first major settlement, the Salesian mission São Gabriel da Cachóeira. Here we were greeted by seven elderly priests, two of them with flowing white beards, one of whom said he had been there for forty years. They gave us a room in the small hospital and we dined simply with them in the refectory. Nuns in flowing white habits flitted around and one came to sit and talk with us. She told us that an Englishwoman had been staying a few days before but was now out in the forest collecting plants.

NEXT MORNING I was pottering about in our boat, repacking our stores and checking for leaks, when I looked up to see a striking blonde in a bush shirt, her hair an unruly mass of curls tumbling over her shoulders. She was Margaret Mee, the legendary botanical artist, then on the third of fifteen astonishing journeys she was to make into the remotest parts of the rainforest, collecting and painting plants. In her book, published twenty-four years later, she describes the meeting:

When we landed in Uapés, I saw to my astonishment a rubber boat with two powerful outboard motors tied at the bank among the other river craft. On further examination I noted a couple of crash helmets [she must have imagined those. We never had crash helmets], British and Brazilian flags and a nice Paisley scarf, so by deduction I concluded that the boat was British owned. A blond, suntanned young man came up to greet me as 'the English woman they have been telling me about'. Who was he, and where was he going? I wanted to know. His name was Robin Hanbury-Tenison and his companion was Sebastian Snow, both young travellers already experienced in exploring the Amazon ... writing a book about the longest river journey on record. That evening we supped together at the invitation of Sister Elza and talked late into the night.

Robin Hanbury-Tenison and Sebastion Snow on their Amazon expedition

Margaret Mee – back in the Amazon in the 1980s

Margaret had been having an exciting time. After a week botanising far up a tributary of the Negro and climbing a small mountain, which had probably not been visited since Richard Spruce had been there a hundred and twelve years before, she had spent a few days at an Indian village recovering. While she was there a rough party of prospectors had arrived by motorised canoe and the leader had made a pass at her, which she had repelled. When he and his companions returned drunk, she was ready for them. With her money, camera and her mother's engagement ring hidden in the hut, she was sitting on a chair with her loaded revolver in her hand. Laughing at his agitated retreat with his hands in the air, she chased him back to the boat and they drove away. I was impressed.

We needed a guide to show us the way through the rapids and the tangled mass of islands and sandbanks which lay downstream of us. The only problem was that there was barely room for another body on board our heavily laden little boat and extra weight made it difficult to get it to 'plane' and so go at a decent speed. Sebastian and I achieved this each time we started by having one of us scrambling over the petrol containers to the bow and bouncing up and down while the other gunned the engines at full throttle. We would need a very small guide. Margaret said that she knew just the man, and he happened to be the best pilot on the river.

Manolo el Tucuma was a wizened old person who claimed to be seventy-three, but he had a saintly nature, a large black umbrella, which he opened against the spray, and a good sense of humour, which he maintained throughout the dramas we endured on the way to Manaus. These included discovering that we had been sold kerosene instead of petrol at São Gabriel. Of course, we only found out when we had refilled the tanks and so this necessitated Manolo and me struggling forty miles back upstream with coughing motors to remonstrate with the trader from whom we had bought it. We left Sebastian, who was no help in a crisis, at an Indian village, to be collected later.

My bonus was that I got to spend another evening listening to Margaret's extraordinary adventures. She was then fifty-five years old and still very good-looking, with her striking hair. She completed her fifteenth collecting expedition in her eightieth year and her Amazon Collection of sixty paintings and many plants new to science are now housed at Kew. When my old schoolteacher at Eton, the distinguished art critic and historian Wilfred Blunt, brother of the spy Anthony Blunt, first saw Margaret's superb botanical drawings, he said: 'They could stand without shame in the high company of such masters as Georg Dionysius Ehret and Redouté.'

Manolo and I duly collected Sebastian and made our way to Manaus. There Manolo met his son, whom he had not seen for twenty years, and Sebastian flew home. It turned out that he was suffering from Ménière's disease, a disorder of the inner ear, which causes dizziness and loss of balance. This was cured and, he told me later, it was confirmed that my injections had also done the trick. I continued alone through the rivers of South America and eventually reached Buenos Aires about two months later.

BACK IN LONDON, I was invited to lunch at Buckingham Palace, where I found myself seated next to Prince Philip, who grilled me about the point of this journey. 'Does it have any economic significance?' he asked. Floundering to give a positive answer, I explained that many of the rivers I had traversed had been very shallow and interspersed with sandbanks and rapids. 'The only boat that could take passengers would be this new thing I've heard about called a Hovercraft, as that would skim over all obstacles and so everyone could go and see what I have seen,' I said, rather unconvincingly. To my genuine astonishment he turned to the man on his other side and said, 'Mr Cockerell, you had better give this young man one of your machines!'

The man who invented the Hovercraft, later to become Sir Christopher, was not best pleased with what sounded like a Royal Command, but that conversation did result in the first major Hovercraft expedition in 1968, when with twenty-two assorted scientists, journalists and film-makers we took an SRN6 off its day job as the Isle of Wight ferry and followed my route from Manaus to the mouth of the Orinoco in reverse. When we reached Uapés I told the captain that we had our first dangerous rapids to ascend. He had a look at them and opined that he didn't think they would pose much problem to a craft that rode a metre above the rocks and waves. I suggested that, as a special favour to me, he requested the services of the best pilot on the river, who happened to live in nearby São Gabriel.

There I tracked down Manolo el Tucuma. He now looked the old man he was and I found him living in severely reduced circumstances in a hovel, where his family brought him food from time to time. I explained that his special skills were once more required. Carrying his battered old black umbrella and walking tall, Manolo passed through the crowd surrounding the beached hovercraft and shook the Captain's hand. With a mighty roar the engines were started up and the great machine slid onto the surface of the water and forged easily up the cataract, as the crowd ran along the bank cheering. Manolo stood in the front indicating the safest route, as he had so many times in the past. I like to think it was his finest hour.

Twenty-four years after our meeting, in November 1988, Margaret Mee gave a talk at the Royal Geographical Society in London, at which her superbly illustrated book, *In Search of Flowers of the Amazon Forests* was launched. I arrived late and sat in the gallery enthralled both by her pictures and the passionate way Margaret described what was happening to her beloved Amazon as loggers and cattle ranchers destroyed great swathes of it. At the end, I decided not to fight my way through the crowd of those congratulating her, but to renew our friendship later. I bought a copy of the book and was astonished, when I arrived home and read it, to find how much she had written about our chance encounter so long before. I was about to try and contact her when I heard that on the 30th of November, the anniversary of our last meeting, she had been killed in a car crash in Leicestershire.

RAJA SHEHADEH

With Eyes Wide Open

RAJA SHEHADEH (born Ramallah, Palestine, 1951) is the author of three highly acclaimed memoirs, **Strangers in the House, When the Bulbul Stopped Singing** and **A Rift in Time**, as well as a travel book, **Palestinian Walks**, which won the Orwell Prize in 2008. He is a Palestinian lawyer and writer who lives in Ramallah – his family were forced from their home in Jaffa in 1948 – and is the founder of the pioneering, non-partisan human rights organisation, Al Haq (Law in the Service of Man).

With Eyes Wide Open

RAJA SHEHADEH

The electric kettle and coffee mugs rattled in their plastic bag as we drove up north. We hadn't bothered to pack them well, our trip was just a short hour and forty-five minute drive. Now we worried they might break but decided not to stop. We wanted to get to the Galilee hills in time for an afternoon walk.

The route we took went through the Jordan Valley – part of the Great Rift Valley that extends from the Taurus Mountains in Turkey to Central Africa in the south. Here is one of the best places to observe how the Rift majestically meanders along the fault in the earth formed millions of years earlier by the movement of the tectonic plates deep in the ground.

The hodgepodge of stuff we were carrying did not all fit in the trunk. After placing the two pairs of walking boots and sticks, a suitcase with our bed clothes and toiletries, and our two backpacks, there was no space left. The books, towels, swimwear, packed lunch, kettle and coffee things had to go on the back seat. By the time we finished hauling in our stuff, the car was quite a sight. But we didn't mind. It was but a short hop to the Galilee.

What a relief it was, we thought, to take a holiday that did not involve flying, with all the hassle of airport lines and searches. We looked forward to the drive down the *wadi* to the cultivated fields on this clear, crisp winter morning. My wife, Penny, and I had for several months been working long hours, hardly leaving our house in confined Ramallah, and we needed time, as Penny put it, to air our brains. A breezy walk along the hills of the Galilee was sure to accomplish this. If not, then surely sitting in the quiet serenity of the large stone patio overlooking Lake Tiberias at the pilgrims' retreat would do the job. The only fault in this otherwise perfect refuge from the turbulence of life in our region was that it had no room service and did not offer the possibility of preparing coffee in your room. And Penny cannot wake up without her morning coffee. Which was why we were travelling with our coffee-making gear.

THE IMPOVERISHED PALESTINIAN farming villages we passed on the sides of the road were a sharp contrast to the highly subsidised Israeli settlements with their red-tiled roofs and spacious gardens, established since Israel occupied the West Bank on confiscated Palestinian land.

Three-quarters of an hour after we started we had already passed the first three of the four checkpoints along the way. At every stop we had to present our Israeli identification cards. The profiling Israeli officials practise at airports is not necessary here. These variously coloured and coded IDs tell everything about their holder, creating segregation amongst the Palestinian population that mirrors the fragmentation of the land by borders, checkpoints and settlements. So far, though, we were doing well and getting waved through without any question asked. And we were not unduly concerned about the last checkpoint ahead – the one separating the West Bank from Israel – because we had often passed it without incident. We were enjoying the drive, too, along a narrow two-lane road; we both dread highways where we find the zooming cars speeding on both sides of our slow-moving vehicle nerve-racking. So we were in a tranquil state of mind.

This was soon to end. We had just passed the Palestinian village of Zbeidat when we came upon an installation that felt stridently out of place in the midst of this beautiful valley. A large sliding iron gate, the width of the road and painted yellow, was flanked on both sides by high barriers of barbed wire. To one side was a prefabricated structure that I had often noticed as we passed but to which I had never paid much attention. We slowed down and stopped at the barrier, rolled down our windows, greeted the soldier and presented our identification cards like all the other travellers.

After inspecting them the soldier did not hand them back but said: 'You go there,' pointing to the prefab. As we pulled over to the right we heard him call out in Hebrew to the soldier standing in the sun that he is sending him 'more Palestinians to check'. I now surveyed the scene and saw one young man carrying a machine gun, with three bullet magazines stuck in his belt, standing ready to shoot, a woman with long black hair holding a black dog by his collar, and a very young-looking man with a fleshy round face wearing a black cowboy hat who approached the first soldier and received from him our documents.

The young man now asked us to switch off the engine and leave the car, after opening all four doors, the hood and the trunk. Then he politely asked that we take out our stuff from the trunk. We unloaded two bags and placed them on the ground, then waited for the next order. The young man said: 'You must take everything out of the car. Leave nothing inside.'

I looked at our plastic bags, boots, sticks, towels and said: 'You can't be serious. Why do you want us to take these out?'

'They have to pass through the machine.'

'What machine?'

'The inspection machine over there,' he said and pointed to the prefab.

'But this is not an airport and we are not taking a flight from here. All we're doing is driving a short distance to the Galilee. What is this about?'

'These are my orders. You have to do what I ask you.'

'But this is ludicrous. Your orders make no sense. When one is taking a flight I can see the logic of searching. But here, in this green valley, in the midst of these cultivated fields, it makes no sense.'

'Do you need a trolley?' the young man asked as if he had heard nothing of what I said.

I didn't feel like accepting favours. I said, 'No thanks,' and proceeded to lift as many bags in my two arms as I could manage, slinging a backpack on each shoulder, Penny trailing behind me with the rest. We must have looked ridiculous but I didn't care. I was getting angry. Then I stopped, dropped my heavy load and eyeing the young man with the cowboy hat said: 'Can't you see that your orders are ridiculous?'

He muttered: 'I'm just obeying orders,' as if to imply this has nothing to do with either of us.

'Hasn't it occurred to you how dangerous it is to obey orders without thinking about them?' I responded. 'Don't you know what this can lead to? Think for yourself. For God's sake, think.'

I heard the young man mutter: 'You don't want to know what I think.' Then after a short pause and in a lower tone, he added, 'Of you.'

But I pretended not to hear him. I suddenly felt my years, an older man concerned about – or perhaps afraid of – what the thoughtless behaviour of the younger generation, in this case one in control of my life and movements, could do.

'Here we are in the middle of nowhere, in the Jordan Valley's fertile cultivated fields, and you are acting as though we are going to board a plane when all we're doing is taking a drive along this two-lane road, don't you find all this bizarre?'

He remained silent.

I don't often act paternal but I somehow felt responsible for this young man's fate. He had an innocent face with big eyes and a silly hat and I could not let this pass. I kept on repeating, rather stupidly now, imploring him to think, think, just think.

'I am here to protect my country against terrorism,' he said to shut me up.

How could he believe this, I thought to myself. Doesn't he realise that anyone interested in smuggling explosives can just cross through the low hills west of here where the border is open? Could he not have thought of this? But when I looked straight into his eyes, I could see he had not given any thought to what he was doing or to the strong possibility that his mission could so easily be thwarted. He was just a well-trained operative in a system far stronger than himself. So for the moment, I gave him a break and stopped bidding him to think, turning my attention to transporting my various items of luggage to the inspection machine which he was now manning.

As I stood looking at my suitcase and plastic bags, my hiking boots and the wooden stick that I found one day in the

Ramallah hills, all riding down on the conveyor belt into the scanner, my anger began to dissipate. I felt that my words were being blown away by an indifferent wind that swept through the Rift Valley, all the way from the north of Syria to Lake Tiberias, in the midst of which he and I stood like specks in a gorgeous landscape that will endure beyond the short span of our lives and that of the political entities to which each belonged.

My attention was then directed to my car which now had a crucified look with all its doors open. The woman with the long black hair was directing the German shepherd where he must sniff. The dog did not seem enthusiastic but his nose was being led to the carburettor, the battery, the various tubes and plugs. When he finished one round he was taken again for a second one. Then came the turn of the guard with a pen light who opened the glove compartment and flashed his light inside it. Then he dived under the seat and inspected there. Like the dog he also repeated his round twice. I wondered whether this was what he was instructed to do or if he was just taking a personal initiative.

I was pondering the futility of it all and thinking about how the repressive system of occupation that has been in operation for over forty years was now being sub-contracted and commercially exploited. This young man with the funny hat was merely an employee of a business, a security company that needs to show its muscle to win more contracts in Israel and elsewhere in the progressively more paranoid world. Israel's domestic security technologies are now amongst the country's biggest exports with more than four hundred Israeli companies exporting $1.5 billion annually in domestic security goods and technologies which are touted as field proven, tested on the nearly-human Palestinians.

I did not notice the other Palestinian who had been detained until he was standing next to me, whispering in my ear. 'What happened?' he asked. 'I always go through here, it is never like this.'

I said I didn't know. Perhaps they were testing a new security system on us, one that they were preparing to offer for sale to Western countries enamoured of Israel's expertise in security matters. As we spoke I looked at the cars of the fortunate ones – the Jewish settlers – as they whizzed through.

WITH THE NEXT SUSPECT on hand, I realised my time would soon be up. Now they had another customer to keep them busy lest their employer should appear and find them idle. The man with the cowboy hat came towards me. Before he handed me our IDs I implored him one last time to think. I said: 'Please, for my sake, think of what you're doing. It is too dangerous to obey orders without thinking.'

He answered: 'Give me your mobile number. When I do, I will call and tell you.'

I said: 'I don't want you to call me. I only want you to think.'

I was getting ready to get into my car when he approached, handed me our IDs, and, without taking his eyes off mine, a Swiss penknife that I was not aware had been in my backpack. It was a kind gesture on his part. I know of Palestinians who have been charged with possession of a knife while passing through an Israeli checkpoint. He nodded knowingly as though to let me know that sometimes he does think about what he is doing.

I was taking my time putting my ID back in my wallet when Penny cried: 'For God's sake, hurry up! I want to get out of here.' I did and we were soon on our way through a Rift Valley that was now carved up by barbed wire in double rounds cutting through the hills, breaking their natural continuity. Tall cement blocks like gravestones were placed side by side, emblematic, I felt, that this has become a cemetery of a land.

As we drove away, I remembered a sculpture at the Kishon Gallery in Tel Aviv – a life-size, soft plastic replica of Ariel Sharon, with his eyes wide open and a stomach that moved up and down at regular intervals. It was the myopic Sharon as Prime Minister of Israel who was responsible for erecting over five hundred checkpoints throughout the West Bank and who began the construction of the abominable wall. For the past five years he has been lying in bed comatose after a massive stroke. The curator of the exhibition described the sculpture as an allegory of Israeli society that, like my young man, has wide open eyes that cannot always see.

Janine di Giovanni
J.D.G.
J.D.G.
Janine di Giovanni

Decide To Be Bold

JANINE DI GIOVANNI (born New Jersey, USA, 1961) is a journalist and author who has reported conflict and humanitarian crisis for nearly two decades. She is the author of five books, including **The Place at the End of the World**, about Sarajevo, and, most recently, a memoir of life as a war reporter, **Ghosts by Daylight** (Bloomsbury, 2011). She lives in Paris.

Decide To Be Bold

JANINE DI GIOVANNI

O'f all the hundreds of photographs of war and conflict I have sifted through over the years, the one I cannot forget, the one that gives me nightmares still, nearly two decades after it was taken, is the one that epitomises the terrible phrase 'ethnic cleansing'.

The French photojournalist, Alexandra Boulat, who died in 2007, took it. It is a photograph of a family, or what was left of a family, in Sarajevo during the bloody backyard war in the early 1990s. The 'liberators' – the Bosnian Serb Army who burnt down the houses, killed and plundered villages, raped and destroyed a society – had found a family photograph inside one of their newly acquired houses. It's a typical photograph that any of us would have in our memories, or in our photo albums. It looks like the late 1970s. There is a neat little mother, a neat little father, two neat little children. They are wearing their good clothes and standing proudly in front of a neat little square house with a neat little fence. Before the war, they probably had a neat little life.

But this photograph is cursed. Because before the ethnic cleansers destroyed everything, one of them took the time to

Sarajevo family – photo courtesy of the estate of Alexandra Boulat

painstakingly scratch out the eyes and the faces of each member of the family. So what remains are heads and bodies, but no faces, just blank, scratchy, chilling lines. Lives utterly and completely deleted, completely denied existence. What was before will never come again.

HAD MY LIFE taken a different route, as it was perhaps meant to, that photograph would have meant nothing to me. But now, in many ways, it represents my life, and what I do, and what I hope to do.

In the late 1980s, I was a postgraduate student. My field was obscure – Chekhov's influence on Katherine Mansfield – and limited. I spent all my time in the British Library in Bloomsbury and on my sofa, with a book and a notebook. My plan was to finish my thesis, start a PhD in Comparative Literature and spend the rest of my life teaching at a university. I was very young, very naïve, and very protected. I lived in the ivory tower of academia and rarely, if ever, picked up a newspaper or watched the news. I was perfectly happy for my life to stay that way.

But one freezing cold December day, visiting my then-husband's family in Chicago, I idly picked up a newspaper while eating my breakfast. The cover story was an article about the outbreak of the first Palestinian *intifada*, or uprising. The photograph was of young Israeli soldiers who looked no older than teens, sitting in a bulldozer burying alive some teenage Palestinians. The picture horrified me, as did the article, which was about a Jewish lawyer who defended Palestinians in military court.

According to the article, the lawyer – Felicia Langer – had fled World War II from her native Poland, where her family were incarcerated in the camps, for Israel. She had been a life-long Communist, and, after having her son, put herself through law school. Unable to bear the injustice of the treatment of Palestinians following the 1967 war, she became one of the few lawyers who would defend their rights.

Her life was a misery because of it. She was spat upon, bombed, tormented, and hated. But she kept doing it, despite the fact that she lost nearly all her cases and that she was exhausted by the system, the process, the fact that she was one of the very few up against a huge machine. Every morning she got up and did it, over and over again, knowing she would lose, knowing she was Sisyphus pushing a rock uphill, only to have it roll down.

That winter morning in Chicago, my life changed forever. I stopped eating my toast and decided to become a journalist. I did not know how, but I had always believed in what Goethe said: when you decide to be bold, great forces come to your aid. In my case, they did: a newspaper launched in the UK called the *Sunday Correspondent*, and an editor named Henry Porter believed in me enough to send me to the West Bank to find out who Felicia Langer was.

I WAS SURPRISED how easy it was to meet her. I simply found her number from the International Operator – this was long before the days of Internet – and rang her. She picked up the phone, and in halting English, invited me to come and see her. 'If you really want to know what this is about,' she said, 'you have to come to Israel.'

I arrived in the spring. The *intifada* was in full force, the young men – known as *shabbab* – hurling rocks with slingshots at Israeli tanks. People were dying in Gaza, in Ramallah, in Jerusalem. Children were being shot with rubber bullets. Unbearable torture was taking place at secret prisons in the Negev.

When I arrived at Langer's office in West Jerusalem, she was sitting at her desk, crying. It was a dingy place, and there was a dying plant on her desk. She herself was in her fifties at the time, pretty, plump, wearing lipstick. Her skin was very good – later she showed me the exact sun block I should be using, by Lancaster, to protect myself from the Middle Eastern rays – and she looked utterly exhausted.

That day, Langer became my guide into a world I never would have known. My trajectory of life was meant to be simple: marriage to a wonderful man; children; an academic life and then comfortably settling into retirement without war and conflict and torture and columns of refugees touching me. It touched some people in some part of the world, I knew in some part of my brain, but certainly not me.

Langer was crying over a case she had just lost, the murder of a teenage Palestinian boy by Israeli Defence Forces. But of course, it was not called murder; he died 'in detention'. She was trying to get the body exhumed. Her requests to the court had failed. She looked up from a huge stack of files, and invited me to sit down.

I did not really know how to interview someone, was not really a professional journalist, but I had my notebook and I began to listen. At some point she told me something that resonated so strongly with me that I literally felt as though I had touched a live electricity wire: if you have the ability and the power to go places where other people don't go, she said, and you have the courage to give a voice to people who do not have a voice, then you have an obligation.

She took me to refugee camps. I had never seen people live without water, without sanitation, and behind barbed wire.

She introduced me to torture victims who jumped when I walked too quietly behind them. She introduced me to people who had lost limbs in Mossad car bombs, to Jewish left-wing activists who had spent time in jail for treason against the Israeli government, to doctors and psychiatrists and politicians in Gaza and Ramallah and Jenin and Nablus.

That trip lasted three weeks, but I flew back to London an utterly changed person. I finished my thesis but the trajectory on which my life was meant to go was dismantled forever.

THE ARTICLE CAME OUT on 19 November, 1989, an issue celebrating the fall of the Berlin wall. I had written about Felicia with the same passion she possessed, and although I did not know how to write a magazine article, it was as though I too was possessed by the same demons that had gripped her. I would never be able to live the way I had before.

The rest would never have happened if I planned it, a bit like falling in love – if you look for it, you never get it. But an agent saw the article. She got me a book deal. I went back to Palestine and stayed for several years interviewing victims on both sides of the conflict. I would return over and over again to that country and remember that first time, the way the pink light hits the white buildings, the way I felt when I first felt the bitterness of injustice in my throat, and my desire to do something about it.

After that, I went to Bosnia and witnessed the dismembering of Yugoslavia. Then to Africa. Liberia, Somalia, Congo, Ivory Coast, Sierra Leone. Chechnya, Kosovo, East Timor, Iraq and Afghanistan. My quest was finding people who did not have a voice, and giving them the chance to speak. To shine a light in the darkest corners of the world, to quote a colleague. Sometimes it worked and sometimes it didn't. Sometimes the people I thought were good betrayed me, or the victims weren't really victims. But most of the time, I sat on the floor taking notes and listening.

Of course, along the way, my marriage broke up. No one could sustain that lifestyle, least of all a husband who wants a wife. My vision of a life with five kids in the suburbs went out the window. I slept in sleeping bags for years, lived on the road, survived on cigarettes and alcohol and stale bread and chocolate and vitamins.

But the occasional victories – the people I managed to get safely out of war zones, the children who grew into beautiful adults and were not scarred by war, the policy makers I got to confront and attack, the way I could channel my indignation at injustice into words – were worth it. I believed in the power of words. In Chechnya, as Grozny was falling and I was trapped by Russian forces pummelling the hell out of me and a group of Chechen soldiers, I thought, This is it. I really am not getting out this time, so say your prayers.

I was mind-numbingly frightened. I did not want to die, least of all a violent death in a frozen and god-forsaken country. I had not yet become a mother. There were too many unspoken things between me and people I loved. But out of the fear came a little voice inside which said: but at least you died believing in what you do. That's not nothing. After that, an incredible calm came over me. The brutal bombardment went on, but I eventually got out.

I LAST SAW Felicia Langer during the first Gulf war. We lost touch. But I never forgot her, never forgot what she gave me. In a sense, I should curse her: my life, of course, would have been simpler had I never seen that photograph of the bull-dozer and the Palestinian teenager, never went into her office, never saw the tears running down her face. But I guess that was not how I was destined.

So when I see photographs of ethnic cleansing – Alexandra Boulat's classic photo of that family – or hear about rape in the Congo or child soldiers in Somalia or abused sex workers in India, I feel sad or despair at the state of the world. But I also feel indignation, anger and the twitchy feeling that something can, and will be done, and that human beings, sometimes, can save each other. And I owe that to Felicia Langer, and that day in West Jerusalem.

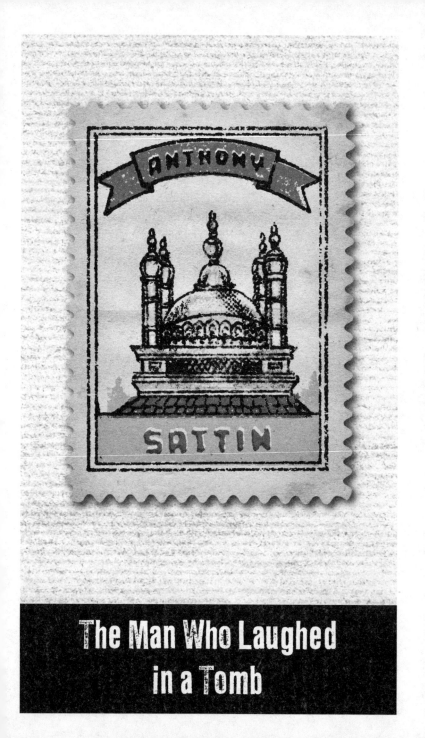

ANTHONY

SATTIN

The Man Who Laughed
in a Tomb

ANTHONY SATTIN (born London, 1956) is a specialist on North Africa and the Arab world and the author of several books of history and travel, including **The Pharaoh's Shadow** and **Lifting the Veil**. He discovered and edited Florence Nightingale's letters from Egypt, which inspired **A Winter on the Nile**, an account of parallel journeys to Egypt by Florence Nightingale and Gustave Flaubert. He writes regularly for the Sunday Times and Condé Nast Traveller and presents features for BBC radio. He is currently writing the biography of an early traveller in Arabia. He lives in London.

The Man Who Laughed in a Tomb

ANTHONY SATTIN

I had never met Saïd before, but his friends assured me that he was a wonderful guy, always lively, happy to get involved. He had been a regular at the café for as long as anyone could remember. On weekdays, he went home from work, saw to his wife and kids, had something to eat and then took up his place in the café, ready to share a joke or a trouble. On Friday, he came directly from midday prayers, shaved, washed and in a pressed white *gallabiya*.

When he died suddenly, Saïd was wrapped in a winding sheet and his family and friends brought him to his favourite table while they went to prepare his interment. He lay stretched on a board, resting over a couple of chairs, a green cloth laid over him, while we drank tea and chatted. When the time came, we all stood up to support him on the first few steps of the final journey. To me, this was extraordinary. But there was nothing unusual to people in this part of Cairo about the presence of death in a lively café, just as there seemed also to be no surprise at the idea of life in the cemetery, the realm of death.

The café stood just outside the Gate of Victory, whose towering blocks of stone were built against the arrival of Crusader knights and Mongol hordes. At that time it marked the passage between the city and desert though, as the city grew and a cemetery spread outside the walls, it became the link between the city of the living and that of the dead. Modern Cairo has now become so large and so confused, there is no longer any demarcation. The living have engulfed everything and even parts of the old cemetery have had to make way for apartment buildings and workshops.

A huddle of black-robed women was hanging around at the corner of the road that led to the burial grounds. They were professional mourners, waiting for a funerary procession to pass, so they could tout their trade. Nearby, a flower seller had arranged sprays of palm fronds and gladioli: funerary flowers. A man who turned out to be a reciter of the Koran tried to take a cigarette off me – sorry, *o ma'alim*, I don't smoke – and extracted one from a passing friend. Then I met Abdu.

There were many unexpected things about Abdu, not the least of which were his size – he was very tall and very broad – and the fact that he lived in a cemetery. But what disconcerted me more than that was the fact that he thought we had met before. 'Really?' I asked.

He laughed, assuming I was teasing, showing his broken teeth. I was not teasing.

He scratched his grey stubble. 'But we know each other.'

Given the way the day was going, I half expected him to tell me we had met in another life, but he assured me we knew each other here and now in this one. 'In Cairo, only last year ... Or was it the year before? But Roberto, why play like this?'

'Roberto?'

'Roberto Cairo.'

I assured him that my name was Anthony, but he was certain that I was joking.

'Come home and say hello to Attiyat.'

Curious as to where this might lead, I followed his tall, heavy figure along the unpaved track, then off it to the right, between a scattering of tombs, ever deeper into the cemetery.

Cairo has been burying people outside its gates for more than a millennium – the unfortunate Saïd, carried from the café, was just the latest in a long time – and among the great domes and religious complexes you might come across the tomb of a companion of the Prophet Muhammad, or a medieval sultan, a nineteenth-century king or a twentieth-century movie star. But the northern part is less illustrious, its tombs mostly flat-topped wooden shacks, and the best you might find here is the tomb of the medieval Islamic scholar Ibn Khaldun, or the Swiss traveller Jean Louis Burckhardt. Abdu led me past these, weaving his way across the sandy ground to his home.

This turned out to be a patched-up wooden shack, built over a single, simple grave. Slight frills around the edge of the wooden roof were Turkish in style; the house was at least nineteenth century, maybe much older. Abdu and his family had made the area their own by putting out some rickety wooden benches, stringing an awning above them and hanging washing lines between the markers of other tombs. When we arrived, Attiyat, his wife, was making tea over a two-ring stove installed on the raised bench of another grave.

She was a solid, fleshy, no-nonsense sort of woman, her hair inside a plain dark scarf, her eyebrows plucked far apart, gold hoops on her ears. She sat me down on one of the wooden benches and poured a glass of black tea.

I discovered, as we slurped the scalding sweet liquid, that Roberto Cairo wasn't a name Abdu had made up: he had mistaken me for a Spanish actor whom he remembered from a film he had seen long ago. I insisted that I was no actor and that we had never met before. I asked him what he did.

'I am the guardian of this part of the cemetery. I used to live in a place called Hassaniya, but when our house fell down, we moved to the tombs. I've been here forty years now, so it's part of my life. My mother and father are here as well: we are on top of them all the time.'

It took a moment for that one to sink in. 'What do you mean?'

'My brother Bulbul lives in a house over their grave.'

Twenty-six years earlier, Abdu had met Attiyat. 'Before that, I was married twice. Or was it three times?'

'You don't remember?'

'Maybe there were more than three, I really can't be sure.' He roared with laughter, a devilish sparkle in his eyes. 'One wife was scared to live in the cemetery, so I divorced her after a month. Another wife didn't want me to work. Well that was no problem – I wasn't going to object. But then someone had to make the money, and she didn't. This one,' he said, winking towards Attiyat, 'bears with me. We have been through the sweet and the dark. One day we eat chicken, another day bread and salt. She is prepared to live according to the wind.'

I had difficulty talking to Abdu that first time. It was too strange to be sitting in a tomb, with someone buried beneath me, someone else beneath Attiyat's cooker. I struggled to reconcile the marble-topped monument with the fridge, beds, cupboards and photographs. Macabre shadows – the word echoes the Arabic *maqbar*, tomb – hung over my thoughts.

Abdu was more pragmatic. 'The dead, may God protect them, they are finished. They don't want anything from us or from the world. No matter what you offer – the wealth of the world – it is of no concern because they are with God. We respect the dead.

They are under the ground now. People like us, who live in the tombs, must believe in God and live rightly, because we are living on sacred ground, but we don't worry about the dead.'

Attiyat, who had been listening to us as she cooked, said, 'But if we invite someone at night, they are scared and we have to go and pick them up.'

'What are they scared of?'

'*Afarit*, *djinns*, the ghosts of dead people,' she listed as easily as ingredients for the dish she was preparing.

'There aren't any *afarit*,' Abdu insisted, starting to laugh. 'None of that is true. It's just something we tell our children. But other people believe in all that, and sometimes we make fun of them when they pass at night.'

'What do you do?'

'We put on masks of devils and appear out of the dark. It always scares them.'

Attiyat laughed with him and said it was time to eat. It was also getting dark. Not wanting them to go to the expense of feeding me, and not wanting to be spooked, I made my excuses and left.

THE NEXT TIME I saw Abdu, a week or so later, it was again at sunset and the muezzin were calling from the old city's many mosques. Night falls quickly in Cairo and I was surprised to see so many people out among the tombs. 'Where are they all going?'

'There are many people in the cemetery at night,' Abdu explained. 'Some are lovers looking for a quiet spot. We tell them to go away, because this is sacred ground. Sometimes there are thieves, but we always catch them. And there are other things.'

'Such as…' I prompted, remembering that the last time we met, he had insisted that there was no such thing as a spirit or *djinn*.

'Once,' and his voice was serious, 'when I had been out working and I was coming home, I saw someone wearing a white suit. I ran after him and eventually chased him into an alley. The alley was blocked at the end, so I thought, 'Aha, I've got you.' I was going to find out who he was. But do you know what happened? He just disappeared. Gone. Vanished. I was scared after that.'

'Scared of what exactly?'

'I can't talk about it. The whole cemetery is full of secrets. There are angels and *zahira* [visual phenomena] and other things that I can't tell you about.' What he could, and did, tell me about, was the city beneath the city, a mirror to the living world, a mythical place that only a remarkable few were ever allowed to see. Abdu assured me that Napoleon had been taken there after he had captured the city. I knew better than to hope to see it for myself.

I VISITED ABDU on many occasions over the space of a year or two and he was always welcoming and playful. He owned very little, had no savings, no idea of exactly where the next meal would come from, but he also had an unshakeable belief that it would come. Then, on one occasion when I turned up unexpected, he and Attiyat and their children had gone. The neighbours told me that they had agreed to be rehoused in a new project far from the city centre. But months later they were back, complaining that whatever the shortcomings of making a home in the cemetery, at least they had electricity, and neighbours, and water, a souk and a café nearby.

Sometimes I took pastries or other food, and Attiyat always offered me tea while Abdu told me something I didn't know. He explained the hierarchy of the place, the bosses, the guardians and tomb diggers, the stonecutters, Koran reciters and all the others who made the cemetery work. The list was very similar to a head-count one could have taken in an ancient Egyptian cemetery, even down to the people Abdu didn't mention, the outlaws, the draft-dodgers and the people who hung around in the hope that the mourners' charitable instincts would provide them with a hand-out.

Abdu lived in a tomb that belonged to the family of an Egyptian diplomat. 'He's an ambassador, so he is always out of the country, but his family look after us when they come to visit. We eat well after that, cook rice, *kofta*, chicken and other good things, and instead of two kilos of meat, we might buy three or four.'

He was always keen to talk about the ways of the world, the corruptness of officials and the hardships of life. He taught me that life could be enjoyable even if it was unjust. And he came to personify for me that most common and most called-upon of all Cairene virtues, the ability to laugh at misfortunes. There was always a long list of those, at the top of which he placed the threat to his job. 'The government wants us out. They say it doesn't look good to have people living in the tombs. We say that we keep the place clean and safe. But they sent someone to count us and look,' he said, pointing to a number that had been painted on his front door, 'now we have also been counted.'

There was always a surprise with Abdu. On our first meeting, it was the fact that he lived in the cemetery and that he thought he knew me. On another occasion, when I had come to terms with who he was and where he lived, there was the surprise of a photograph, hanging on his wall, in which Abdu appeared alongside a famous Egyptian actress.

'That is my other work.'

'As what?'

'A *kombarsi*, an extra in the cinema. I've been doing it for years, since I was fifteen or sixteen. I got into it thanks to a man from the studios whose mother is buried here. He sat with me as you are sitting with me and he told me I was good to do cinema. So the next day I went to the studios and since then I have appeared in about fifty films and plays and TV soap operas.' He went over to the only cupboard in the tomb and came back with a plastic album full of pictures of himself arm in arm with some of Egypt's most famous movie stars. 'Am I not famous?'

'You are a star, Abdu.'

'So now you know,' and he pulled a strong-man pose, flexing his considerable biceps, a hand on his head, which is how I left him. 'Come back soon, Roberto Cairo,' he said, laughing, as I went.

That is how I remember him. I never sat in a café with another corpse and I never saw Abdu again. The next time I went to the cemetery, the tomb was still there, but the shack was empty. Abdu and Attiyat had gone. For me, at least, the two worlds of the living and the dead separated themselves back out.

HORATIO CLARE

A Villain

HORATIO CLARE (born London, 1973) is an author and journalist. He has published two memoirs – **Running for the Hills** and **Truant** –and a book of natural history travel, **A Single Swallow**, following the birds' epic migration from South Africa to South Wales. His first novel, **Clip's Truth**, will be published in October 2011. He currently divides his time between London, the Black Mountains of South Wales, and Verona, Italy, where he writes, teaches and tries to avoid the local staple: horse with gnocchi.

A Villain

HORATIO CLARE

This happened in another country, in a town of low hills and hard times. The people on the train were very polite. At each stop the doors admitted hot rectangles of orange sun; cramped passengers made careful space for each new arrival. In derelict acres beside the track the buddleia bloomed, still fountains of purple scent and flies. We passed cracked concrete, shuttered warehouses and cars which looked abandoned, as though their drivers had given up on some shady business and walked away. The little train swayed exhausted into the station and we disembarked with many after-yous. The taxi drivers wore *jellabas*. There were two mosques and shops which smelled of spice.

In the months I lived in the town I came to know the sky-line: the roofs of bankrupt factories; the chimneys which sprouted plants; the volleys of birds and the low heads of the surrounding hills. I found the people very friendly. My friends were teachers, several men who did odd jobs, small traders and a woman who sold food. They were a close and kind society. On Friday evenings we all gathered in a dusty garden where men and boys played boules. It was here, I think, I met him.

'Where are you from then, mate?' he said. His voice was soft. His eyes were the first thing you noticed. They were slow and brown and bright. They considered you with a gentle sort of sadness which made you want to see him smile. The second thing you noticed was the way he listened. He did not wait for you to finish so that he could speak. He did not follow your words for the hook which would give a starting point for his reply. He just listened, his head angled down slightly so that his eyes tipped up, as if he watched you over the top of invisible spectacles.

The third thing you noticed was the effect he had on women. 'Oh, I just love him!' one said. 'He's absolutely *gorgeous*,' agreed another, her mouth enjoying the word. 'Such a good man – such a *beautiful* man.'

Even on the slightest acquaintance with him one felt one-self agreeing with her. He was not a George Clooney type: not tall or pretty-featured, not thick-haired. He had an air of competence and he was strong-framed. If you were asked to guess his profession you might say builder – possibly a specialist, perhaps a craftsman, but then there was that slow gaze and those listeners' eyes. Could he be a detective? And there was the contained, quietly watchful worldliness – a soldier?

He never stayed for very long. After he had gone the women discussed his girlfriend. It was quite a recent relationship and when it was beginning the women had felt they needed to say some things. They took this girlfriend aside and warned her: 'Now you just make sure you look after him, right? Because he's gold and we love him and we wouldn't want to see him hurt...'

The girlfriend had not taken kindly to the implications in this, but it was all sorted out now, and the women had decided they liked her and that she was good for him.

'And what does he do?' I asked, intrigued by the jealous care he inspired among them.

'Oh! He's a man of mystery, isn't he?'

'He's a naughty boy.'

'Oh he is ... !'

No one actually came out with it but over time the whispers left no doubt.

HE NEVER TOLD me either. We became friends in spite of the little time we spent together. Sometimes my phone would ring and he would invite me bird watching. He seemed to love the creatures in the same way I do: not as collector's items, not as trophies, but for exquisite things in themselves, for the way they focus the world around them, for the integrity of their magnificence. One day he proposed we take a bike ride over the mountains. It was exceedingly hot. He appeared with a van. Bikes were loaded in and he drove us up into the hills: I was struck by the speed and competence with which a proposal turned to action. We set off, riding towards the sky. He was very fit.

'I don't do any drugs now,' he said, when the subject came up (a lot of our mutual friends did). 'It's like I found my calm. I do yoga. I'm into balance. And cycling. I'd like to do a really long ride, across countries. My girlfriend's into it, too. It's given her the perfect arse!'

We rode between white rocks, and along stony paths, and then the rocks were black. The sky was still and the hills shimmered. We stopped on a bluff, overlooking a green valley, and he began to tell me a story about a trip to one of the less secure parts of Africa where he fell into the hands of corrupt policemen. He described a cell, or some sort of holding room in some police station, in the throat of a hot mad night. Here and there the shapes moved in the gloom. Now and then they dragged him to the tiny light for more questions. Sweat ran down faces, down arms. There was the smell of bodies, breath and alcohol, the smell of smoke and men's darkness.

'I tell you...' he said softly. He described fear. Fear of rape, of murder, of the kind of beating you carry all your life, if you escape with your life – they were all there, leaning against the walls, waiting for their signal. His captors spoke languages he did not know. The not knowing, the confusion, the frigid terror in the heart of that thick heat: I felt I could see it all, though he told it without drama.

Later, after we had parted, I thought about why he should have told that story. I think it was a kindness; a leveller. He knew I was a traveller so he told a traveller's tale. He chose one that emphasised his vulnerability, describing the kind of nightmare I have occasionally fallen into, when your masculinity is nothing, when the strength in your arms is nothing, when your derring-do, your chutzpah and your cunning are all useless. You do not escape, so much as luck-out. They free you, by the grace of God and one of their superiors, when they have taken whatever they can get. In this way would I emerge from such a Hell, as did he, that time – but relying on luck to liberate him was not my friend's usual method.

'HE'S BEEN IN JAIL in about eight countries,' someone said. 'He had some very dodgy friends – I mean scary people.'

'He escaped from a lot of prisons,' said another. 'He told me one story about when they were under arrest somewhere, being held in a hotel, waiting to be deported. He worked out that it was possible to get out of the room by jumping off the balcony into the swimming pool, and that you could climb back in. So they jumped out, went round the corner and stuck up a bank. They always used fake guns. Then they stashed the money and climbed back into the hotel. The police may have suspected them, but they had a good alibi...'

No doubt I should feel guilty for the amusement lurking behind the disapproval with which I listened to this story. Fake weapons or not, it must be horrific to have someone threaten you with what you believe to be a gun. For all that some bankers may not be admirable people (indeed, some are thieves enfranchised by lax laws and empowered by inadequate oversight, as entire nations have learned), for all that, bank tellers and clerks, surely, are innocent. They are merely employees doing an honest job for employers whose higher crimes and machinations are committed in those glittering dagger-towers which hover high over the hearts of the great capitals, rather than over the counter in some local branch.

But I fear that hearing this story made me picture it from my friend's perspective, as he planned his raid. The only people who can actually be hurt (if indeed their guns are fake, and it is hard to see how they could not have been, if my friend was under arrest) are the robbers. They will take terrifying risks, which, if they are lucky, will be rewarded in bricks of cash. It will be horrible for the tellers, but the tellers must know that robbery is a possibility. They will have a procedure and follow it. The difference, of course, is that while I cannot contemplate holding up a bank, my friend apparently made a career of it.

ANY BOOKSHOP OR DVD RACK tells you how our culture regards bank robbers. We may couch it in 'moral' tales, in which they get their 'just deserts', but as long as they are played by handsome actors, as long as the good end happily and the bad unhappily, we adore this sort of criminal. An old-fashioned, glamorous sort of villain is the bank robber, in popular culture at least. How else to account for the millions of words and weeks of film we devote to heists?

Ideally, we want the bank to be owned by someone unequivocally bad and robbed by someone unrelentingly ingenious. Perhaps the most perfect example is Spike Lee's *Inside Man*, in which Christopher Plummer's ex-Nazi-turned-banker is stripped of his evilly-gotten diamonds by Clive Owen's anarchically moral thief. It seems a ludicrous, contrived scenario, but having met an otherwise entirely decent and moral person who happens to have been a thief, and knowing, now, how banks have been conducting themselves, one does begin to wonder whether it is necessary to distort and contrive in order to tell a story that reflects our ambivalent relationship with financial crime.

On a book tour in America I travelled the eastern seaboard at the height of the credit boom. In towns like Greenwich, Connecticut and Wilmington, Delaware, my hosts pointed, with breathless admiration, to the greater-than-Gatsby's palaces of their local heroes: hedge fund stars and credit card chiefs whose wealth was wild beyond dreaming. In Delaware my hostess was an employee of a credit card company. She drove me through the white streets of Wilmington and proudly presented her skyscraper, the global HQ of a corporation called MBNA.

'I know you!' I exclaimed. 'You used to send me credit card applications every other month. I never had any money and I never knew how you got my address but you never stopped sending the application forms. They're still coming, in fact.'

'Well,' she said, and dropped her voice, 'that's actually our secret. We just don't take "no" for an answer. And we never give up.'

It was true. For a decade the offers of silver credit cards, gold credit cards, even black credit cards, promising terrifying spending power and limitless status, should I choose to draw one, shining, from my wallet, slid through our letter box (which is pretty well hidden by ivy, and located in the depths of Wales). I buckled once, wanting insurance for a long journey. When the expedition was over I paid off the bill and asked the provider to cancel the card.

'I can't actually do that,' said the man on the phone.

What did he mean, can't?

'I mean,' he said, 'I have no way of taking you off the system.'

I complained to my bank, which had provided the card, but there was nothing they could do. I was in the hands of their sub-contractor. My credit card, and therefore the details I had given to obtain it, belonged to MBNA. I do not mean to imply that this company is especially devious: it just happens to be the one that I encountered. I am sure there are others from which there is no hiding, which do not take no for an answer, and which never let you go.

IS THERE A MORAL HERE? We have two entities which have both made money by immoral means. One, by ruthlessly exploiting people's desires and gullibility; the other by pointing a cucumber at them, wrapped in a paper bag. Let us imagine both have seen the error of their ways. Suppose they have both reformed, and now go about their business in a moral and plain-dealing fashion. Disregard the comparative numbers of their victims: do not try to measure the relative terror of a dozen bank clerks against the misery of thousands, even hundreds of thousands, living near or beyond bankruptcy. Only answer me this: which entity, do you suppose, gives the greater portion of its wealth and time to charity? I do not know the answer, but I have reason to sadly suspect.

Now that the credit boom is over, and my friend retired from crime, it might be instructive to know how our principals are behaving today. The banks and credit card companies have a double strategy: put on the frighteners and apply for bail-out. So hundreds, perhaps thousands of householders no longer answer the door or the phone, while bailiffs' calling cards pile up on their mats. At the same time, the companies appeal to the courts to bankrupt their creditors, which will trigger corporate insurance pay-outs.

As for my friend the villain: you will not drive past any villa of his on the Costa del Sol. But you just might find him in a far country, in a dilapidated town, in an anonymous house. He gives to charity and does voluntary work with the sick and the old. This is all perfectly true.

TOM BULLOUGH

TB

TB

The Zoo from the Outside

TOM BULLOUGH (born Hereford, 1975) grew up on a hill farm in Radnorshire. He has worked as a sawmiller, a travel writer and a Zimbabwean music promoter, and is the author of three novels: **A** (2002), **The Claude Glass** (2007), and the forthcoming **Celestial Mechanics**, based on the life of nineteeth-century Russian space pioneer Konstantin Tsiolkovsky. He lives in the Brecon Beacons with his wife Charlie and their son Edwyn. **www.tombullough.com**

The Zoo from the Outside

TOM BULLOUGH

G'ito-Bass stood near the back of the narrow stage. A thick-built man in jeans and a neat black T-shirt, he played with eyes sealed, the coloured lights dancing from the streaks of sweat on his big, shaven head. Around him, unseen, the horns blew skin-tight waves, the backing singers howled, the guitar chopped Afro-beat through the reeling thunder of his bassline. Down on the dance floor, the drag queens shrieked in netting vests and beehive wigs, while women girned and touched their toes and the men behind them mimed sexual ecstasy.

It was four o'clock in the morning when Xitende finished their final set. Aside from the taxi drivers who had woken to service the emptying club, Maputo was quiet. The windows of the bakers' and hardware shops on Avenida Eduardo Mondlane reflected the yellow streetlights – a body or two among the shadows in the doorways – but with the police as much of a danger at this time of night as any tsotsi, Gito-Bass, my friend Selemane and I turned into an unlit alley and worked our way between the small white houses of the back streets, the shed-like churches built by officials looking to salve their souls, the yards where women still shook their hips and men with battered acoustic guitars played skipping *marrabenta*: the great dance music of Mozambique.

Gito-Bass lived on a square of white-socked trees and straggling piles of rubbish. In the hallway of his tower block, three old women were sitting round a candle, giggling and gossiping, each with a plume of loaves in a basket on her head. It was hard to tell how many floors we climbed. Once, in the faint grey light that leaked from the derelict lift shaft, we met a woman coming the other way, who screamed invisibly and fled towards the ground. At last, we emerged on the flat, tarred square of the roof, where a concrete hut once used by the building's janitor stood alone above the streaming, rippling lights of the city.

The hut was small but homely, with a single chair, three cassettes, a battery-powered cassette player and a narrow bed where a boy of about fourteen was asleep with an electric guitar. Smiling hospitably and gesturing for us to sit down, Gito-Bass prodded the boy awake and set him to work on a long and complex jazz scale. He removed his T-shirt to reveal a glistening belly and the words 'Gito-Bass' tattooed on his right bicep, threw his arms around my neck to make it quite clear that I was welcome and retrieved a bottle of vodka from underneath the bed. Then, to the skittering grooves of Wes Montgomery, we settled down to consider which bands to include in my chapter in the *Rough Guide to World Music*.

At dawn, the three of us went outside onto the roof. We stood unsteadily a few feet from the edge and stared past the silhouettes of the treetops at the blossoming sky, the end of the headland where the Presidential Palace met the pink-fringed Indian Ocean. On one building, a beige-skinned woman was laughing into a mobile phone. On Avenida Eduardo Mondlane, a taxi passed the Taqwa Mosque, moved slowly between the jacaranda trees and the still-burning streetlights and vanished into the darkened reaches of the ghetto.

Gito-Bass said something in low Portuguese, which I had to ask Selemane to translate. 'He say,' said Selemane, after a moment. 'He say that here we just care about the music. That is why it is so hard.'

'I FIRST HEARD the word *marrabenta* in 1946,' recalled Dilon Djindji, leaning back in his plastic chair. 'Back then, I was young and strong. I was always invited to play at parties, and at the end of the party I would always come home with one or two women... It was then that "Marrabenta" became my nickname, because the *marrabenta* was the one who was always last to leave the party. The word comes from *rebentar* – "to break" in Portuguese – but in our slang it also meant to party. So, I was the one who never got tired, who would always go until it was morning!'

Dilon was a small, white-haired figure with a Latin moustache, a baggy grey suit and sharp little eyes which would emerge from their wrinkles whenever a woman passed on the neighbouring footpath. We were sitting outside his bungalow in Marracuene – a village fifteen miles north of Maputo – and ever since Selemane and I had arrived in this dusty, overlooked patch of bush Dilon had been lauding himself, libelling his manager, slating the government for paying him insufficient attention and keeping a very close eye on posterity. The claims of singers like Fany Pfumo, Maekwana and Xidiminguana to a place in Mozambican musical history had received not a mention. Dilon was the King of Marrabenta: an 'elephant' of strength and endurance. He railed, cursed and boasted. He slipped randomly between Portuguese and Shangaan, and even when Selemane and I picked back over my recording that evening it proved far from easy to decipher.

'I am original music!' Dilon declared. He received a file from one of his thirty-two grandchildren – several of whom were milling around us – and rifled through a pile of old 7-inch record sleeves until he found a thesis from the University of Vienna. 'Look! You see? The Austrians understand, even if the government doesn't!'

He jabbed a finger at a list identifying the seven key figures in twentieth-century African music. There was Fela Kuti. There was Franco. There was Thomas Mapfumo. And there too was Dilon Djindji, who had, it seemed, invented *marrabenta* in 1952. Dilon brandished the paper triumphantly, then collected a steel-string guitar which was leaning against a tree and picked his way through a jaunty tune.

Besides the milling of the grandchildren, not a lot seemed to happen at Dilon's house. Back in 1982, the Congolese superstar, Sam Mangwana, had made a kind of pilgrimage here – his song 'Marrabenta' was written in Dilon's honour – and Dilon mentioned the fact so often that it might have happened that morning. A hundred yards away, the EN1 fed north towards Xai-Xai – the link between Maputo and the rest of the country – but only the footpath made its way to Dilon's door. On our journey from the city, Selemane and I had had to walk over a mile from the nearest bus stop.

'So when did you first learn to play?' I asked him.

'I started to play in 1938,' Dilon replied, concluding his song. 'Back then I had a guitar made from an oil can, with only three strings, and when I wanted to practise I would have to go off into the bush because my father didn't like it. As a boy, I would carry the instruments for musicians at parties. I would sit there all night, just watching them. Those musicians were playing traditional music, of course. It was not until 1947 that I began to play a five-string guitar, and that was when I invented *afina cãomatola*, my own tuning system, which is the basis of *marrabenta*...

'In those days, I had a very sexy style!' He sprang to his feet and performed a series of pelvic thrusts. 'Later, when I came to play in bars in the city I had to learn to behave, but back then I would *rebentar* all the women! You see that sexy style in the clubs? Well, that was me who started it! Back then, I was the greatest because only I had the *marrabenta* juice, and the same is true today!' Again he jumped up. 'Even at this age, I am still Marrabenta!'

LEAVING THE TIDES of Japanese saloons and minibuses on Avenida Vladimir Lenine, the building sites and the salesmen waving ground nuts and plastic dogs with marching feet, Selemane and I passed beneath a sign reading 'Associação Moçambicana de Músicos' and arrived in a garden of fruit trees and gaudily painted walls, where a hundred or so musicians sat on rows of metal chairs, eating chicken, drinking beer, nodding along to a knocked-together band, which was playing 'Georgia On My Mind' on a low concrete stage in the corner.

The craze for these public jam sessions had begun in Maputo back in the late 1990s, with the Big Jam at Club Tchova Xita Duma – birthplace of Kapa Dêch and Timbila Muzimba, two of the biggest groups in the country. At the time, Mozambique was the poorest country in the world – crippled first by a ten-year war of independence, then by a fifteen-year civil war in which a million people had been killed. Like all of its industries, many of which had been destroyed by the Portuguese colonials on their departure in 1975, Mozambique's music industry was almost non-existent: a handful of clubs and a single, state-owned recording studio. With the jam sessions, the musicians of Maputo had found a place to play, to fraternise, to innovate, for the first time in a generation.

'When we first went to Tchova,' Tsetse, the leader of Timbila Muzimba, had told me a couple of days earlier, 'we were really just looking for somewhere to practise. Back then we were basically a traditional *timbila* ensemble, like any other group from Inhambane Province. But at the Big Jam we found ourselves playing with Cuban drummers, and in a few months we had an electric bass, a jazz drummer, a saxophonist, even a rapper!'

Looking at the musicians waiting their turns at the Associação Moçambicana de Músicos, it was not hard to imagine how such a transformation might have taken place. There were teenaged hip-hoppers and ageing *marrabenta* guitarists, pianists with beards like Thelonious Monk and bassists with waist-long dreadlocks – although, as I had seen on an excursion to Zimbabwe, the alchemy that would allow them to bring their talents together was not to be taken for granted. In Harare, I had encountered musicians of all these different types, but such was the economic despair and political intimidation that there was just no energy, no appetite for fusion. In Mozambique, on the other hand, a new generation was growing up in a climate of peace and optimism – a parallel, perhaps, to Britain in the 1960s – and the one thing that everybody wanted was change.

As 'Georgia On My Mind' came shuddering to an end, the musicians on-stage set down their instruments and returned to the audience – with the exception of a skinny little boy in a red T-shirt and oversized leather shoes who appeared to have been playing the drums. He was clinging to the drum sticks, arguing with the sound engineer, glaring at him, furious, and when the man tried to lift him from the drum stool he darted suddenly beneath his arm and secured the bass guitar before anyone else could reach it – tightening the strap as far as it would go.

'The kid is playing bass!' remarked Selemane approvingly, as the boy launched into the bassline to 'Smokestack Lightning' – throwing in trills and fragments of the melody.

I stared at him in amazement.

'For Christ's sake!' I said. 'How old is he?'

'Sufixo…' Selemane pulled down the corners of his mouth. 'Sufixo eight years old.'

The boy was playing with absolute absorption, grimacing, rolling his head. He seemed barely to notice that his shoulders were crumpling, his legs collapsing with the weight of the instrument, and finally the sound engineer went to fetch a small amplifier, which he pushed beneath him so that he could sit down.

'Who the hell is he?' I persisted.

'Sufixo, he is a street kid,' Selemane shrugged. 'He come here four years ago. We used to send him to buy weed for us… Oh, but he never smoked it! People here, they are looking after him. They are paying his school also.'

'Has he got no family?'

'He has one grandmother, but you see this boy! Nobody can stop him from making noise! The womens here they are saying, "Oh Sufixo, it is time you go to sleep," or "Oh Sufixo, it is time you must wash." But Sufixo, he is playing drums. He is playing bass, piano, guitar, *timbila*… Sufixo is making noise! That's what we do here in Maputo. We make noise!'

THE SMALL, BEACH-FRONTED town of Catembe lay on the southern side of Maputo Bay, where it was visited every forty-five minutes or so by a fat old ferry with a jungle of weeds below the waterline. The ferry carried commuters, traffic for Ponta d'Ouro on the South African border and tourists on day trips to the various bars and restaurants on the beach, and one day it also carried me and Selemane. Jumping from the jetty, we set out along the rubbish-strewn sand, handing a bottle of vodka between us and talking, as usual, about music. From here, you could look back towards Maputo and almost see the city as a whole. A mile distant, the arms of cranes stretched above high-floating freighters, loading goods from the factories of Johannesburg. Beyond them, grid-faced tower blocks stood over their reflections, waist-deep in churches and tenements, while out to the east there were parks and gardens, embassies and hotels, the ocean empty all the way to Madagascar.

Jangada was an open-air restaurant where Chico Antonío, King of Maputo Fusion, held court every Saturday afternoon. As Selemane and I climbed the steps to the verandah, we arrived among waitresses, tourists eating seafood and Chico fans waiting for the next set – although the larger crowd was at the back, where a group of the capital's foremost musicians were sitting among ashtrays, wine glasses, beer bottles and coffee cups, the floorboards around them having something in common with a moat. There was Carlitos, founding member of Ghorwane, the biggest group in the country. There was Jorge Domingos, who had been playing with Gito Baloi when he was shot dead in Johannesburg. There was Roberto Isaias from Kapa Dêch, and Dino, mercurial bassist of the Pazedi Jazz Band. And there, at the head, was Chico – his short grey dreadlocks spilling round his ears, his eyes black and mesmerising, his teak-coloured face consumed in moments by a grin of perfect white teeth.

Selemane and I pulled up a couple of chairs.

Like Sufixo, Chico had once been a street kid and had learnt his various instruments at the São José de Lhanguene mission school in the ghetto. He had gone on to play trumpet with the Orchestra Marrabenta Star de Moçambique, and to become head of the local Alliance Française, but even today he had the look of a vagrant – his trainers worn bald, his clothes eclectic enough to have come from an aid agency. As Selemane would often observe, music in Maputo was all about freedom, and Chico was like the music personified. Just to get here, he had walked five miles along the shoreline, his guitar on his back, his trousers rolled up to stop them from dragging on the ground.

'In the past it was colonial time,' Chico told me, when we were sitting together later that afternoon. 'The colonials didn't give us space to play. They banned *marrabenta*, and they closed down the venues because they realised that the culture was bringing people together, fuelling the revolution. That was a hard, bad time. It's been more than thirty years now since we won our freedom. That is a long time, of course, but you must think of it within the context of Mozambican history. Right now, culturally, it's a transition time…

'We know who we are. We are African people. But we are African people who are mixing with Europeans, Americans, Chinese… So, to express who we are we must bring our traditional music together with the music of all these other places. We must be Africans, but Africans open to the world!'

As the clouds turned fiery, Chico sat on-stage with his acoustic guitar, singing in his rich, haunted voice, throwing jagged chords into the blend of jazz, heavy metal and traditional rhythms that his band was generating behind him. He stared beyond the city, turned in moments to usher in a drum fill or to conduct a spiralling guitar solo, smiled his magnificent smile – although a handful of people were bouncing up and down in their seats, yelling 'Bravo!', and those few tourists who had remained for the evening were nodding politely if they were listening at all.

'You must be wise, cool, kind... but the devil too!' Chico continued, as we were walking back towards the ferry that night, the rest of the musicians stumbling drunkenly behind us. 'Life, you see, is like a zoo. A bar-zoo! You see chickens, lions... And some of us must escape!'

'And what are you?' I asked.

'I myself am a bull!' Chico's grin flashed in the darkness. 'A red bull! I see the zoo from the outside!'

The crossing to Maputo took only twenty minutes, but there was a bar on-board, and it was here that we gravitated, clambering round the lovers canoodling on the staircase, emerging on the top deck as, with a groan from the engine, the nose of the ferry turned into the bay and the city appeared from the rolling superstructure: a line of light the breadth of the horizon, punctuated by a floodlit cathedral the shape of a rocket, by red-tipped radio masts, advertisements for soft drinks and the brilliant strata of the tower blocks.

'Okay, maybe you have a wife and kids,' said Chico softly, a beer in his hand, a hat on his head on which he had crossed out the word 'Safari' and written the word 'CHICO'. 'Wife, kids, money... These things aren't important. There is only the music! You have to see the zoo from the outside!'

SARAH
MAGUIRE

Divan

Meetings with Remarkable Poets

SARAH MAGUIRE (born London, 1957) is a poet and translator, and director of the Poetry Translation Centre. Her interest in Arabic literature led to visits to Palestine and Yemen, and to her c0-translating the Palestinian poets Mahmoud Darwish and Ghassan Zaqtan; the Sudanese poet Al-Saddiq Al-Raddi and the Afghan poet Partaw Naderi. She set up the Poetry Translation Centre in 2004 – and it is through their tours, bringing poets to the UK, that she has her most remarkable meetings. **www.poetrytranslation.org**

Meetings with Remarkable Poets

SARAH MAGUIRE

I f you scroll through the photos of the Poetry Translation Centre's first World Poets' Tour in 2005, you'll notice that the photographer suddenly rotates his camera from landscape to portrait mode – at the moment when Maxamed Hashi Dhamac 'Gaarriye', the astonishingly famous Somali poet, invites 'the tallest man in the world', fellow Somali Hussein Bissad (8' 1"), to join him on stage. The capacity audience at London's Brunei Gallery – half of them Somalis – exploded, while the British poet, David Harsent, who'd co-translated Gaarriye, looked on wryly from the sidelines. 'I had a suspicion,' David told the audience when he came to read his translations, 'that sharing a stage with Gaarriye might be a tall order ...'

When Sir Richard Burton visited Somalia in 1854, he was immediately struck by the Somalis' devotion to poetry. 'The country teems with poets,' he wrote, 'the fine ear of this people causes them to take the greatest pleasure in harmonious sounds and poetical expressions, whereas a false quantity or a prosaic phrase excites their violent indignation.' Nothing since then has changed – other than the fact that Somali became a written language in 1972 – and poetry is still the supreme achievement of Somali society, wielding a power and fascination that's difficult for us Westerners to grasp.

I'd never before been in such close proximity to someone as famous as Gaarriye. The experience, I imagine, is something akin to being on tour with Michael Jackson: the instant he's spotted, he disappears into a scrum of delighted Somalis of all ages, who crowd around him, chattering, eager to shake his hand, touch him, be photographed next to him. In his late fifties, small, balding, wearing oversized glasses and sporting a Daallo Airways T-shirt, Gaarriye is a man most non-Somalis would walk past in the street without a second glance. Look more closely and you'll see that he's never at rest: his expressive face is electric with animation; his eyes dance; he fidgets constantly, gesticulating, grimacing, grinning, scowling – and that's when he's 'at rest'. On stage, he is a consummate performer, carving his poetry into the air with startling gestures that so powerfully articulate the meaning of his verse you almost begin to think you can speak Somali. Gaarriye is nothing short of a showman: hence his co-option of Hussein Bissad. Had a performing bear been available, there's no doubt it would have ended up sharing his stage.

The UK is home to the largest Somali community in Europe: an estimated 100,000 Somalis were thought to be living here in 2010. They routinely feature at the very bottom of all those indicators of well-being: health, housing, employment and educational opportunities. I yearn for the day when – instead of Somalia being a byword for instability, ceaseless war and piracy – the country's exceptional poetic tradition brings it universal renown.

I founded the Poetry Translation Centre in 2004 (thanks to the Arts Council's generosity) with two aims: to ginger up poetry in English through translating contemporary poetry from Africa, Asia and Latin America; and to engage with the countless thousands of people now settled here for whom poetry is the highest art form, as it is for anyone from an Islamic background. The zeal for poetry is far from confined to Somalis: the many Sudanese, Afghans, Pakistanis, Kurds and Iraqis living here are equally fervent in their devotion to poets and poetry. So what better way to make them feel welcome than to translate their most highly esteemed poets into English, using the skills of talented linguists working closely with leading British poets (such as Jo Shapcott, Sean O'Brien, Lavinia Greenlaw and W.N. Herbert), with the additional hope that brilliant translations might engage English-speaking audiences too? And that meetings between these remarkable international and local poets might change their writing and, perhaps, their lives?

The tours are the thing: there is nothing like having the opportunity to witness a poet such as Al-Saddiq Al-Raddi from Sudan (arguably, our 'star poet') bewitch an audience with the precise music of his intensely lyrical Arabic. The polar opposite of Gaarriye, Saddiq on stage is preternaturally still, focused, heartbreaking. And yet his hugely complex, gorgeous poetry is equally popular with the Sudanese community here, and the poor man can't get from one end of Queensway to the other without being set upon by admirers.

Just as famous with the Persian-speaking communities of Afghanistan, Iran and her own native Tajikistan (and to many

Russian-speakers in the former Soviet Union, where her work is widely translated), is Farzaneh Khojandi, who is generally acknowledged as the best woman poet writing in Persian today. Performing, she stands with her hands clasped together and, looking upwards, recites her playful, haunting poetry in a voice verging on a whisper, as though praying to someone whose attention she is certain she can claim.

The night I met Farzaneh, for our second World Poets' Tour in 2008, she was white-faced from the exhaustion of her interminable journey from the remote Khojand province – and from the shock of finding herself in such an alien place. Her translator, Narguess Farzad, had found Farzaneh and her husband (a renowned Tajik musician whose stage name is 'Mr Lightning') sitting in their hotel room in the dark. At first Narguess thought they'd not yet grasped how to use those slot-in cards to activate the electricity in their room. But, in fact, supplies of electricity being so random in their part of Tajikistan, and light bulbs (when they light) so weak, they preferred the familiar comforts of darkness to the glare of their hotel.

At the dinner we held that evening to welcome all our poets, Farzaneh was seated next to the Somali journalist and translator, Maxamed Xasan 'Alto' – the first African she had ever met. Alto, like seemingly all Somalis, a supremely gifted linguist, began speaking to her in Russian: the one time in my life I actually saw someone's jaw physically drop. And then Farzaneh broke into a luminous smile: looking round the restaurant for the first time, she made it clear she knew she was with friends.

TIM BUTCHER

Letting Greene Go

TIM BUTCHER (born Rugby, 1967) is a journalist, broadcaster and author. His first book, **Blood River** (2007), is an account of an epic journey through the Congo to unravel the region's turbulent history. For his second book, **Chasing the Devil** (2010), he trekked 350 miles through Liberia, Guinea and Sierra Leone. On the staff of the Daily Telegraph from 1990 to 2009, he specialised in awkward places at awkward times, reporting on conflict in the Balkans, the Middle East and Africa. He lives in Cape Town with his girlfriend and their two children.

Letting Greene Go

TIM BUTCHER

IT WAS not just mist that hung over the Freetown peninsula when my ferry approached the coast of West Africa back in the dry season of 2009. The aura of the great English author, Graham Greene, was also strongly there, framing my hazy view of the mountain skyline and timeworn foreshore of Sierra Leone's capital city.

Always before a journey I read up on a place and when it comes to this part of Africa Greene dominates, after writing so authoritatively about his numerous visits. His first trip was back in 1935 when Freetown was the launching point for an overland trek he immortalised in his first published venture into non-fiction, the travel classic *Journey Without Maps*. He came back for a calendar year as an MI6 spy in the Second World War, an experience he famously used as the backdrop for what I regard as his best novel, *The Heart of the Matter*. And so strong was his association with Freetown that at the height of his literary fame a British newspaper flew him back to write a post-independence piece on the city in the late 1960s.

I had devoured it all: the search for seediness both physical and moral, the acid wit and the heaving sexual undertow. But although I had used his work during my numerous Freetown trips to better understand the country's colonial history I had never met anyone in Freetown with any clear connection to Greene. Civil war in the 1990s had destroyed the city's libraries and driven away many of the country's best academics, so I was convinced those links had died with the author back in 1991. How wrong I would prove to be.

A SETTLEMENT FIRST founded by mariners in the 1500s is still best approached by water. Those early sailors from Europe had crept south from the Straits of Gibraltar in their tiny ships, picking their way down an African coastline that offered inhospitably arid desert at first and then, as they ventured into the tropics, nothing but low-lying, disease-ridden mangrove swamps.

What a miracle it must have been to round the northern headland into the Sierra Leone river estuary, Africa's greatest natural harbour, a freak combination of powerful tidal currents that prevent silting in a deep channel tucked behind a long mountainous peninsula that curves up into the Atlantic, acting as a bulwark against the motion of the ocean. Better still, freshwater streamed all year round down the flanks of the peninsula, water so sweet it was used to fill the casks of seventeenth-century pirates, eighteenth-century slavers and nineteenth-century humanitarians.

The twenty-first century ship that delivered me to Freetown was a superannuated Greek ferry that had been pensioned off after decades of service in the Ionian Sea to work the daily crossing of the Sierra Leone river estuary. I had taken the dawn service and as we set off from the northern shore the blast from the ferry's horn bounced back from thick sea fog making my chest shudder. The other passengers barely noticed, carrying on chatter that sounded like tuning a short-wave radio, a babble of foreign sounds every so often crystallising into a familiar word. They were speaking Krio, the broken form of English with roots reaching back to those early mariners and which is still the main language of Sierra Leone. I heard *tok* for talk, *aks* for ask and *pekin* for child – derived from *piccaninny*.

Down on the car-deck every inch between the vehicles was taken up by passengers, mostly women hawkers with cotton *lappa* wraps pulled tight around their shoulders against the damp air. At their feet were baskets heaped with produce to be sold that day on the streets of Freetown; cairns of bananas, peanuts bundled by the handful in knotted twists of plastic, portions of fried yellow plantain freckled with tiny black seeds and tinged red by the palm oil they had been cooked in. Young men sat astride motorbikes, cheap Chinese-made models with the excess of chrome common to second-rate machinery.

After an hour or so enclosed in our cloud capsule there was movement down on the car-deck. The motorbikers had begun fidgeting with their kick-start pedals and the women were standing, stretching out of their *lappa* cocoons. The ones who had heavy loads to carry on their heads fashioned hand cloths into quoits to cushion their scalps. I peered ahead and could see why they had stirred. Freetown was coming into view.

At first it was like a watery Japanese print as I could make out only the blurred loom of mountain ranges overlaid more and more faintly, one behind the other. It was by ship that Greene first reached here in January 1935 and saw this same view, one that he would later describe as 'an impression of heat and damp'. As we crept closer, the mist dissolved and the focus sharpened to reveal under the hills a shoreline of buildings, rooftops, tower blocks and the occasional startled outline of a leafless cotton tree. From a distance it looked like ports the world over, a bit old perhaps, but a functioning port nonetheless. I knew this sense of normalcy to be an illusion.

As the ferry reached the Kissi ferry terminal, the lowering front ramp scoured the concrete slipway to a standstill and the passengers spewed out as grain spills from a split sack. After the relative cool of the early morning crossing, I stepped off the ferry and felt the true mugging weight of West Africa's climate. By the time I found a taxi, an old Mercedes estate still bearing a German number plate, I had already begun to flag. Wilting into its saggy front seat, I groped for the window handle but found only a knurled, rusty stub. Taking pity on me, the dreadlocked driver, George Decker, leant across and slapped the flat of his hand against my window with such force he could shudder the glass pane downwards.

Traffic oozed like treacle along clammy, narrow roads stiff with pedestrians, livestock and hawkers. Street-sellers had plenty of time to catch up with scarcely moving vehicles whenever a passenger showed interest in the local newspapers, knock-off DVDs, plastic bags of chilled water or other items for sale.

I could barely see through the web of cracks in our windscreen but George kept up a sotto voce commentary on local landmarks, almost all of which were connected to Freetown's peculiar history as a laboratory experiment for early British philanthropy. After centuries of active involvement in slaving, it was here, at the start of the nineteenth century, that Britain sought to redeem itself. Britain would not just end its own involvement in slavery but do everything in its power to stop other nations' slaving by unleashing the Royal Navy. Britain's maritime might would be used to intercept slave ships crossing the Atlantic and, for want of anywhere else to bring them, the freed slaves would be brought here to a settlement whose name celebrated the act of liberation – Freetown.

We inched past Cline Town, one of the larger suburbs, named after Emmanuel Cline, a freed slave originally from Nigeria who made enough money as a trader in the mid-nineteenth century to buy what was then empty land near the shoreline on the eastern approaches to the city. And we paused at what was once Cline Town's largest building, Fourah Bay College, the oldest university in colonial Africa. Founded in 1827 to train freed slaves as teachers and chaplains, it produced a stream of alumni who took their qualifications far beyond Freetown – the first cohort of modern black professionals to spread across Africa. It earned Freetown the soubriquet of 'The Athens of Africa' and a suitably grand three-storey college hall was constructed close to the shoreline.

Built out of quarried blocks of laterite, the pinkish-coloured stone that is common on the Freetown peninsula, it would, in its day, have looked at home in the grounds of any Oxbridge college. Its portico was framed by elegant cast-iron columns, Norman windows lined its flanks and its grounds were tended by a staff of gardeners. But by the time I saw it the elegance was no more. Abandoned when Fourah Bay College moved to other premises, the college building was a roofless ruin, its floors concertinaed into a heap of broken masonry and its walls scorched with fires lit by squatters who overran it during the civil war.

George followed the drove through the city centre where the main artery, Siaka Stevens Street, passes under the spreading boughs of a cotton tree. Cotton trees are common across West Africa but this huge specimen in the heart of Freetown commands a special position in the history of the country, protected as a national monument. It was under this tree, in 1792, that a service of thanksgiving was held by an early group of freed slaves, as they sought God's blessing for their new life in Africa.

They used the tree as the centrepoint when they laid out Freetown's original grid of streets leading down a gentle slope to the shoreline of the Sierra Leone River estuary, a grid that remains largely unchanged today. As we drove slowly by I looked up and saw thousands of large bats, each the size of a rat, hanging from its branches in furry, twitching bunches, unmoved by the street noise below.

War and decay meant Freetown was a city that did not wear its age lightly. There were a few tired-looking tower blocks in the city centre, many with their own generators noisily providing a private electricity supply to make up for the lack of mains power. Rivers – the ones that brought those early sailors here to replenish fresh water – were clogged with raw sewage and discarded rubbish, vermin-infested mats of filth rucked occasionally by large, malodorous pigs. Near a bridge over one stream I saw a sign that said *nor pis yah*. As so often with Krio I had to speak the words out loud before I could work out what they meant – 'do not urinate here'. A gaggle of women going about their ablutions in the streambed suggested the ordinance was not much heeded.

Statues erected to Sierra Leone's post-colonial leaders, the ones who guided her through independence in 1961, were in dire need of attention. Noses had fallen off, lettering had faded and ceremonial fountains had dried up. One of Freetown's oldest buildings, St George's, the Anglican cathedral built of red laterite which Graham Greene described as dominating the city centre, is now dwarfed by hulking 1960s structures hung with rusting air conditioner units, paint flaking from the walls.

And down on the water's edge stood Connaught Hospital with its nineteenth-century foundation stone bearing an inscription that spoke eloquently of the British imperial chutzpah behind the creation of Sierra Leone. It said: 'Royal Hospital and Asylum for Africans Rescued From Slavery by British Valour and Philanthropy'. Looking around the ruined hospital, that boast rang hollow. The Connaught's pharmacy had been raided by corrupt civil servants and its roster of doctors had been emptied by a steady exodus to Europe, America and elsewhere. It did not feel like much of a 'rescue'.

As a journalist I had covered the war that did so much damage to Sierra Leone between 1991 and 2002 but what I found disturbing was that since the fighting ended my various visits had shown scant sign of progress. The spirit to survive was strong in the million or so Sierra Leoneans who now live in Freetown's crowded, unserviced shanty towns. But the spirit to thrive, to develop the city, was not.

I turned, once again, to Greene and went in search of the City Hotel, a place he visited each time he came to Freetown and which he often wrote about, most famously when he used it for the opening of *The Heart of the Matter*. His City Hotel was a forlorn place of ambitions run to waste or, as he put it: 'a home from home for men who had not encountered success at any turn of the long road and who no longer expected it'. Through Greene, the hotel became a literary leitmotif for the late colonial age not just in Sierra Leone but across Britain's declining Empire.

The hotel had ceased functioning in the early 1990s and was gutted by fire in 2000 but I wanted to see if the façade was still there. In my pocket I had a photograph of Greene

The City Hotel in the 1970s (top) and (below) after the war in the 1990s

taken outside the hotel, hands in pockets, feet in sandals, leaning on the stone balustrade at the bottom of a flight of steps leading up to a verandah shaded by a floor above supported on pale stone columns.

I was four days too late. A gang of men was just completing the demolition of the building. Without cranes or power tools they had done it in the most basic way possible, knocking it down stone by stone with sledgehammers. In spite of the hard labour and dry season heat, the foreman, in a floppy tweed cap that made him look like a 1920s American golfer, had not a drop of sweat on him as he clambered about the mound of masonry shouting instructions to his colleagues. In the wreckage I spotted one of the distinctively shaped capitals that topped the columns behind Greene in the picture.

'Can I help?' The voice was friendly, with just the faintest of Krio lilts, as I turned and met a man who introduced himself as one of the owners of the site. 'My name is Victor Ferrari – my granddaddy, Freddie, used to manage the hotel.' I recognised the name immediately. Greene had written in the 1960s about 'the kindly sad Swiss landlord' who ran the 'home from home'.

Victor was the first person I ever met in Sierra Leone with a connection to Greene. He knew all about the author, had read everything he ever wrote about West Africa and even had a video of the 1953 film of *The Heart of the Matter* starring a very sweaty-looking Trevor Howard. Victor invited me that evening back to his home and brought the hotel bar back to life for me with a collection of old photographs. There was no power so we had to sit outside in the twilight as he told how his grandfather, an Italian-Swiss from Locarno, arrived in Freetown as a child in the 1920s before taking over the City Hotel and running it for decades.

Victor, now thirty, had grown up there, its bar his childhood playroom. The pictures were taken from the 1950s onwards, some time after Greene first visited, showing customers – all white men – enjoying a drink. Fashion changes were obvious with the men in the older pictures wearing collared shirts and ties, their hats hanging behind them on hooks, while in the more recent snapshots there were T-shirts and sunglasses. But the bar appeared just as crowded as in Greene's description, with bottles of iced beer set up on the bar's curved counter, the faces of the customers sweaty with a mix of alcohol-infused conviviality and climate-induced torpor.

In part there was sadness about his family story. Freddie had died in the 1990s, a year or two after Greene, and the business had fallen on hard times during the war. Victor himself had left Sierra Leone and set up home in London. But there was also a hint of rebirth, hope even, about his story. A city council decree had demanded all city centre buildings either be used or redeveloped. The fire had destroyed the City Hotel so the decision was taken to knock it down and the site's owners were looking for potential investors for redevelopment.

Hearing the spirit in Victor's voice, the enthusiasm with which he dwelt on the Greene connection, with which he thought through ambitious ideas to take the site forward, I was left thinking, for the first time since arriving back in Freetown, not so pessimistic about the city. Now might be the time to free Freetown of its colonial baggage. Now might be the time to let Greene go.

DAVID SHUKMAN

Heat of Darkness

DAVID SHUKMAN (born London, 1958) has been a BBC television news reporter for more than three decades. He reported live from East Berlin during the fall of the Wall, and was the first journalist to film Soviet nuclear weapons. He became Science & Environment Correspondent in 2003, after years covering conflicts such as Northern Ireland, Bosnia and Tajikistan. He has authored several books, most recently **An Iceberg As Big As Manhattan** (2011), an account of his travels on the new frontlines of environmental science.

Heat of Darkness

DAVID SHUKMAN

The sunlight vanishes, the temperature soars and a lot of hysterical screeching begins. I know that's what's meant to happen in rainforests and for years I have been vaguely sympathetic to the idea of saving them. But now I'm inside one, I'm uneasy.

Up until this moment, everything I know about this cause has been second-hand – the singer Sting touring the television studios with the saucer-lipped chief of the threatened Yamomami Indians; the almost monotonous invocation of Belgium or Wales as the area logged every year; the wildlife documentaries with lingering beauty shots.

Among the well-aired facts I've picked up is that one third of the world's different species exist here, making the Amazon the uber-hotspot for biodiversity. The only hitch is that biodiversity means all creatures great and small, a wonderful thing and vital for a healthy planet, no question, but some of those creatures are, let's face it, pretty revolting. You don't hear much in the conservation conferences about fighting for the tape-worm or that squirmingly malicious little fish, notorious here, with a fondness for the odours of the urethra.

What everyone knows about the rainforest is that it rains, often every day, sometimes almost all the time, rather like standing in a sauna under a hot shower. A soaking is pre-ordained, as is the resulting soupy mess of rainwater mingled with sun block and insect spray and lots of sweat. On my first day, I realise that it's uncomfortable doing anything other than inhaling air conditioning and, if none is available, then fantasising about it.

But what no one tells you about rainforests is that they feature another form of rain as well: a gentle but constant precipitation of ants, bugs and assorted wrigglers tumbling from the dark heights. Whole ecosystems flourish in the canopies – their existence in the tree-tops is one of the wonders of the natural world – but, unfortunately, not all of them are very good at staying up there.

On our way to a research camp, riding on the back of a quad bike, I happen to glance down at my shirt. It's heaving with a mass of creatures, mostly tiny, but one particularly assertive ant seems the size of a paper-clip. And because I'm looking down while I frantically swat away these invaders, my neck is exposed and it becomes a landing-zone too. I react with horror and manically flick and brush. Initially I seem to be winning this struggle. But then I notice that a few of the pluckier arrivals are roaming freely over my hands, untroubled by the sheen of insect repellent.

We stop at a tiny clearing. Suddenly I hear a loud yelp and spin round to an extraordinary sight. Cameraman John Boon is twisting in pain. Flavio, our guide, is thrashing him on the back with his hat.

I run up, confused.

Has John caused offence? Has Flavio been in the forest too long?

The answer lies on the ground. Reaching down, Flavio picks up a red-and-white-striped insect the size of a wasp.

It's a type of mosquito, he says. It was on John's shirt and trying to punch through. If it had stung him, you could forget filming for a few days.

He points out the insect's proboscis: it's thick and sturdy like a hypodermic needle, so out of proportion with the insect's body it's like a child holding a rifle.

We shudder, but time is short so we press on. But then we're shaken again by another surge of primal fear as a familiar black shape scuttles towards us: it's a scorpion, several inches long, tail poised.

It's okay, says Flavio. You only need to worry if it's got a red dot. Otherwise it won't actually kill you.

I can't tell if it has a red dot. All I know is that I'm sure the rainforests need saving – in theory. But saving this bit, in practice, right this minute, every creature? Up to a point.

A BUMPY TRACK leads us towards what I'm told is a fresh example of deforestation. I think I know what it will look like – I've seen pictures of this kind of thing: the lone tree, the miles of bare dry soil, the forlorn trunk on its side. Deforestation has been in and out of the news for at least two decades so, as we lurch along in the heat, I wonder if there's any chance of discovering a fresh angle. Can this new environment correspondent find anything new here?

But as we turn a corner, I enter a scene where I realise my assumptions could not have been more wrong. Huge stumps lie in their thousands, many of them charred, and the red earth beneath them is churned into ugly ridges. The clearance is like a giant prairie heaped with junk timber. Nothing seems left alive. Amid the shattered trunks, their branches twisted, there are no birds. Countless wisps of smoke turn the sky grey. None of the images I'd seen before remotely captures the enormity of this destruction. And there's something unimaginable in the Amazon: the insects seem to have vanished. Of course, I realise – there's no canopy for them to rain down from.

In one of my newspapers cuttings, a journalist had likened the deforestation to the horrors of the First World War, the fields ravaged by craters and trenches. Standing here now, I'm not convinced the writer had left his desk. The atmosphere, particularly the silence, reminds me more of urban warfare, battles waged in streets. The wrecked trees, even lying on their sides, are as tall as buildings and are grey like concrete. I recall the fighting for control of the scarred town of Gornji Vakuf in Bosnia. A mini-Beirut, its inhabitants were stunned after each spasm of violence. Like the destroyed forest, the town had thin columns of smoke twisting into the air, the whole place seemingly winded. What I'm looking at now resembles the same kind of carnage except that it wasn't caused by tanks and artillery.

It was bulldozers. Linked by chains.

I'm with an environmental officer, Ernesto, one of a small band of officials trying to stop deforestation: seven men equipped with a handful of vehicles and just one week's use of a helicopter every year to defend an area about the size of Britain and France combined.

The bulldozers, Ernesto explains, are brought in on trucks and at the edge of the forest the heavy chains are slung between them. The vehicles then advance side-by-side, in military formation, and everything in their path gets torn down. The trees are felled, the stumps uprooted. The wreckage is then set alight and eventually ploughed ready to be used for agriculture – either as pasture for cattle or fields for cultivating soya beans. From land that's dirt cheap, beef and beans fetch high prices on the global markets.

But surely it's illegal?

Yes, says Ernesto, but there are loopholes. Virgin rainforest has the strongest protection in law but to retain that status it has to remain untouched; once it's been tampered with in any way, it's classified differently and enjoys less protection. So landowners encourage small-scale loggers to push into the virgin forest and extract the most valuable trees. When the work of the loggers is 'discovered', the landowner can exclaim in horror that his forest is no longer 'virgin' which just happens to mean, rather conveniently, that the penalties for any further deforestation are much lighter. And that's when the bulldozers are brought in.

JUST AS ERNESTO is explaining this, we spot a truck in the distance, parked close to the edge of the remaining forest. He's immediately suspicious and we race over. In the front of the car is our escort, a policeman, who's armed. Confrontations can turn ugly. Local campaigners, including a priest in this very area, near the town of Santarem, have been warned to shut up on pain of death. In another region, an outspoken American nun was murdered for resisting the loggers. The land beneath the trees can yield so much money that it's triggered an equivalent to a gold rush, anarchic and unrestrained.

When we reach the truck, a battered old thing, there's no one around. But loaded onto it are four freshly felled trunks. I notice sap, almost colourless, dripping from one of them. I reach out and let my finger stick to it; it's surprisingly watery. I realise that while the massive scale of the deforestation is shocking, touching the life force draining from just one tree provokes a different sentiment: it's just plain sad.

The policeman checks his revolver and goes off in search of the loggers. He enters the forest, calling out, pushing through the undergrowth. We follow him, past a severed stump – the newly-exposed wood seems unnaturally pallid, almost naked, and heaps of bright sawdust are scattered nearby. It's like stumbling into a crime scene just minutes after the act. We press on, the policeman's shouts echoing off the wood. And the din soon produces a result.

One of the loggers appears, dressed in a stained football shirt, a sheepish grin on his face. The game is up.

The ringleader stumbles out too, hot and irritated, shirt slung over his shoulder, brushing flies from his bare chest. He's been caught red-handed and admits it. Two more trunks and his truck would have had a full load. Now he knows that the timber will be confiscated and that he'll be fined. He's so resigned to his fate that even the presence of a questioning British television crew doesn't faze him.

Do you know what you're doing here is illegal?

He nods, and Ernesto, translating, confirms that he knows the logging is wrong.

So why do you do it?

To make money, he says.

But what for?

He and Ernesto engage in a long discussion. It turns out the logger is trying to pay off a fine.

What for?

For a previous time he was caught logging.

So this is a way of life, and he's just one of thousands of men, pushing into the jungle, carving new inroads, paving the way for the big agro-industrialists. It's a march on countless fronts and seems unstoppable. It occurs to me that the annual comparison with Wales or Belgium underplays the point: the total area of forest cleared so far is about the size of three United Kingdoms.

And the reference to the UK has another relevance too. Much of the soya grown where the trees once stood is shipped across the Atlantic to Merseyside. It's used in everything from chicken-feed to margarine. The soya cultivated in the Amazon has a particular attraction: it is not genetically modified. Soya from the world's other big producer, America, is GM. So, as long as we choose to avoid GM food, the processors and supermarkets opt for Amazonian soya rather than American, a choice with a consequence. Standing by the four dripping trunks, I realise that their felling did not happen in isolation.

I think back to my cynicism on arriving. Maybe the chant, Save the Rainforest, has been repeated so often that its message had left me cold. But talking to Ernesto and seeing his

An illegal logger – working to pay off his fines ... for illegal logging

team in action – tackling impoverished foot-soldiers – strikes a chord. The statistics may be numbing but they're easier to grasp knowing our encounter stopped, or at least delayed, the felling of another couple of trees.

Ernesto instructs the gang to drive straight to the environmental police compound. There's a standard procedure to follow and they know it well. The trunks will be impounded and added to a stack, several storeys high, of thousands of others. More fines will levied. The men look miserable, their day's labour wasted. Their truck starts up in a cloud of smoke. It will be impounded too. They crawl towards the main road for the two-hour drive to Santarem, the prized logs now a burden. It'll be dark by the time they reach it and I surprise myself: I actually feel a bit sorry for them.

JAN MORRIS

The Fourth World

JAN MORRIS was born of a Welsh father and an English mother in 1926, and lives with her partner Elizabeth Morris in the top left-hand corner of Wales. She has written studies of Wales, Oxford, Venice, Manhattan, Sydney, Hong Kong and Trieste, besides a Booker-shortlisted novel about the imaginary city of **Hav**, the **Pax Britannica** trilogy about the British Empire, and the autobiographical **Conundrum**. Earlier in life she spent ten years as a foreign correspondent of The Times and The Guardian, and was the only reporter with the expedition that first climbed Everest in 1953.

The Fourth World

JAN MORRIS

he place is bloody, reported a perhaps apocryphal dispatch sent by a British imperial administrator after a visit to one of the Empire's less desirable possessions, *and so are the people*.

I know how he felt, being myself of a politically incorrect generation. Places can often be bloody, and God knows so can people – but to my mind, never all of them! My own experience, after seventy odd years of the meandering life, is that scattered throughout the far reaches of our planet, in slums as in palaces, in deserts and suburbs and great cities, there exists a kind of vast supranational community whose citizens may indeed be bloody-minded sometimes, but who are essentially *kind*.

A hazy adjective I know, but then the qualities of this virtual nation of mine can be elusive. Its members may not be brave, may not be selfless, may not even be generous. Sometimes they seem silly, sometimes rather arrogant. But I know them by now, and I recognise them in all their myriad guises. I have recognised the signs in statesmen as in housewives, in taxi-drivers as in actresses or tycoons – a look in the eye, a smile, a gurgle of laughter is often enough. I knew I was in the presence of an initiate when, one day in the high Himalayas, alone in the high snows, I met a wandering holy man with whom I shared not a word or even a gesture, only an instinct. And slowly, over the years I have come to realise that these people constitute a vast and powerful freemasonry. They have no secret handshake to identify them, they speak in many tongues, they believe in many gods or in no gods at all, but I think of them one and all as constituting a Fourth World of their own

Here are some of the characteristics that qualify them for its conceptual citizenship: They may be patriots, but they are never chauvinists. They share with each other, across all the nations, common values of humour and understanding. When you are among them you know you will not be mocked or resented, because they will not care about your race, your faith, your sex, your age, your colour or your nationality. They suffer fools, if not gladly, at least sympathetically. They laugh easily. They are easily grateful. They are seldom mean. They are not inhibited by fashion, public opinion or political correctness. In short, they are kind. Not always, not every one of them, and some are kinder than others, but in general the Fourth World of my experience, and of my imagination too, is a diaspora of kindness; and having encountered its citizens wherever I go, I have come to think that the identification of kindness is the ultimate achievement of the human and animal kingdoms, the one high ideal we can all understand – and better still, perhaps, harness.

For consider the potency of kindness. By definition it cannot be a force for evil, but it constitutes an incalculable force for good. If it can instantly bond total strangers to one another in empathy, whatever their religions or their loyalties, even a Welsh agnostic and a guru meeting near the top of the world – if it can do all this piecemeal, so to speak, just think what it could do if all its disparate energies could somehow be united! Organised religion, as we know too well, has often exerted its power balefully. Love of country can curdle into selfish pride and aggression. Pride of club, pride of school or social class, pride of race can all turn nasty. But an association as wide and varied as my Grand Diaspora, bound only in decency and humour, could surely be unconquerable, if only its citizens knew it.

For long years of contact with the people of the Fourth World have persuaded me that the power of kindness could be a vastly potent political asset. Think of it! It is not just that kindness is non-religious, or inter-religious. It is omni-religious! Omni-national, too! Omni-taste! Omni-purpose! Everyone understands the meaning of kindness, and all the great faiths pay service to it. We need no theologians to explain it to us. The least literate of tabloid readers know what it is about.

Every political party, democratic or despotic, everywhere in the world, claims to be the Party of the People, the Party of Progress, the Party of the Future. Seldom, though, do any of them dare to propose any transcendental, fundamental solution for life's problems. When did you last hear a mention of kindness in any political speech? But there is no political context, in my opinion, in which the Kindness Factor could not play a winning role. There is a vast putative electorate waiting to vote for it. Kissing babies has always been a messy and unconvincing duty of electoral candidates: extending the same techniques into the proportion of a political manifesto, preferably with a more sincere enthusiasm, could sway the opinion of millions. The kinder the party, the bigger its majorities would be!

In a bar in Edinburgh one day I embarked upon an impassioned spiel concerning the grandeur of the notion and the latent force of the Fourth World, and in my somewhat heightened condition told the waitress that one day there would be a plaque above the seat where I sat, commemorating the birth of the International Coalition of Kindness.

'Is that so,' she simply said. 'And in the meantime, shall I fill your glasses while we wait?'

RORY STEWART (born Hong Kong, 1973) is an author, academic and – since the last election – the Conservative MP for Penrith, in Cumbria. He grew up in Malaysia and Scotland and served in the Army and Foreign Office before setting off, in 2002, to walk across Pakistan, Iran, Afghanistan, India and Nepal, staying in more than 500 different village houses. **The Places In Between** (2006) is the account of this journey. **Occupational Hazards** (2008), his second book, describes his time as a coalition forces governor in Iraq. **www.rorystewartbooks.com**

The Wrestler

RORY STEWART

Most charities are founded rather differently but ours began with a wrestler. Aziz had won the Afghan national wrestling championship in 1963, gaining a broken nose, cauliflower ears, damaged knees and the title Parwan or 'Wrestler.'. His speech was composed of boasts and scandalous revelations, interrupted by grimaces provoked by his bad knees. 'I will make your project work. I challenge anyone to say I have ever taken a bribe,' he told me, and added in a stage-whisper, 'But I am a bandit.'

I had originally set up operations in the front room of a tailoring shop with two chairs, a frayed pink Bokhara carpet, a safe, a feather-duster, six glasses and a thermos of green tea. There was also a laminated brochure, whose opening paragraph I had written on the plane, promising that the Turquoise Mountain project would conserve a threatened section of the medieval city of Kabul, improve living conditions, restore ancient buildings and create an academy to preserve and develop traditional skills.

On the back page it said: 'Presidents: HRH the Prince of Wales and HE President Karzai'. Prince Charles had sent me to Afghanistan because he wanted to help retrain Afghans in traditional crafts. I picked Kabul because I wanted to combine his interest with my own desire to save a poor community I had first encountered after the fall of the Taliban. The Prince had raised seed money for the first six months of operations. Thereafter, we would largely be on our own. I was listed in the brochure as Chief Executive. I was in fact the only employee.

THE AREA IN QUESTION was called Murad Khane and my guide was Uncle Khalil. He invariably wore an old dark *shalwar kamiz*, muddy white gym-shoes and a tweed jacket and, because he was a pigeon-master, his hands were scarred by beak marks and by the sharp thread with which he pinioned his pigeons' wings. There were three rose bushes in the courtyard of his house, standing in pools of muddy water, and an art deco balcony, built by his grandfather in the 1920s. Khalil was from the Qizilbash Shia minority which had been persecuted for centuries, but like most of his neighbours he was a house-owner. All but one of the houses in the district had been inherited father to son for over a hundred years.

We followed some children chasing a dog through the wasteland of mud that formed the centre of Murad Khane. Two old men squatted in the open to relieve themselves. Nearby, three cooks were peeling onions. I watched a woman in a *burqa* clamber over a heap of rubbish into her courtyard because the garbage had submerged her entrance. Four acres of Murad Khane were covered in rubbish. There was no electricity, no water, no sewerage. One in five children died before they were one; most of the population could not read or write; and the life expectancy was about forty. Around the edge of the central land-fill site ran a narrow bazaar, a couple of mosques, some bath-houses and about sixty mud-brick courtyard houses, crammed between the river and shabby six-storey 1970s shopping arcades.

Uncle Khalil seemed confident that the bazaar could be easily rebuilt. Down a lane was an old mud-brick mansion, where three goats browsed in a courtyard littered with crates of bananas. The wooden shutters were carved with Mughal stars and floral arabesques, delineated with delicate lattice-work. The wood was unpainted, and the plaster patterns lightly washed with lime.

Back in the bazaar, I was introduced to Master Abdul-Hadi, one of the greatest carpenters in Afghanistan. He was seventy-six years old and had been selling fruit in the market for fifteen years. He had no students to whom he could pass on his skills. This was the area I wanted to restore; these were the people I had promised to help.

OFFICIALS FROM SEVEN Afghan ministries, eight foreign embassies and four charities told me our plans were unwise and possibly illegal. Although Kabul was in ruins and had ballooned from less than a million to more than five million people in five years, the consensus was that too much had been spent on the capital city already. The European Community wanted programs only in 'gender, rural development and governance'; the military focused on the unstable areas of the south and east; and the Afghan government demanded that all funds be placed in the central budget of the Ministry of Finance.

It was illegal to demolish a building in the old city; it was also illegal to rebuild there. Only charities could export tax-free traditional crafts; but charities were not permitted an export licence. The best craftsmen were semi-literate descendants of traditional craft families but vocational craft qualifications could only be given to those who had graduated in Persian literature at high school. There was demand for carved cedar and replicas of Afghan jewelry but the Interior Ministry banned the purchase of cedar and the Culture Ministry banned replicas. A senior Pashtun lawyer confided that the real problem with Murad Khane was that the inhabitants were 'dirty, illiterate, superstitious Shia criminals, who would be better pushed out of the area'. He called them foreigners, as 'they only moved to Kabul from Persia in the eighteenth century'.

The new Mayor had also been Mayor of Kabul in the 1970s. He had spent fifteen years in Canada but had not learnt English. One of his first initiatives was to try to stop the women's hour at the municipal swimming pool on the grounds that women could not swim. When I mentioned Murad Khane he pointed to a map behind his desk, inscribed in Cyrillic *Master Plan for Kabul 1976*. This scheme, drawn up by Soviet and East German planners, remained his dream for the old city. He wanted to demolish the ancient streets and courtyard mansions and replace them with concrete blocks. The next official I met was equally determined to flatten the historic site. His resolve was apparently strengthened by understandings with property developers eager to launder their new – and often heroin-derived – wealth through the construction of skyscrapers.

But local people liked the idea that we believed traditional Afghan art and architecture were beautiful, worthy of international admiration, and could create jobs. I was determined to press on with the project, even if it seemed contrary to public policy, private interest and municipal regulations. The only way to do so was to make rapid progress and then dare the government to demolish what we were rebuilding.

'We are the original inhabitants of Murad Khane,' Parwan Aziz roared when I went to see him, at Khalil's insistence, to get support from the community. 'Only one house in the area has ever been bought or sold. I will not let the government touch it.' I explained that I wanted to rent the mansion with the banana boxes and to restore it. He told me instead that I should rent two houses. 'I will place you – the foreigner – at each corner, so the government will not send in the bulldozers. If you take the centre, the government will demolish the edges.'

I proceeded to recruit staff. Even an uneducated Afghan who had attended a development training course and could speak passable English could earn more than a thousand

The Wrestler – Parwan Aziz

dollars a month. I could not afford those salaries. My first employee had worked as a salesman in a Pakistani carpet shop and in the 'informal export sector' during the Taliban period, which seemed to involve carrying semi-precious stones across mountain passes. But an old friend had employed him as a driver and said that he had once risked his life to save her from kidnapping. Within a week I had added an Afghan woman, a young radio operator from the north, a fifty-year-old white-bearded engineer, a one-legged horseman, a high school literature teacher, a woodworker and a physically handicapped academic administrator. Thus, respectively, I had appointed my logistics manager, office administrator, finance director, chief engineer, guard, calligraphy master, woodwork master and office manager.

None had had senior jobs in an international organisation; none spoke fluent English; the majority had not completed a high school education and I suspect they would not have been employed in any formal recruitment process. But I believed I could trust them.

Each employee began to build their own team. Within three weeks we didn't have enough space for our growing staff. An Englishman called David suggested that I could occupy and restore a nineteenth-century fortress, set above two acres of gardens. The original owner's widow now lived in Delhi and David and his friends lived in the only occupied wing. We replaced ceilings and windows, installed loos and repaired the underfloor heating system of the nineteenth-century bath-house so that we could bathe in the winter. In the garden we set up an office and the carpentry and calligraphy school and began building a new school to teach ceramics.

The early staff came from different social classes and from ethnic groups that had recently been at war. Each favoured their own: the manager from the persecuted Hazara minority hired a Hazara cook and translator; while Panshiri Tajiks came to dominate the driving pool. My personal relations with each, stretching back over years or through mutual friends, made it almost impossible for me to fire anyone. I had to spend a great deal of time at weddings, lending money, trying to help relatives and paying medical bills from my own pocket.

But it proved a wonderful team: each was bound to me by some form of personal loyalty, in a society where institutional loyalty was scant. Their eight separate origins meant that they kept an often jealous eye on each other, ensuring that as the organisation grew it could never be dominated by a single cabal. I decided to launch a cultural foundation by hosting a play and was delighted to see how everyone threw themselves into the preparations. Just before the start I watched the guard, the finance director and the driver each fixing lights and carrying plates of food.

I HAD RESERVATIONS about appointing the tailor's brother to oversee restoration work, not only because he had little formal education or knowledge of architectural conservation but also because he came from a different ethnic group and a different sect of Islam from that of the community. But when he walked over the rutted mud lanes of Murad Khane and met Parwan Aziz he seized him by the biceps and began a mock re-enactment of a wrestling match, laced with jokes and elaborate compliments. It was he who negotiated with the wrestler and who convinced me to follow the wrestler's housing plans. We were rewarded by a petition signed by the fifty most senior members of the community asking us to work in the area. Henceforth, community support was our greatest defence against the municipality and mayor, international policy shifts, vagaries of funding and greedy developers.

We decided it would be strategic to begin by shifting rubbish. The engineer conjured up a workforce and began. At this point the municipal director appeared with police and a document ordering us to stop. The police advanced with Kalashnikovs; the labourers fell back; I rummaged for dogeared registration documents and the director wrote in bold strokes on a clipboard. Behind me, I sensed a gathering crowd. An old man who I had not met before stepped forward and shouted, 'How dare you stop these men? I remember when you last cleared the garbage: I was ten years old and it was 1947.' The wrestler shook the hands of the now-smiling police. The engineer put his arm around the director's shoulders and walked him out of Murad Khane. The next day we received a letter from the municipality authorising us to proceed.

Parwan Aziz went to the President's office; the Minister of Urban Development was invited to a service at the shrine; and when the police intervened again, the community laid a new concrete forecourt for the police station. Foreigners had told me that Afghans were slow and inefficient. That was not my experience. Over the next eighteen months, the engineer cleared over 10,000 trucks of rubbish, dropping the street level by more than seven feet and creating near total employment. Then he levelled the streets, dug drainage and wells and laid paving, and began emergency repairs on fifty houses, making them water-tight, propping walls, installing lavatories.

People began to come back into the area and drug pedlars moved elsewhere. But the engineer's real genius was political, in defusing the conflicts over jobs for relatives, fights over wages and over which properties should be repaired first. He dealt with things in his own style, grabbing an angry mullah by the beard after we had accidentally brought down the mosque wall. Astonishingly, the mullah laughed and forgave us.

Meanwhile, in order to cope with demand, our lack of funding and the shortage of professionals, I brought in more than a hundred international volunteers over two years. Enthusiastic amateurs mingled with serious experts. Many lived three to a room and we all ate together at a common table.

Where we had no expertise we had to be inventive. I had started with a few prejudices: I wanted the repairs to build-ings to be visible but not too obvious. But that was hardly a coherent conservation philosophy. I thought the high tem-peratures in electric kilns eliminated all that was intriguing in the low-fired pots but that didn't help us win contracts from suppliers who wanted less fragile glazes. I didn't think we should pay too much for international volunteers but what about providing life insurance? Should the financial year start in January or April? Should we have a substantial document detailing our plans for urban regeneration and who should lead it: an architect? A planner? A property developer? Me?

It was clear we needed to work quickly to prove to the gov-ernment that the area and crafts were worth saving and to the community that we were serious, competent and serving their needs. Our initiatives multiplied, responding to sudden crises or the shifting expertise of our volunteers or the community's demands. We produced a traffic plan for the northern bank of the river, took an exhibition of calligraphy to a museum in Bahrain, built different designs of self-composting lavatories (one under a 'Nubian vault') and fitted earth buildings with new types of mud brick, solar panels and elaborately carved calligraphic doors. We created factory management systems around new carpentry equipment; launched IT and business courses for students; developed partnerships with Pakistani art schools, opened a rural museum for potters and sold an Afghan-carved suite to the Connaught Hotel in London. Anna, our plucky development director, recorded the recipes of the old city and designed a restaurant in a historic building which would provide employment and draw Afghan visitors back to the old city with good, affordable food.

Some of the best ideas came from the community itself. Like the primary school. Education is bad in Afghanistan: perhaps a quarter of teachers are illiterate and as recently as 2001 girls were not permitted to attend. Children in the old city needed a safe-haven during the day from homes often marked by domestic violence and drug abuse. But we were overstretched and I was reluctant to launch a new initiative. We compromised: the community provided the space while we focused on the teaching.

We began in a single room with a couple of teachers and within an hour of opening the doors we had 160 boys and girls, most of whom had never been to school before. Their smiles alone made me feel our project was worthwhile. Yet it was no easier than anything else in Afghanistan. The school would have remained second-rate if we had not hired better teachers, negotiated with the Ministry of Education, built new classrooms and introduced local history and art classes, city tours, adult literacy classes and mathematics. And much of this depended on foreign staff. The curriculum was reformed and the teachers were trained by the head of science from an inner city school in Boston.

The Institute for Traditional Afghan Arts began as little more than an apprentice workshop with people huddled on rough benches watching Master Abdul Hadi. A year later, there was a full timetable for the students including IT, English, business studies, Islamic art history and design.

Our new business development section launched catalogues and websites of our work, won commissions from embassies, represented us at international trade fairs, sold coasters in Canada and a wooden library to Japan. Monsoon had given us money to train women in embroidery to sell in their stores. We had begun to plant trees to make our timber source sustainable. We had built a girls' school for a fraction of the cost of a concrete building. At the start of the second year we had 650 applicants for 33 places.

It was only once we had succeeded in each case that the relevant Afghan ministry began to support us. A new Minister of Education recognised the degree certificates from our school and registered us as a national higher education institute. Two decrees were issued to register the area as a protected historical site. Our architects provided training for the Ministry of Urban Development and they in turn worked with us on land-use plans for the site. The media became excited and flattering profiles appeared. We were often on the Afghan evening news.

I WAS THE ONLY PERSON aware that we were dangerously short of cash. I needed to raise thousands of dollars a day. I began to lend more of my own money to try to keep things going. Many had trusted us: donating land for our schools, working long hours, enrolling to learn complex skills in traditional crafts and architecture. But we had to slow the building projects, which meant laying people off at the onset of winter. I began to wonder what might be raised by selling our minivan or carpets.

By November 2006, I had two weeks before I would have to give everyone a month's notice. I woke at three in the morning and felt very afraid. No one was used to giving to a brand-new organisation that had grown at this pace or was operating on this scale. Most donors required two years of audited accounts. As I walked to work, I was greeted by people – the gate-guard who had lost his leg to a landmine; the receptionist who needed a heart operation and the driver who had been the first to leave his job to join us – and when they smiled or thanked me, I felt like a fraud.

An objective examination of the costs and probabilities suggested we should shut down. Continuing was a gamble: an attempt to bend the world improbably to our dreams. I continued through stubbornness not reason. I flew back to Britain and left behind the conversations and the crises that I had loved in the old courtyards of Kabul in order to fundraise around the world. I made it a rule to return to Kabul every fortnight but I was on almost three hundred flights over the next two years.

In countries I had never visited I waited for meetings that never happened. Once, when I made it past a secretary in a Gulf state, I was accused of terrorist financing and shown the door. Some of the wealthy would only support us if we changed what we were doing: to advocacy for women, or schools for the blind. If by luck they would support something we were doing, they could change their mind and suggest something that we were not. I was hopeful about our chances with foundations created by young dot-com leaders and dedicated to 'social entrepreneurs'. But they wanted synergies and income streams and compared us on cost per unit metrics. They did not want to be distracted from their 'core mission'.

But we didn't just do one core activity. We believed, for example, that to regenerate the bazaar we had to clear garbage and develop attractive sites for visitors, we had to train craftsmen to manufacture products to sell, teach the shopkeepers to read and write and count, give incomes to women, provide shelter, water and electricity. Our strength was our local knowledge: we had been in every house, employed someone from every family, worked alongside them, negotiated, tussled, shaped their aspirations and were shaped in turn. But there was no universal model: what worked for us might not work elsewhere.

The only way to convey our work was to get donors to visit. One of our best supporters was an eighty-four-year-old American woman who almost immediately on arrival forced senior ministers and generals to act: establishing an orphanage, providing razors for troops, bringing equipment to eliminate water-borne diseases. She clambered up stairs, over danger-ous gaps in the roof, trudged through mud, interrogated our female students, watched the customers buy the products that provided the income to sustain the project and listened to the community itself. But very few people dared to come.

One foundation boasted to me that after an exhaustive analysis of proposals he had ignored us and instead allocated hundreds of thousands of dollars to an Afghan woman who was running thousands of girls' schools. I knew these schools did not exist.

In the end we were saved by private generosity. An Afghan nightclub owner crossed a street in Washington to give me a thousand dollars because he had heard about our work from his family in Kabul, a Swedish woman cycled up to our office to give us fifty dollars, our English volunteer did a skip-a-thon with an Afghan friend in Dorset. And Prince Charles remained our chief supporter and champion.

Our largest donors gave from their private accounts, because their foundation bureaucracies were too restricted to be able to support us. Some had heard of us, others gave randomly with no prior contact. A lady talked to me about Afghanistan for twenty minutes over lunch in California and later sent a million dollars. Then she visited us and sent another million. The Afghan government is now putting its own money behind us and we now have 350 employees.

Recently, I stood in the central square of Murad Khane. I could move without sinking into the mud because the drainage and stone-paving has worked. I noticed that the carving on the windows of the upper gallery needed to be redone: the Nubian vault had been removed from the loo because of a rumour we were building a pagan temple. I heard that the Mayor might have agreed not to build the threatened road. There was a new community box, outside the women's clinic, and people had put in thirty dollars which would cover prescriptions for the next two months. Three streets had agreed to take over the cost of garbage clearance from us; one had not. I noted that the students at the primary school had new uniforms.

Western bureaucracies seem to exist to stop this kind of project. If it succeeds, it will not be a neat lesson in 'social entrepreneurship', in management, or a new model for international development. Rather, it is a story of sudden expressions of faith, acts of generosity and amateur flair. Ours was a local project in a mud city spun by an ageing wrestler, teased by volunteers, tugged by a grey-bearded engineer, deconstructed in conversations around a table at mealtimes. My hope is to return in thirty years and admire the old city's arts and architecture and encounter a community which is more just, prosperous and humane. There is no guarantee.

COLIN THUBRON

ตราสำปั้

In Mandalay

COLIN THUBRON (born London, 1939) is a travel writer and novelist. His first books were about the Middle East – Damascus, Lebanon and Cyprus. In 1982 he travelled by car into the Soviet Union, a journey recorded in **Among the Russians**. From these early experiences developed his classic travel books on China, Russia and Central Asia: **Behind the Wall: a Journey through China**, **The Lost Heart of Asia**, **In Siberia**, **Shadow of the Silk Road** and most recently, **To a Mountain in Tibet**. He has won many prizes and awards. In 2010 he became President of the Royal Society of Literature.

In Mandalay

COLIN THUBRON

It is thirty-five years ago now, and the time has faded to a sepia strangeness, lit by a few sharp surviving details: a man's pained smile, a shelf of mouldering books. It was a time when Myanmar – old British Burma – was even more constrictive than now. Travellers were permitted seven days in the country, and in that tense span might attempt the gruelling 450-mile railway journey from Rangoon to Mandalay, returning down the Irrawaddy by steamer past the long-ruined capital of Pagan.

I had driven out from Europe through countries which were less dangerous then – Afghanistan, Pakistan, Kashmir – and across northern India. But the Burmese border was where the overland journey had always stopped dead. I ditched my car in Calcutta and flew south-east, bypassing the jungled tribal hills of northern Myanmar, to land at last in a sequestered Rangoon.

I remember the city in grand decline: shrubs sprouting through the Victorian stone, a black market thriving among people who lived by a private economy, the otherworldly beauty of worshippers processing round the Shwedagon pagoda, as if nothing for centuries had changed. It was a land and people whose infinite appeal to the camera barely softened a harsh poverty. The junta of General Ne Win looked set to rule forever. The democratic heroine Aung San Suu Kyi was still a wife in Oxford. The country lay in a time-warp, charming the fleeting foreigner, who knew nothing.

The only domestic air flights had been commandeered by the army, so it was by the steam-train that I laboured north to Mandalay. I cannot remember how long it took, or how often it broke down. The train was so crowded that people clung to its foot-rails and squatted on its roofs. For an interminable night I sat wedged among betel-spitting farmers above the clanking buffers linking two carriages. Whenever we stopped, the villagers waiting on country platforms stormed through the windows (the glass had long ago gone) or charged through the jammed doors; while those inside – already half suffocated – slammed down the window shutters and fought to keep them out.

IT IS EVENING, in my memory, as we grind to a halt in Mandalay station. Mandalay! It was the last royal capital of the Burmese kings, the city of Kipling and Orwell. In 1885 its heart – the royal palace – had been looted by the invading British, and its library burnt to the ground. Then the Japanese occupied it in World War II, and the allies bombed it to a wasteland.

Pandemonium broke out in the station as the bleary passengers descended. A horde of bicycle rickshaw drivers was waiting to transport us through the city, and I was encircled by bellowing cries for custom. I remember no faces at all, only the clamour of these voices rising in a raucous plea from men whose lives might last only as long as their stringy bodies held up.

Suddenly, at the back of the crowd, a quaintly pedantic suggestion floated: 'Excuse me, sir, would you care for a rickshaw?' I hunted for the source of this, and saw a face whose gentle features were inexplicable among those around him: the hair curly and barbered, the bones more delicate. He bowed slightly. 'My name is Tun.'

He pedalled me out into the city whose markets and monasteries seemed scattered at the end of the world. Mine was the only white face. Tun recounted the town's history in soft, studious English. He wore an immaculate sarong and a skimpy vest. I felt guilty for using him.

Beyond the moated palace – brick palisades pierced by flimsy gates and turrets – lay the wasteland left by the British. It looked pathetically vulnerable – a medieval world levelled by aircraft. I wandered through it with uneasy fascination at what had been lost. Some weed-glazed canals survived among the overgrown terraces, where humps and ridges marked the course of vanished passageways and rooms. A harmless-looking cannon pointed at nothing. I remembered illustrations of Burmese soldiers in quilted armour and leather helmets. But Tun spoke only with hardy irony that he and I – Burmese and British – should be walking here at peace. 'Things were different then. Those were cruel times.'

I thought: but he is still living in such times. His government was a tyranny. His city was poor and decaying, its infrastructure collapsed. Its streets were tracks. Yet he retained this curious refinement. As we emerged through one of the toy-like gates and over the moat, he said: 'Will you come home with me? I will learn good English.'

'You already have good English.'

I was waiting for him to explain why – was he a disgraced teacher, a journalist? – but he only said: 'It's too long forgotten.'

HIS HOME LAY behind a stockade spiked with palm trees: a wooden house with a flaking white balcony and a roof of falling tiles. Three small, fat children sat in its entrance, dressed comfortably in woollen jumpers, cramming their mouths with rice out of an aluminium bowl. Their sleepy eyes looked at me in mute bewilderment. Their mother might have belonged to another race from Tun's. Her furious cheekbones and jutting teeth gave her a look of inadvertent wildness. She smiled an artless welcome at me.

Their home held almost nothing. A watchdog crouched under the steps. The inner walls were woven palm leaves. The bed where I slept that night was a wooden frame clouded by mosquitoes. A single shelf held mildewed books, which might have been salvaged from somewhere grander. I noticed Dickens' novels, Alistair Maclean's *The Dark Crusader* and the stories of Rudyard Kipling.

No, Tun said, his wife did not read. She was illiterate. 'She is not very clever, but she is very good.' After a while he said: 'Will you meet my other relatives?'

I imagined them living as he did, in modest suburban poverty. Instead, to my astonishment, he bicycled me to a ponderous Edwardian mansion. Without knocking, we entered dust-filled rooms lined with teak furniture, where his aunt and uncle – inscrutably old and courteous – rocked in padded chairs and mewed out greetings.

Walking in their garden, lost under honeysuckle and weeds, my pent-up curiosity at last spilled over. Why was Tun not living like them? What had happened to him?

Momentarily he winced, then settled into a story that filled him with self-wonder, as if he were talking of somebody else, or of somebody long ago.

He came from a good family, he said, old Burmese aristocrats. Some years ago he had started his career as a soldier, and was one of a handful selected to go to England for officers' training. There, with his quick ear, he had picked up the language.

'After I came back I was a favoured cadet, of course, and in time I found myself serving as a captain on our north-east frontier. In those days it was filled with Chinese bandits, and we were trying to eliminate them.' These bandits, he explained, were the remains of Chinese Nationalist armies who had fled the Communist victory of 1949. At first they had lingered on the frontier, hoping to reoccupy their homeland, but were each time repulsed. So at last they became little more than outlaws and drug traffickers, and the Burmese army moved against them.

'I was young then. I was in charge of a platoon dug in above a ridge near the Chinese positions. I confess I was frightened.' He was walking fast along the weed-sown paths, almost marching. 'One night our sentries had fallen asleep. But I was still awake, reading an Alistair MacLean novel in the moonlight. It was very bright. Suddenly I heard a clink in the silence, and I looked up to see the slope below swarming with Chinese. They were climbing towards us and already so close that I could see their teeth gleaming in the moonlight, smiling.'

His expression on me was one of faded horror. He said: 'I managed to wake up my platoon in time. Then we mowed them down. All of them. It seemed like hundreds. We were concealed above them and they didn't stand a chance.'

I said lamely: 'So you did your duty.'

He shook his head. 'Then something happened inside me. Something I don't understand. In those days officers wore long swords. I pulled mine out and climbed down the slope.' He lifted a ghostly sabre. 'Then I went mad. I started hacking at the dead and wounded, the dying. I couldn't stop. It was a kind of frenzy. On and on, in their blood. Slashing …'

We had arrived back at the gate now, where his rickshaw stood comfortingly with its twin wheels and padded carriage.

'After that I wasn't the same. I was revolted at myself.' He turned towards me. 'Was this myself? I decided to leave the army. I tried to resign. But they had spent too much money on me, and wouldn't let me go. It was only later that General Ne Win demanded all army officers sign an oath of allegiance to him. I took my opportunity and refused, so they sacked me. And no other employer would touch me then, of course.'

He mounted his bike, while I sat behind, wondering, ashamed again that he was toiling for me. He ended: 'So I became a rickshaw driver in Mandalay.'

IN THE DAWN LIGHT I woke to catch the steamer south to Pagan, and Tun pedalled me unspeaking to the wharfside. He may have regretted his sudden intimacy, I don't know. He looked quiet and worn. Only as the tottering, two-storey steamer pulled from the quayside, he raised his hand at me departing over the flood-waters, and went on waving for a long time, as if he were saying farewell to something else, until the swell of the river took him from sight.

A Cave on the Black Sea

PATRICK LEIGH FERMOR (born London, 1915) is widely regarded as 'Britain's greatest living travel writer'. At eighteeen, he set out to walk across Europe to Constantinople, a trip recalled in the masterful **A Time of Gifts** and continued in **Between the Woods and the Water**. But Paddy had made his mark on travel and literature long before their publication, notably with his books on Greece, **Mani** and **Roumeli**. As an SOE officer, he was, famously, parachuted into Crete in World War II, where he led the capture of the German commander, General Kreipe. Knighted in 2001, he lives mainly in Greece.

A Cave on the Black Sea

PATRICK LEIGH FERMOR

A Time of Gifts and Between the Woods and the Water tell the story of Paddy's youthful walk 'from the Hook of Holland to Constantinople', but the latter ends at the borders of Romania and Bulgaria, and a third book remains unfinished. This story – which might form a part of it – takes place in December 1934, when Paddy was travelling down the Black Sea coast of Bulgaria. Istanbul was less than 110 miles away to the south but somewhere between Varna and Burgas the path petered out just as night was coming on.

This was Europe's easternmost rim; but it was hard to remember that the ocean-like sweep that flashed from the cliffs of Bulgaria to the bare horizon was inland water: Tcherno More, Kara Su, Marea Neagra, the Euxine, the Black Sea ... Constantza, Odessa, Batum, Trebizond, Constantinople ... the names were intoxicating. Due east, the Caucasus lay; Asia Minor to the south; north, the Danube and Rumania, and north-east, the Ukraine and all the

Russias. The chill that crackled in the December air was a hint to a traveller of those limitless impending snows.

Inland, to the north-west, rose the Great Balkan range. At the other end of this brilliant morning I could just see the ice-bright and blue-shadowed snows and, to the south-west, a faint gleam of the Rhodope mountains. Perhaps it was just about here that the migrating storks I had seen pouring over the Stara Planina four months before had struck the Black Sea coast on their way to Africa. The tiers that rolled inland, so arid then underfoot, were feathered now with young grass. The Bulgarian winter had not yet begun and the emerald and moss-bright froth across the russet soil spread a fiction of early spring. The hills were empty. Glimpses of villages soared inland, their chimneys balancing above them veils as thin and blue as un-inhaled tobacco smoke. Slow threads rose swaying and expanding from distant bonfires, as though Mohicans were signalling. The hillsides uncoiled red scrolls of plough; beehives, muffled for the coming winter, stood in cataleptic kraals; and only the far-sounding bells told that the flocks were grazing their way across Bulgaria at a glacier's pace. Magpies fidgeted about the landscape and an unstable confetti of gulls whitened the grass and the furrows.

When the track dipped steeply into a coomb, streams curled to the sea over a crescent of sand and the ravines that twisted inland were filled with bare, silver walnut trees and the spidery winter distaffs of poplars. Hundreds of hooded crows were settled along the boughs and a clap of the hands would shed them deafeningly into the sky as the branches sprang free, sending them up the valley in a drift of soot for a league or two; then back they swung to plunge the spinneys into raucous mourning again. Some people say that these birds – suddenly ominous by their numbers – live for more than a hundred years; a number of these might have pecked at the dead in the Crimean War; a few Methuselahs could even have flown south across the Ukraine after following the Grande Armée from Moscow.

In an inlet, close to the sand's edge, an old man was smoking a *nar-ghileh* on the doorstep of a hut beside a little boat beached among the rushes. His high-cheeked face was a benign skeleton leaf of wrinkles. In faulty Bulgarian on both sides, we talked of the coldness of the day and the brightness of the sun. He was an old Tartar fisherman, the only human being I saw all day.

For, as the miles mounted up, the scene grew emptier until rising woods concealed the interior. Trees sank to the sea's edge and the path curled across tilted glades full of white and red anemones. The smell of herbs filled the air. Myrtle, bay and arbutus – dark green leaves crowded with berries as big and scarlet as strawberries – sank seaward. Blue-black ilexes jutted among them, their roots looped in plaited arches like the roots of trees in Japanese paintings.

Downhill, at the end of plunging tunnels of evergreen, the European continent disintegrated in tufted spikes and islets standing in green water as translucent as glass, darkened, as it receded, to the blue of a peacock's neck as it fled away to the skyline. Creases slight as a breath on silk stirred the almost still water just enough to ring these spikes with a bracelet of white. Headlands followed each other in a south-westerly recession of plumed capes dwindling at last to dim threads that could belong equally to the sea or the sky.

In the late afternoon, sunbeams filled the tilted clearings and struck the tree boles and the leaves with layers of wintry gold. Rafts of light hung in the leaves, fell through the woods in spokes and broke up the loop of shadow over the water with windows of radiance. The solitude and the hush were complete. A promise of the Aegean and the Greek islands roved the cold Bulgarian air, sending a hint of their spell across the Propontis and the Bosporus to the shores of this huge barbarian sea.

A trio of cormorants had flown across the Tartar's cove and I had seen their craned necks, beaks swivelling like periscopes, sticking out of the water farther south. On the rocks a dozen were standing now with wings heraldically half-open, as though hung out to dry. I followed a path downhill towards them, but they took flight in an urgent wedge over the water, which was now patterned with streaks of zinc and lilac. The track grew thinner; by dusk all trace of it had vanished and I found myself climbing through undergrowth and rocks: leaping from slab to slab, dodging pools, bestriding fissures and ledges, hoping for a gap that might lead uphill again. When it was dark I went on by torchlight, negotiating the water and the steeper confusion of boulders, determined to turn back if it grew worse.

Then I lost my footing on a ledge and skidded, with a screech of hobnails, down a slant like a barn roof. A drop and a jolt threw me waist-deep into a pool. Jarred and shaken, with a gash on my forehead and a torn thumb, I climbed out, shuddering with cold. At the bottom of the other end of the pool, about two fathoms down, the torch was sending a yellow shaft through sea anemones and weed and a flickering concourse of fish. I wondered what would have happened if in my rucksack and overcoat and heavy boots, I had followed the torch into the depths. Should I take off my heavy stuff and dive for the drowned light? I was shaking and my teeth were chattering. The sun had only just set: waiting till dawn meant twelve or thirteen hours in the freezing dark.

In case there were someone on this empty-seeming coast, I decided to shout. But what? I had forgotten, if I ever knew it, the Bulgarian for *Help*. All I could think of was the formal cry of 'Good evening' – *'Dobar vecher!'* I shouted for a few minutes but with no reply. My stick was floating on the shallower part of the pool, so I retrieved it. With a reluctant look at the lost torch and the glittering mob of fish now going mad round that fallen portent, I began to fumble my way forward, tapping and feeling a way along the rocks: sliding, crawling on all fours, climbing ledges slippery with bladder-wrack, wading up to my armpits and sounding ahead with the stick for fear of a sudden drop. Now and again I sent up my cry of inappropriate affability. Stars dimly indicated distant masses in silhouette. After a long slithering advance, a few constellations, appearing in front where all had been black before, indicated that I was reaching the cape.

I crept on, preferring to wade now; the water was less cold than the night air. When I crawled on the rocks, the air embedded me in icy plate-armour. Within a few minutes of each other, as though by collusion, both my bootlaces broke; the boots became loose, dragging anchors under water and heavy fetters up and down the blades of rock. Breathless and exhausted, I lay on a ledge until spurred on by the cold. At last, lowering my half-shod foot on to what I thought was the surface of a pool, I felt the solidity of sand and the grate of pebbles. Another pace confirmed it; I was on the shore of an inlet. Round a buttress of cliff a little way up the beach, a faint rectangle of light, surrounded by scattered chinks, leaked astonishingly into the darkness. I crossed the pebbles and I pulled open an improvised door, uttering a last *dobar vecher* into the measureless cavern beyond. A dozen firelit faces looked up in surprise and consternation from their cross-legged supper, as though a sea monster or a drowned man's ghost had come in.

Ten minutes later, in gym shoes, canvas trousers, two shirts, several layers of jersey and a shepherd's hirsute cloak, with three or four slugs of *slivovitz* burning inside me, sipping a second glass of tea brewed from mountain herbs and two inches deep in sugar, I was crouched in front of a blaze of thorns stacked as high as a bonfire. I was still shuddering. One of the inhabitants of the place had washed the blood off my face and feet, another had plied a towel. Recovered from their surprise at the apparition of this sodden and bleeding spectre, they had leaped to my help like Bernardine monks.

It took some time to focus and segregate the figures moving about in the firelight and the smoky shadows. They were wild-looking men. Six were dressed in the customary earth-brown or dark blue home-spun; patched, tattered, cross-gartered with thongs over their felt-swaddled shanks and shod in canoe-tipped cowhide moccasins. Knives were stuck in their wide red sashes and, like me, they were hatted in flat-topped sheepskin *kalpaks* that had moulted most of their fur. An old man with a tangled white beard seemed to be the leader of this group. Four others, equally torn and tattered, wore blue jerseys and seamen's peaked caps set askew. Shepherds and seamen, in fact. The oldest of the sailors had only one hand, with a star tattooed on the back of it.

Gradually the surrounding firelit hollow resolved itself into a long cave, arching high overhead but not burrowing very deep. Blades of rock formed much of the outer wall, unmortared masonry filled the gaps, and branches and planks and flattened petrol tins stamped with *Sokony-Vacuum* in Cyrillic characters, completed it. The flames picked out fans of shrub springing from the rock and a high cluster of stalactites; they also summoned from the shadows a scattering of gear which told of the cave's double function: a boat tilted on its side, oars, rudders, huge carbide lamps, long-shafted fishing spears, tall multi-pronged tridents with barbed spikes like eight-toothed combs, anchors, geometric fishing traps, creels, bait baskets, corks, gourd floats, wedges, coils, drooping russet festoons of net and links of rusty chain. A small anvil topped an embedded tree stump.

The other side of the fire displayed a set of conflicting clues: wicker cheese baskets on planks, a leaning sheaf of crooks and a grove of white, hanging globes – cheese that had been poured liquid into dripping goatskin bags, hairy side innermost. A cauldron of whey simmered over a second fire, and the stooping Cyclopean greybeard stirred and skimmed. Across the dark reaches at the far end ran a breast-high wall of bleached stones and furze, and the mystery of an abrupt and derisive cachinnation beyond.

The old man took a brand from beneath the cauldron and flourished it with a possessive smile. The lasso of radiance that his flame looped into the murk lit up a thicket of spiralling and bladed horns and the imperial beards and matted black-and-white pelts of fifty goats; a wave of the torch kindled a hundred oblong-pupilled eyes, provoking another falsetto jeer, a click of horns and the notes of a few heavy bells. A patina of smoke and soot polished the walls of the cave. Jags of mineral were tables or sideboards for these troglodytes. Half a dozen dogs slept or foraged around; a reclining white mongrel with hanging tongue and forepaws crossed observed the scene through close-set eyes, the left one of which was surrounded by a black ring. The sand and the pebbles underlay a trodden crust of goats' pellets and fish scales, and the cavern reeked of fish, goats, curds, cheese, tar, brine, sweat and wood-smoke. It was an abode harmoniously shared by Polyphemus and Sinbad.

Supper was finished but they ladled me out the last of the lentils while one of the fishermen poured oil in the frying pan, laid a couple of mackerel across it and, in due course, whisked them out sizzling by their tails and put them in the tin plate the lentils had that instant vacated. I must have been coming to; these delicious fish were demolished at speed. What were they called? *Skoumbri,* one fisherman said; no, no, cried the others: *skumria.* There was some friendly teasing about this, for the shepherds were Bulgars and the fishermen were Greeks, members of the Greek community scattered all over southern Bulgaria. I was surprised to see these irreconcilables in each other's company. One of them apologised, saying they had finished the *slivo* and wine. I dug a contribution out of my rucksack: two bottles of raki from Tirnovo, one safe in a wooden flask, the other mercifully intact. In spite of an occasional shudder and a rattle of teeth, my spirits, as the food and drink piled up, began to rise. The circulating raki ignited a mood of nautico-pastoral wassail and by the time the second bottle was broached the wind-battered and weather-chipped faces were wide-mouthed in song.

A goatskin, which I had taken to be a vessel for milking the ewes, turned out to be a bagpipe. But when the old man puffed it full, the drone through the horn trumpet died in a wail that called forth an answering howl from the white dog, briskly silenced by a backhanded cuff. A crease in the cracked parchment had split. I patched it up, to everyone's applause, with a criss-cross of adhesive tape. As the sound swelled again one of the fishermen began a burlesque Turkish belly dance, called the *kiitchek.* He had learned it, he said, in Tzarigrad, the Bulgarian for Constantinople, the town of the Emperors.

It was very convincing, even to the loud crack that accompanied each spasmodic wrench of the haunch and the midriff, produced by the abrupt parting of the stiff interlocked forefingers of both hands as they were held, palms joined, above his head.

The comic effect was enhanced by the fierce and piratical looks of Dimitri the dancer. 'He needs a *charchaff*,' one of the shepherds cried. He wrapped a cheesecloth round the lower part of Dimitri's face. The rolling of his smoke-reddened eyes above this yashmak turned him into a mixture of *houri* and virago. Meanwhile Costa, another sailor, advanced into the firelight with the same rotating motion as Dimitri. Uninhibited laughter broke out. A third fisherman tied a two-foot length of rope into a ring, made Costa step into it, then lifted it to the level of his thighs and made him stretch his legs apart. When the rope was taut he inserted a heavy log which he turned over several times, till the log in the twisted rope could be made to lift or drop like the beam of a siege engine. The comic impropriety of this vision brought the house down. (I wonder whether Aristophanes knew of this device? It would have been handy for the *Lysistrata*...) A mock pursuit of the veiled Dimitri began, with Costa moving by leaps: the ithyphallic gait of a pasha-like grasshopper bent on rape. To drive this fierce aspect home, he pulled out one of the shepherds' knives and held it between his teeth.

The bagpipe howled with growing stridency and the spectators jovially clapped out the time. Dimitri oscillated with lumbering skittishness; the uncouth chase brought the sweat to Costa's brow, while monstrously enlarged shadows of their evolutions loomed about the cave. Finally a long scream of the pipe propelled him, with his legs splayed and knees bent, round and round his partner in mock-lecherous leaps. Cheerfully goaded by the onlookers the bagpiper blew faster and faster until the panting pibroch mercifully ended at last with the diminishing wail of an ox under the knife: my running repair had come unstuck. Laughing and out of breath, Costa collapsed with mock melodrama. The raki travelled round the cave in a hubbub of laughter, and the flames threw a beltane chiaroscuro over hilarious masks.

Another bottle was miraculously discovered. Panayi, the fourth of the fishermen, lifted a long object from the boat. When he rejoined us on the floor, the unwinding of the cloth revealed an instrument halfway between a lute and a mandolin. Ivory and mother-of-pearl inlaid the sounding board, and ivory and ebony ribbed its gleaming bowl; but the great length and slenderness of the neck which slanted from his cross-legged lap, while he screwed the pegs into tune and plucked the eight wires with a hen's quill, gave it the air of a court minstrel's instrument from a Persian painting: an incongruously delicate and skilfully wrought thing for this rough den.

When it was in tune, the player showered an intricate pattern of minims and crotchets into the falling hush of the grotto and then plaited a flowering wreath of chords in different keys which cohered, after a short halt, in a tune whose slow, heavily stressed and almost lurching beat fell between metallic cascades of short notes and defined a rhythm that slid insidiously into the bloodstream until even the musician himself, stooping over the strings or gazing into the flames with large grey eyes, seemed to be mesmerised by his own music.

Panayi the lutenist was a tall and muscular man and the slender *bouzouki* looked frail in his great hands. He and the older man began a song that sounded like a lament. It was full of repeated phrases and Oriental modulations, and at moments it was designedly strained and grating. Oddly placed pauses syncopated the run of the words. The older man marked the beat by slapping the side of a gourd with his star-backed hand, steadying it with the stump of the other.

The night moved into a different gear. Linked at arm's length by a hand on each other's shoulder, Costa and Dimitri were standing side by side; their feet were together and each unsmiling face hung, chin on breast, like that of a gallows-bird. This initial immobility thawed into movement as slight as the bending and straightening of the knee; the feet, flat on the ground with heels together, opened at an angle, then closed and opened once more. Both right feet were then lifted and slowly swung backward and forward. A left-foot jump brought their torsos seesawing forward in a right angle to balance a simultaneous kick on the ground behind them with their right. Then the dancers swept forward for an acceler-ated pace or two, braked and halted with their right bent legs, from the knee down, lifted parallel to the ground and sweeping in slow scything movements and falling again. An unhurried flick sent both right feet soaring, and their hands smote together under their knees in a sudden clap; then they were almost on their knees, hands on each other's shoulders again, gliding sideways, then rolling forward in a gait resem-bling a sleepwalking hornpipe.

Nothing could have been less carefree or orgiastic than the perverse mood of their evolutions: the subtle and complex beauty of this peculiar dancing, coming, as it did, hotfoot on the straightforward bumpkin commotion of the first perform-ance, was as much of a surprise as would be the discovery, in a collection of folk verse, of a contorted metaphysical jun-gle of conceits, tropes, assonances, internal rhymes, abstruse allusions and concealed acrostics. At the end of the dance, Dimitri joined us by the fire and swelled the accompaniment with his own voice and another gourd. The next dance, on which Costa now embarked solo, was, though akin to its forerunner, odder still. There was the same delay and deliberation, the same hanging head with a cigarette in the centre of his lips as he gazed at the ground with eyes nearly closed and rotated on the spot with his hands crossed in the small of his back. Soon his arms lifted above his head and slowly soared in alternate sweeps before his lowered face, like a vulture rocking on a slow breeze, with an occasional carefully placed crack of thumb and forefinger as the steps evolved. The downward gaze, the precise placing of the feet, the sudden twirl of the body, the sinking on alternate knees, the sweep of an outstretched leg in three quarters of a circle with the arms outflung in two radii for balance – these steps and passes and, above all, the downward scrutiny were as though the dancer were proving, on the trodden fish scales and the goats' droppings, a lost theorem about tangents and circles, or retracing the conclusions of Pythagoras about the square of the hypotenuse.

But more striking still was the tragic and doomed aura that invested this dance, the flaunting so quickly muffled and the introvert and cerebral aloofness of the dancer. Absorption lifted him so far from the others in the cave that he might have been alone in a distant room, raptly applying ritual and undeviating devices to abstruse and nearly insoluble conundrums or exorcising a private and incommunicable pain. The loneliness was absolute. The voices and hands had fallen silent, isolating the wiry jangle of the strings.

On a rock, lifted there to clear the floor, the round, low, heavy table was perched. Revolving past it, Costa leaned forward: suddenly the table levitated itself into the air, sailed past us, and pivoted at right angles to Costa's head in a series of wide loops, the edge clamped firmly in his mouth and held there only by his teeth buried in the wood. It rotated like a magic carpet, slicing crescents out of the haze of smoke and soon travelling so fast that the four glasses on it, the chap-fallen bagpipe with its perforated cow's horn dangling, the raki flask, the knives and spoons, the earthenware saucepan that had held the lentils and the backbones of the two mack-erels with their heads and tails hanging over the edge of the tin plate, all dissolved, for a few swift revolutions, into a cir-cular blur; then it redefined itself, when the pace dwindled into a slowly revolving still life.

As the dancer sank gyrating to floor level, firelight lit the table-top; when he soared into the dark, only the underside glowed. He quickened his pace and reduced the circumference of the circles by spinning faster and faster in the same place, his revolutions striking sparks of astonished applause through the grotto: cries which rose to an uproar. His head was flung back; muscles and veins corrugated his streaming features and his balancing arms were outflung like those of a dervish until the flying table itself melted into a vast disc twice its own diameter and spinning at such a speed in the cave's centre that it should by rights have scattered the still life that it bore into the nether shadows.

Slowly the speed slackened. The table was looping through the smoke five feet from the floor. Soon it was sliding from its orbit and rotating back to its launching rock, unhurriedly alighting there at last with all its impedimenta undisturbed. Not once had the dancer's hands touched it; but, the moment before it resettled in its place, he retrieved the cigarette he had left burning on the edge of a plate. Dancing slowly back to the centre with no hint of haste or vertigo, he tapped away the long ash and replaced the cigarette in his mouth. Gyrating, sinking and rising again, he unwound the dance to its sober initial steps; then, straight as a wand and poised on tiptoe at his motionless starting point, he broke off and sauntered with lowered lids to the re-established table. Picking up his raki glass he took a meditative sip and, poker-faced in the clamour, slowly subsided.

I could catch a loose word here and there in the flow of Romaic as they talked among themselves. How was I to find out, with my clumsy rudiments of Bulgarian, the origin of these dances, the roots of their unique and absolute oddity? Panayi was swaddling his instrument for the night: its incendiary work was done but its message still twanged and hovered in our veins. Dimitri had dropped asleep for a moment, lying with his head on his arm. The one-handed elder clapped the raki bottle to his eye, as an admiral would a spyglass, to see if any was left. Costa the dancer smoked and smiled with the easy air of a geometrician who has proved what had to be proved; *Quod erat demonstrandum,* the silent smile seemed to say under the peak of the old cap tilted rakishly forward to shield his eyes from the flames.

The cave dwellers, after a final gulp of raki, began to settle for the night. I was to sleep at the sailors' end of the cave. Costa and Dimitri hospitably spread new leaves close to the fire, rolled up a coat as a pillow, piled blanket on blanket and laid the old shepherd's cloak on top of me. *'Kryo?'* they asked. *'Studeno?'* 'Cold?' – they had learned four or five words of English on their travels. Only an occasional tremor at wide intervals reminded me of my earlier mishaps; later impressions had snowed them under. There was nothing guarded or apathetic about these particular Greeks; the trance-like melancholy of their steps had evaporated with the last fumes of the dances and the music; their identical grey eyes were filled with humour, alertness and friendly warmth. I thought I had divined an extra feeling in their welcome and in their horny handshakes earlier on, and I had interpreted it as a late symptom of Greek feelings towards Lord Byron's countrymen. I was right. Dimitri said as much. Uttering the words *'Lordos Veeron!'* he raised his bunched fingers in a gesture of approval.

Sleep was long in coming. There was much to think about, especially Greece and the Greeks, which were drawing nearer every day. An occasional clank from the fifty goats at the farther end broke the deepening silence. A few yards off, beyond the twelve adjacent snores, I could hear the gasp of the Black Sea. The light ebbed from the walls and from the stalactites as the fire shrank to a feathery glow. Through a gap in the wall, three quarters of Orion blazed an icy slanting lozenge.

A slight clatter roused me as I was on the brink of sleep. It was the spectral, tiptoe figure, confident that everyone was asleep (ah! but they weren't!), of the dog with the black monocle, tidily licking the last of the lentils and fish gills out of the saucepan.

BARBARA STOCKING (born Rugby, 1951) joined Oxfam as Chief Executive in 2001 and has been travelling to further the charity's work ever since.

Afterword

BARBARA STOCKING

Chief Executive, Oxfam

Throughout my time with Oxfam, I've been fortunate to experience many remarkable meetings, with many remarkable people and in many remarkable places. I've also seen time and again how people's lives can change simply by getting together and talking. It's a privilege I'm careful never to take for granted.

But among all of the inspiring memories, there is one particular meeting I find myself thinking about more than most. It took place in Mali in 2004, when Oxfam was working – as we still do – in the Sahel region, between the Sahara to the north and the sprawling savannahs to the south. Our focus in the country is on girls' education, and we work with nomadic Tuareg communities to develop ways to make it easier for children to go to school.

As with any trip, there are a lot of individual details that stick in my mind. The journey from the capital, Bamako, to our destination in the Gao region was a long one. It started with a day's journey on good quality roads, before we moved briefly onto a ferry and then back into a 4 x 4, from which we watched the roads disappear underneath us as we bumped and jolted our way across the desert.

But what I remember most about the journey isn't the time it took, or the rocky ride. It's the hospitality we were shown by our driver. He would take a break every couple of hours and – wonderful man that he is (he still works for Oxfam, in fact) – at that time the tea ritual would begin. A beautiful red Persian-style rug would be taken from the car boot, swiftly followed by a stove, a teapot and some cups. The stove would be lit, and then would come the most fantastic sweet tea I've ever tasted, poured from a great height into a small cup, then back into the pot, and then down from a great height again, to ensure the sugar dissolved. And there we would sit, seeking refuge from the sun under a tree in the middle of the Malian desert, enjoying one of the finest cups of tea you could ever hope to drink. Those moments were, in themselves, remarkable meetings, as we sat, shared stories and put the world to rights.

But the most remarkable meeting of all occurred when we arrived at our destination, slightly weary and feeling generally crumpled after nearly thirty-six hours of travel. I was there to take part in a workshop the Tuareg community had organised, and the sun was already setting as we pulled up at a small settlement of three or four mud huts. My memory is of everything being brown and blue; the brown being the colour of the earth and the huts, and the blue the wonderful, shimmering shade of the traditional Tuareg robes, which people sweep around their bodies and faces as protection from the sun, sand and dust.

A meal was prepared and we sat down on the ground to eat in the traditional way, around thirty of us sticking our hands into pots and pulling out balls of rice and cuts of meat. By this point it was dark, so we were there under the stars, with just a few torches to light our faces as we ate and chatted. The only sounds were voices and the occasional rustling of robes, as people went to tend to their camels or find something to drink.

The conversation moved to Oxfam's work in Mali in the mid-1990s, shortly after a peace agreement had been negotiated to end deadly clashes between rival Tuareg groups across Mali and Niger. After the fighting had stopped, we were working in Mali, distributing goats, camels and other animals to help people earn a living. And as people shared their memories of this time, one of the Tuareg leaders said something extraordinary.

He recalled that, once the conflict had stopped, he had told Oxfam staff that they should give all of the animals to the Tuaregs who were returning – in other words, to people his tribe had been fighting with only months earlier. His logic was simple – the new arrivals would otherwise have no way of earning money or getting food, and would therefore inevitably end up stealing animals to survive. The only way for the dispute to be resolved permanently and for everyone to settle peacefully, he decided, was for the animals to be given to the returning group.

I found the statement very moving, and remember thinking how different the world would look if more leaders and politicians thought in similar ways. He wasn't being particularly altruistic. He simply looked at the bigger picture and focused on a solution that was most likely to bring lasting peace, even if it meant his people might miss out in the short term. Moreover, his logic has since been proved right. I was there eight years after the peace accord was signed – and the

Tuareg groups were living happily together, side-by-side and without problems.

It was undoubtedly a remarkable meeting. And it's also one of the many occasions that I have spent time with people in poor communities, learning about their lives, their culture and how they cope day-to-day, and have left feeling more informed, more educated and, crucially, more hopeful for the world in which we live.

Ultimately, when you sit down in those situations, all of the trappings of everyday life disappear. It's just people talking about the things which bind us all, the concerns and experiences that everyone shares. And it can be interesting for me because I'm in the privileged position of also being able to do that with political leaders and heads of state, often only a few days after I've been in remote communities like the one in Mali. Those meetings are important too, of course. They give Oxfam the chance to make sure poor people's voices are heard and acted upon.

But if I'm honest, it's those meetings like the one in Mali that I remember more. The ones where the conversation gets right to the essence of people's lives. Where you find out about people's hopes and people's dreams. Where you see how our work has enabled whole families to move away from poverty. And, often, where you meet people who not only renew your faith in humanity, but also remind you of how problems can so often be solved by simply sitting down together and talking.